PARENT-CHILD RELATIONS

PARENT-CHILD RELATIONS

AN INTRODUCTION TO PARENTING

Jerry J. Bigner, Ph.D.

Department of Human Development
and Family Studies
Colorado State University

Macmillan Publishing Co., Inc.
New York

Collier Macmillan Publishers
London

Copyright © 1979, Jerry J. Bigner

Printed in the United States of America

MACMILLAN PUBLISHING CO., INC.
866 THIRD AVENUE, NEW YORK, NEW YORK 10022

COLLIER MACMILLAN CANADA, LTD.

Library of Congress Cataloging in Publication Data

Bigner, Jerry J
  Parent-child relations.

  Includes bibliographies and index.
  1. Parent and child. 2. Child development.
3. Family. I. Title.
HQ772.B477   301.42'7   78-3572
ISBN 0-02-309820-1

Printing: 3 4 5 6 7 8   Year: 0 1 2 3 4 5

To Karl King
for his inspiration and friendship and

to Patricia Ann
for her loving patience and understanding and

to Todd, Shannon, and Kate
for helping me in my growth and development

Preface

The focus of this book is on parents *and* children. The book is based on the conviction that children are influential in the development of adults as parents just as adults are influential in the growth and development of children. The text describes the process of interaction by which parents and children affect each other as individuals and as a family. Factors are examined that influence the parents in their behavior as caregivers to children.

An increasing number of young people today question the assumption of the parenting role as a valuable and fulfilling role in adulthood. The rapidly changing nature of contemporary society has prompted the reconsideration of traditional values and attitudes of the past and whether they have relevance today. These are difficult times that challenge the security and confidence of parents in their ability to raise children in a competent manner. The issues that are examined in the text recognize these concerns of contemporary parents as well as of those who contemplate becoming parents in the future.

This *is not* a book on how to be a parent in the conventional sense or on how to conduct specific styles of parent–child interaction. The text does provide information on parenting by describing the course and nature of parent–child interaction through the child-rearing years of the family life cycle. The book is divided into three parts. The first one explores contemporary issues about parenting and examines the individual roles of mothers and fathers using information from classic and contemporary research. The interactional pattern of parent–child relations described is based on Erikson's theory of psychosocial development and Duvall's explanation of the family life cycle. The second portion of the book introduces the reader to the changing nature of parent–child relations through the years of infancy, childhood, adolescence, and early adulthood. The last part features the effects of differences in family structure and functioning on parent–child relations and the challenges of child rearing for contemporary parents. Each chapter is summarized in the "Points to Consider" section, and references mentioned in the text appear at the end of each chapter.

This text is the result of the efforts of many individuals. Numerous colleagues are acknowledged for their contributions through research. I extend special thanks to Jill Kreutzer, Barbara McCornack, Florence Kerchoff, Lois Mickle, and Vera Borosage for their helpful suggestions in the preparation of the manuscript. John Beck of Macmillan has my deepest appreciation for seeing the promise of my work and for his help in clarifying my ideas into more meaningful formats.

J. J. B.

Colorado State University

Contents

TWO
DEVELOPMENTAL INTERACTION IN THE CHILD-REARING YEARS

THREE
DEVELOPMENTAL INTERACTION: IMPLICATIONS FOR PARENTING

ONE

An Introduction to Parenting

Parenthood:
A Contemporary Choice

Young people today are at a point in cultural history where individual choice plays a significant role in the decision to become a parent. Medical technology provides individuals with the unique opportunity to choose and decide *if* and *when* to reproduce with a high degree of accuracy. These days, individuals become parents by choice, by accident (through contraceptive failure, improper use, or neglect), or by ignorance—all related to the availability and use of a wide number of reliable birth control methods.

Why, then, if there is such control in choosing adult roles in life, does a couple choose to assume the roles of mother and father? Many factors influence this decision. Questions are raised by young people that reflect the influence of several factors in their decision making. The economic contributions of children to a contemporary family are usually ruled out from the start. Having children has evolved from being an economic asset in the past to being an economic liability today. When families were settling this country, children contributed much to the survival and success of the group. Children helped to provide much of the physical labor of the farm-oriented society that existed on such a large scale until recently. With increases in technology and the greater opportunities that were to be found in cities, farming family populations have declined while urban populations have increased. As a result, the extended family group has shrunk to include only a few individuals.

The current estimated costs of raising children in middle-class families indicate the economic demands of children on family income. A report of the Population Reference Bureau (Espenshade, 1977) states that the estimated expense of raising one child from conception to age eighteen is $53,605. When the lost income to a family that results from the woman's staying home to be a full-time mother is included, the figure increases to $107,000. If a family chooses to pay the costs of a private college education for the child, the estimated total figure for child-rearing expenses is almost $125,000. (The largest expenditure included in these figures is for housing costs, accounting for 32.2 per cent of the total amount.)

The success of family life is closely interdependent with the conditions of the larger society. As the extended family has increasingly become a relic of the past, families have changed in their size, structure, composition, and functions. Much of family life in the past focused on fulfilling instrumental functions, those that relate to the survival of the group and especially to the procreation of human beings. The functions of the family today focus on meeting the emotional needs of members, or expressive functions. The smaller group of individuals who compose the families of today find that interpersonal interactions are intense and frequent. The survival of family groups today may depend on how well emotional needs are met as well as on the successfulness of restricting the size of the group, which must be supported on limited financial resources.

These changes in the family have occurred over a relatively short period of historical time. Large numbers of young people, for example, would not have questioned the idea of anticipated parenthood in their future ten or twenty years ago. Today the question that is asked with increasing frequency of young couples is "Are you going to have children?" instead of "How many children do you plan to have?" Concern for the well-being of children in their own future is very much on the minds of young people today. There are many uncertainties about what the future holds based on our experiences in the past. Much publicity about the "population explosion" has made young people think consciously about an overcrowded existence in the future if the population continues to grow as it has in the past. The quality of life in the future may revolve around survival from one shortage of goods and materials to another on a planet that has limited resources. Even if a couple can support a child economically, one hears young people ask, "Who in their right minds would want to wish this kind of existence for their children in the future?"

The period of adolescence as a time of self-discovery and determination of life goals has extended further into the years of what once was considered to be early adulthood. The wide range of possible alternatives in life that are available today make the end of adolescence a questionable event. As a result, young people can be heard to ask, "How can I expect to be responsible for guiding a child's development when I don't have enough of the right answers yet about myself?"

All of these questions, then, about whether to become a parent or not and when may act as a "natural" selection process in contemporary times for those who sincerely wish to do as good a job as possible in parenting roles. Those who choose to have children may find answers to their questions and a rationale for their decision to have children in a number of psychological and social issues. If people have come to realize that children are a very real and heavy drain on family finances, then the reasons for wanting children shift to these other bases. People may have several reasons for wanting to become parents and may be more consciously aware of these reasons today than in the past.

MOTIVATIONS FOR PARENTHOOD

One theoretical explanation for becoming a parent is discussed by Erik Erikson (1950). He believes that when an individual arrives at the adult stage of life, he or she expresses an innate motivation to care for others by having children and assuming the parenthood role. While people do appear to achieve healthy psychological development in adulthood by becoming in- volved in teaching, socializing, and caring for the next generation, we can question Erikson's explanation of the innateness of generativity in adulthood. This idea comes uncomfortably close to suggesting that humans are stimulated by instinct to assume the parenting roles. The presence of any instinctual drives in motivating human behavior was discarded long ago by empirical research that disproved such hypotheses. When we look at the parenting be- havior of lower species, where instinctual parenting behavior in some form exists, we marvel at its complexity and order. Biological evolution in hu- mans, however, has resulted in the replacement of automatic behaviors with individual choice—based on logic and reasoning—to assume the parenting roles.

Motivations for becoming a parent are seen as antecedents of the varying attitudes people have toward this role. Such motivations may be present long before an individual has children and may influence whether or not an indi- vidual chooses to become a parent. When and if children are produced, the underlying reasons for the decision to assume the parenting role may be based on the particular attitudes that the person possesses or adopts about the performance of child rearing. The reasons a person decides to have chil- dren may be closely associated with the experience she or he expects to have in relating to a child. People might desire, for example, to have a child to enhance or ensure their social acceptance or status as an adult. They may choose to have a child because of an interest in nurturing human life. One may choose to become a parent because a child is a concrete symbol of a close, intimate relationship with one's spouse. The implication is that attitudes toward parenthood do not result completely from an ongoing, dynamic rela- tionship after a child is born (see Figure 1-1). These attitudes may have origins prior to the beginning of the parent–child relationship (Rabin, 1965).

Types of Parental Motivations

The idea that some people become parents for *fatalistic* reasons is one of four motivations for parenthood described by Rabin (1965). Some individuals

"YOU SHOULDN'T *SAY* THAT, GEORGE! THE *MITCHELLS* MIGHT NOT WANT
ANOTHER CHILD FOR ANY NUMBER OF REASONS. I DON'T THINK
DENNIS HAS *'SOURED'* THEM ON THE IDEA!"

Figure 1-1.

have children because they believe that reproduction is the reason for their
existence. People having fatalistic motivations believe that to prevent conception is to commit a sin against God because they feel that human beings
should not interfere with the creation of life. These people are motivated by
religious beliefs that are founded on fatalistic ideas about their part and
contribution to a larger, predestined plan for humans.

Another type of fatalistic motivation is to ensure that one's family name
will continue by becoming a parent. This motivation, however, carries a
50–50 chance of not working out as parents wish. This is one of the prime
reasons that boys may still be highly desired by some families and ethnic
groups because of our patrilineal family system, the process in which families'
last names are perpetuated through males. The maintenance of family lines
was once considered to be extremely important. Laws of inheritance were
based on the principle of primogeniture, that is, the inheritance of wealth
through males only. The firstborn son usually inherited the bulk of the
father's estate. By having a male child, the family could rest assured that

possessions would remain intact within the blood lines of the family. Although changes have occurred in such laws and in the feelings of many people about such matters, it is still not unusual for some couples to be very pleased that their family name will not die out because a son has been produced to carry on the name through subsequent generations.

Altruism may be another reason for becoming a parent. This may be the primary motivation for many people to have or adopt a child. The motivation is described as an unselfish desire and need to express affection and concern for children by becoming a parent. Erikson's concept of generativity falls under this classification if we disregard the innate aspect of his explanation.

Parents have a psychological need to be "needed," according to Erikson's concept of generativity. This can be considered a *narcissistic* motivation for parenthood. Narcissism in this context refers to the expectation that having children will reflect on the goodness of the person and serve as a concrete, visible statement of maturity and adequacy as a sexually active adult. This reason for becoming a parent is parallel to a cultural belief that every couple should have children (LeMasters, 1974). It is essential to the psychological comfort of some people not to be radically different from others. Some individuals may feel that becoming a parent is an important initiation into the fraternity of adults.

Another narcissistic reason for having children is the idea that parenthood will provide one with emotional security. This is similar to wanting a pet for companionship. There is no guarantee, unfortunately, that children will provide emotional security for parents in their old age, nor is there any reassurance that "love begets love" within the context of parent–child relations.

There are other reasons for becoming a parent that are *instrumental* in nature, for example, the expectation that children will achieve specific goals for the parent. These goals may or may not have been attained by the parent, such as getting a college education, learning particular skills, or overcoming particular personal problems. The parenting experience represents a second chance at life for some people; some parents may unconsciously believe that they can relive their own childhood through their children. Along these same lines, there is the hope and determination that one's children will not repeat the parent's mistakes.

A woman may allow herself to become pregnant in order to begin a marital relationship. Some people are likewise lured into the mistaken assumption after marriage that having a child will repair a troubled relationship or prevent the dissolution of a marriage. These are desperate attempts to use children in frightening ways to achieve a specific adult goal.

Having a child to please or appease one's own parents also falls into the instrumental category. Parents can place considerable pressure on their adult children to make them grandparents (see Box 1-1). These motivations may be instrumental or narcissistic for both parties. Middle-aged people may want

CHILDLESS COUPLE NEEDS HELP TO FEND OFF CRITICS

DEAR ABBY: My husband and I have been married for three years and have a really great marriage. We have no children because we don't want any. We discussed it before our marriage and agreed on it.

We both work and enjoy taking off for a skiing weekend, or sleeping late whenever we feel like it. It's not that we don't like children—we do, but we just don't want a family.

Our problem: our parents. His keep saying, "You'll be sorry later on. Children hold a marriage together."

Mine say, "Not wanting children is unnatural, selfish and immature."

Our friends who have children keep asking if they can bring their kids to our place so we can babysit since we're going to be home anyway. We've done this a few times (and for whole weekends) and have decided we don't want the responsibility.

Abby, what do we say when our parents hassle us? And how do we tactfully tell our friends, without losing their friendship, that we don't want to look after their kids?

CHILDLESS BY CHOICE

DEAR CHILDLESS: Tell your parents that you appreciate their concern and advice, but you don't feel the need to justify your decision or debate the pros and cons of parenthood with them. And the friends you lose because you refuse to babysit, you are well rid of.

Source: Reprinted by permission of Abigail Van Buren.

to conform with their peers in being grandparents. Their children may give in to their pressures to reduce the guilt that they generate.

Silverman and Silverman (1971) point out that men may have instrumental motivations to become fathers. For example, they may see the fathering role as exercising ultimate power by impregnating women and ruling the home life of the family. Illustrating this point is the saying that men achieve this high social power by "keeping their women barefoot and pregnant."

THE CULTURAL MEANINGS OF PARENTHOOD

Every culture has ideas of the characteristics and functions that are ideal in the social roles of the culture. These ideas are often exaggerated notions that act to shape the thoughts, reactions, and behavior of the individuals who assume these roles. Often these ideal notions are not questioned, and the individual accepts them as valid and true characteristics.

J. E. Veevers (1973) describes the social meanings of parenthood and nonparenthood that exist in our culture. These ideal notions about these roles are derived from behavioral and social science research. The social meanings attached to parenthood and nonparenthood are important to an understanding of their influences on individual behavior. Many individuals may be motivated by their belief in these social meanings of parenthood to assume this role rather than nonparenthood. The social meanings of parenthood may act to place cultural pressure on individuals to become parents.

Veevers uses six main themes to classify these social meanings: morality, responsibility, naturalness, sex, marriage, and mental health. These themes and the relation of each to parenthood and nonparenthood are shown in Table 1-1 and are briefly discussed here.

Many individuals may interpret parenthood as fulfilling a *moral obligation.* According to Veevers, the Judeo-Christian traditions of our culture

Table 1-1. The Types of Social Meanings of Parenthood and Nonparenthood

Category	*Ideal Type of Parenthood*	*Ideal Type of Nonparenthood*
Morality	Parenthood is seen as a moral obligation; parenthood shows morality.	Nonparenthood is seen as rejecting religious authority; childlessness is immoral.
Responsibility	Parenthood fulfills a civic obligation; parenthood shows a sense of responsibility.	Nonparenthood signifies avoidance of responsibility; childlessness shows irresponsibility.
Naturalness	Parenthood is instinctive; parenthood is natural.	Nonparenthood is unnatural.
Sexual Identity and Competence	Parenthood shows acceptance of one's gender; being a parent proves one's sexual competence.	Nonparenthood is seen as a rejection of gender; it implies sexual incompetence.
Marriage	Parenthood gives meaning to marriage, improves marital satisfaction, and prevents divorce.	Nonparenthood decreases the meaning of marriage, increases chances of divorce, and promotes marital dissatisfaction.
Normality and Mental Health	Parenthood indicates normal mental health; being a parent shows social maturity and personal stability.	Nonparenthood indicates abnormal mental health; childlessness indicates social immaturity and emotional maladjustment.

Source: Adapted from J. E. Veevers. The social meanings of parenthood. *Psychiatry,* 1973, *36,* 291–310.

follow the Old Testament directive for individuals to be "fruitful and multiply." Procreation becomes a moral obligation for those who devoutly practice the teachings of their religious group.

Becoming a parent may imply fulfilling a *civic obligation,* according to Veevers. Society depends on parents to replenish the population because governments and culture cannot continue their existence without new members. Veevers states that using the alarmingly high costs of child rearing is not acceptable as an excuse not to have children because reproduction represents a valuable contribution to society. Individuals who have the financial and social resources to be competent parents and choose to remain childless are thought to be selfish and irresponsible.

Parenthood is thought to be an expected and *natural* behavior of adults. This attitude refers, as Veevers states, to the belief that conception is a natural consequence of sexual intercourse between married couples. This idea of parenthood is a residue from the period of time before the appearance of reliable contraceptives. People assumed that those who were childless had some type of physical problem that prevented conception. The childless individual was, according to this logic, an unnatural and abnormal person; something was wrong with him or her. Veevers states that this is an erroneous assumption about many individuals who are childless. If, indeed, there were an instinctual drive in humans to reproduce and provide care for children, according to her logic, then there would be a more common method of socializing children and performing caregiving in every culture. As anthropologists have shown, there is much cultural variation in these parenting functions.

The parenthood role has *sexual* meanings and implies that an individual is an adult capable of reproduction and one who can find sexual identity through reproduction. The psychological as well as physical condition of childless individuals is questioned because of the lack of these proofs. Closely associated with the sexual meanings of parenthood is the notion that parenthood gives meaning to *marriage.* The idea is that children round out a marriage, improve the relationship between couples, help a troubled or stagnant relationship, and prevent divorce. Empirical evidence to the contrary is discussed at length in later chapters. Although children may not necessarily improve a marriage, their presence acts to prolong the relationship. For example, the median duration of marriages among childless couples before divorce in 1969 was 3.8 years, whereas that of couples with three or more children was 13.8 years (Plateris, 1973).

The last idea discussed by Veevers relates to the *normality* of individuals who have children. We have the notion that the bearing of children fulfills a destiny for women more than for men in our society, according to Veevers. Thus the woman who is childless is seen as unnatural, abnormal, and lacking in "normal" mental health. Implicit is the assumption that parents are socially mature individuals. Having a child is considered to be a means of achieving adult status and of being recognized by others as having it. Parenthood carries the idea of caring for others and being concerned for their welfare. Nonparenthood, conversely, implies that one cares more for his own well-being than for that of others.

It is difficult to determine completely the influence of these cultural meanings of parenthood on the general population. As Veevers notes, several organizations have been formed in reaction to these attitudes toward parenthood and nonparenthood. These groups, such as Zero Population Growth and the National Organization for Nonparents, may be indicative of changes in the consensus of opinions about parenthood or may change these attitudes.

THE SENSE OF GENERATIVITY

The years of adulthood represent the culmination of an individual's maturation from our culture's point of view. This is the time when mature responsibilities are assumed, such as earning a living, entering into parenthood, supporting a family, pursuing occupational goals, and making some type of contribution to society. In Erikson's theory of psychosocial development, the adult years constitute a period when the individual is encouraged by society to meet these responsibilities and in doing so to prepare himself for the next and final stage of life.

Our traditional cultural ideas about this time in life address the expectation that when an individual reaches this stage of life he will establish a life-style that is family oriented. People are expected to marry and have children. Statistics from the 1970 national census confirm this belief, showing that approximately 90 per cent of individuals eighteen years of age and older marry at some time in their life. Of these, approximately 60 per cent have at least one child (U.S. Bureau of the Census, 1970).

These figures have implications about people's decisions to become parents. Do people become parents because it is expected and because they don't wish to be different from the majority of people at this time in life? What are the working mechanics that help a sense of generativity to emerge in an individual's development during adulthood?

One explanation of why people become parents is provided by Erikson (1950). He believes that when we reach the adult years we are "triggered" by physical, psychological, and social stimuli to develop a sense of generativity. A central component of this attitude is the desire to care for others. For the majority of people, parenthood is perhaps the most obvious and the best opportunity to generate the attitude of caring.

Erikson believes that a distinguishing feature of an adult is the emergence of an inborn desire to teach. We become aware of this desire when the event of being physically capable to reproduce is joined by the events of marriage, establishing an adult pattern of living, and assuming job responsibilities. According to Erikson, by becoming parents, we learn that we have the need "to be needed," by others who are dependent on our wealth of knowledge—about cultural expectations of behavior, values, attitudes, skills, and information about the world. By assuming the responsibilities of being primary caregivers to children through the long years of social and physical growth, we concretely express what Erikson believes is an inborn desire to teach. We produce, through the reproduction and care of children, a continuation of culture. By doing so, we begin the development of a sense of generativity as adults.

In contrast to Erikson's thoughts are those of social psychologists and historians who believe that the reasons for becoming a parent and the ways someone behaves as a parent are shaped predominantly by cultural influences on the individual at the time he or she assumes this social role.

CHANGING CONCEPTS OF PARENTHOOD AND CHILDHOOD

Two social historians, Phillip Aries (1962) and David Hunt (1970), argue that the nature and quality of caregiving are significantly influenced by cultural values about parenting and the actual historical time in which an individual assumes the role of caregiver.

© 1976 by NEA, Inc.

"Say, whatever happened to the family unit?"

Figure 1-2.

Most people have the idea that our culture values the well-being of children and supports this idea by providing numerous social institutions (the family, the school, social service agencies, and so on) to meet children's needs. We tend to think that we have a child-centered society. We see childhood as a special time in someone's life—a time of preparation and education for functioning in the later years of life and a time for happiness and freedom from anxiety. We believe that children have special needs that are met first through the members of the immediate family and later by other institutions, groups, and agencies.

A primary point of both Aries and Hunt is that our current concerns and conception of the unique nature of childhood developed only as the result of years of social change in Western culture. Contrary to what might be expected, the ideas of childhood, parenthood, and the family have been viewed very differently since the Middle Ages. Erikson's idea of generativity is seen by Aries and Hunt to be characteristic of our times and particularly linked to the manner in which the family's functions have changed over the years. By and large, most social historians would agree that the nature of a sense of generativity as experienced by adults has probably not changed over time but that change has occurred in the way this sense has been expressed by adults through their parenting behavior. In other words, generativity is expressed by parents through the culturally appropriate ways of caregiving to children that are in existence in any particular historical time.

Children in premodern times were raised by parents in a manner that we would interpret today as being indifferent to their special needs. During the Middle Ages and for some time afterward, that nature of an infant was taken for granted by adults. There was no conception in these times that infants needed to learn to trust their caregivers. Assimilation into the adult world came at an early age, sometimes between four and seven years. A child's schooling and probably his only education came from observing and imitating his adult models. A parent in these times probably had the notion that he was a caregiver for his child, but this was only a rudimentary and vague conception at best, compared with our modern attitudes. In the time prior to the Industrial Revolution, caregiving was only one of the many functions of the extended family unit. What most concerned the family was survival and producing the food, clothing, and shelter that would ensure their survival.

Aries points out that in modern times societies have changed from a basic agricultural orientation to being highly complex and industrialized. Changes in societal functioning have prompted corresponding changes in family structure and functioning. The family has reflected these changes by setting aside the large, extended family grouping to become smaller in size and specialized in function. The resulting form is now called the isolated *nuclear family*. The duties, responsibilities, and functions of the family have become more intensely focused on a few issues. Childrearing has become a focal point of the family's attention. The family has come to spend less time in producing the goods and services it needs for survival, as these functions are performed by other agents in society. Interactions have become more concentrated on meeting the emotional needs of family members. These factors have changed family life, the concepts of childhood, and the ways in which caregiving is conducted by parents.

The grandmother was a source of wisdom about the processes of child rearing for young parents several centuries ago (Winch, 1971). The culture entrenched the advice about child rearing and the role performances of parenthood in folklore that was handed down from generation to generation. As a result of the major changes occurring in the larger society, grandmothers became obsolete as a source of knowledge about child rearing because "in a changing culture the elders lose their infallability" (Mead and Wolfenstein, 1955).

The increasing stature of the scientific approaches to child study joined with a rapidly changing and mobile society to produce a phenomenon that is described by Winch (1971) as characteristically American: advice giving by professionals and laymen alike on how children should be raised properly. In our culture, it is these individuals who have replaced the grandmother in advising parents on the problems and methods of raising children.

The Colonial Period: 1600–1800

The cultural conditions in existence at the time the United States was being colonized created a unique notion about the nature of children and the role of parents in caregiving. Children were seen as having an inherent, depraved nature. Parents provided stern discipline through work experiences to ensure that the child became a self-denying and pious adult. Children were prized because of their usefulness in the colonization process. Their value was increased because of the high infant mortality rate in those times.

The notion that children's nature was depraved and sinful stemmed primarily from the Puritan religious orientation of the settlers (Calhoun, 1945). These views were described in the *Day of Doom,* a catechism that almost every child was expected to learn. Parents were responsible for providing rigorous moral training and stern discipline. A primary aim of parental guidance was to help children achieve infantile conversion, that is, to recognize their own sinful nature and to become a Christian at as early an age as possible. The responsibilities of child rearing were accomplished through a coalition with God. Children were taught that to escape the perils of hellfire and damnation they must obey their parents, and especially their fathers, in every possible way. They were taught to curb their "natural" inclinations to commit sins. The things about childhood that are taken for granted today would have been considered the work of the Devil in colonial times. Play activities were sinful, and children read such interesting pamphlets as, "A

Token for Children. Being the Exact Account of the Conversation and Holy and Exemplary Lives of Several Young Children" (Calhoun, 1945).

The role of parents in shaping their child's development was approached with extravagant overconcern in colonial times. The impression we have of colonial parenthood is hardly one of indifference; rather it is a sordid conception of parental overbearance and concern with religious matters. This is a distorted impression. Parents in this period had great affection for their children and showed their sense of generativity by using the culturally appropriate methods of child rearing in vogue at the time. This presence of generativity is shown by letters of John Quincy Adams written in 1774 to his wife:

> Above all cares of this life, let our ardent anxiety be to mould the minds and manners of our children. . . . Pray remember me to my dear little babes, who I long to see running to meet me and climb up upon me under the smiles of their mother. The education of our children is never out of my mind. Train them to virtue. Habituate them to industry, activity, and spirit. [Calhoun, 1945, pp. 115–116]

The Nineteenth Century: 1800–1860

Information given here regarding advice giving during the mid-nineteenth century comes from an analysis of child-rearing literature by Robert Sunley (1955). Focusing on the forty-year period preceding the Civil War, Sunley notes that there were contradictory views concerning the nature of children that prompted three different theories about how parents should raise their children.

CALVINISM.   The strongest theory, which received the most attention, was the Calvinist approach advocating stern discipline and strict moral training. This approach illustrates a belief in a cause-and-effect relationship between the manner in which a child was trained and his personality as an adult.

During the first half of the nineteenth century, a shift occurred in family life from that of colonial times. The father's central role had consisted in these times of performing the religious and moral instruction as well as the discipline of the children. Mothers began to assume these and other responsibilities that directly related to the character development and socialization of the children. Fathers began to take jobs that placed them away from the home for the majority of their time. The mother came to be considered the best instructor and the central figure in developing a child's character during the first six years of his life, as is shown in the following quotation from Allen (1848, p. 98): "Especially a mother cannot act without leaving an impression on the child . . . by the mother's forming hand it receives shape to a great extent, for all its future existence."

As a consequence of the increased participation of mothers in the care-giving activities for children, the literature encouraged the abandonment of physical punishment, a practice that was formerly under the father's administration. Children were encouraged to become independent of the parents as soon as possible. Toilet training, weaning, self-feeding, and walking were encouraged in children at an early age (some training was recommended to begin at the age of one month). A compulsive attitude and a preoccupation with cleanliness and personal hygiene were evident: "For dirt and indelicacy are frequent companions, and a disregard for the decencies of life is a step away from its virtues" (from Sunley, 1955, p. 158).

As early as 1820, maternal associations were formed in the larger cities that addressed the Calvinist idea of "breaking children's wills." Editorial space in newspapers and magazines occasionally was devoted to discussions of techniques that would result in children's submission to the authority of the mother. Infantile conversion was still a topic of concern during this era. When a child was able to accept the religious principles of his parents and to begin to pray alone or read the Bible, he was considered to be showing his independence as well as the socialization efforts of the mother.

ENVIRONMENTALISM.   A second approach that appeared during this time was influenced by the writings of John Locke (1699) and Jean Jacques Rousseau (1763). Locke is best known for his *tabula rasa* theory, which states that children are born with their minds like "blank slates" and that the experiences they have as they grow and develop "write in" their adult personalities. This was a departure from the Calvinist approach, which viewed children as innately evil and gave attention to the environmental experiences a child had while growing up as the crucial factor of development. Experiences were described in the literature that encouraged the "hardening" of children's characters. Examples of such experiences called for cold baths and plunges (DeWees, 1826).

EARLY DEVELOPMENTALISM.   The third approach during this era was similar to the viewpoints that have been found in more recent years. Stemming in part from the movement in Europe that advocated early childhood education through nursery schools and kindergartens, this approach held that children were "ignorant of right rather than bent to wrong" (Sunley, 1955). Parents were advised not to be so concerned about breaking a child's will nor to be fearful of indulging their child. Obedience was valued, but it could be obtained by firmness, persuasion, and reward rather than by physical punishment (Mann and Peabody, 1863). This viewpoint can be considered the first type of developmental attitude toward children in modern times as it emphasized (1) the presence of children's developmental needs; (2) the emerging personalities of children, which parents helped to shape into full development; and (3) the effects that resulted from neglect and harsh punishment as well as from gentle care and nurturance.

The Twentieth Century: 1890–1950

Content analyses have been performed on advice-giving literature that appeared between 1890 and 1950. The most comprehensive account is provided by Celia Stendler (1950), who analyzed articles appearing in three popular women's magazines (*Good Housekeeping, Ladies' Home Journal,* and *Women's Home Companion*) during each decade of the period from 1890 to 1950.

One of the most prominent findings of Stendler's investigation is the documentation of the wide swings in advice giving that occurred during this period. Stendler's data indicate that between 1890 and 1920 writers reversed from encouraging the indulgence of children to advising a more restrictive pattern of child rearing. This period of restrictive advice continued to be in vogue until the middle 1930s, when the trend was reversed to urge parents to be less restrictive and more child-oriented in caring for their children.

The factors that brought about mothers' increased involvement in child-rearing activities during the nineteenth century continued to be in effect at the turn of this century. The prominence of the mother in caregiving activities is explained by Stendler as being due to the men's preoccupation with materialism and capitalism during this time. The country was experiencing a rapidly growing economy that depended extensively on industrialism. The father was removed even further from participation in family life as compared to the Calvinist era. Indulgence of the children by parents was particularly evident early in the period. Children were said to be "smothered" with maternal affection and attention, and if the family was wealthy, a governess or nursemaid fulfilled these functions.

During the early years of the period from 1890 to 1920, considerable immigration took place from European countries. The immigrants brought with them the hope of achieving the American dream. Children were taught to take advantage of the numerous opportunities for advancement and to attempt to rise higher than the father in occupation and social status. The use of children in the labor force increased dramatically with the expanding industrial economy. It declined in later years because of an increased concern with children's health and welfare. Laws were later enacted to restrict the use of children as laborers.

The 1920s through the 1930s ushered in a highly restrictive era in the parental role and caretaking activities. The 1923 edition of *Infant Care* (a serial publication of the Children's Bureau) advised strict, consistently regular scheduling of infant care routines and encouraged rigid methods of early toilet training. An author writing in *Ladies' Home Journal* in 1920 predicted that a parent could achieve proper training for a baby if "everything done for him were so regular that one could tell time by what is going on in the nursery" (Coolidge, 1920, p. 44).

Although no one factor accounts for this dramatic change in child-rearing attitudes, a contributing factor was the writings of J. B. Watson, known as the father of behaviorism. Watson's views on child training are best illustrated in the following excerpt from his widely read book on children published in 1928:

> There is a sensible way of treating children. Treat them as though they were young adults. . . . Let your behavior always be objective and kindly firm. Never hug and kiss them, never let them sit in your lap. . . . If you must, kiss them once on the forehead when they say good night. Shake hands with them in the morning. . . . In a week's time you will find how easy it is to be perfectly objective with your child and at the same time kindly. You will be utterly ashamed of the mawkish, sentimental way you have been handling it. [Watson, 1928, pp. 81–82]

Watson warned parents against the dangers of too much "mother love" and believed that too much coddling and attention in infancy resulted in a child's being a "psychological invalid" in adulthood. The belief that infants and children should be ignored and not picked up when they cried can be traced to Watson. He cautioned parents that a child could be conditioned to expect too much parental attention.

Another compounding factor was the great concern over the physical development and well-being of children. "The up-to-date mother was one who knew her calories and her vitamins, who fed her children scientifically, and who saw that her baby had fresh air (however cold) and sunshine" (Stendler, 1950). Infant mortality rates were very high, and doctors campaigned for healthier babies by advising strict feeding schedules and regimented caregiving activities.

Clark Vincent (1951) states that while the 1920s and 1930s were known as the "parents' decade," the next period, from 1935 to 1945, could be termed the "baby's decade." Vincent's terminology refers to the swing from the doctrine of the previous era that obviously was parent-oriented to an attitude that was child-oriented and advocated self-regulation by the child as well as permissive caretaking practices by parents. The influence of Freudian psychology with its heavy emphasis on the importance of infantile experiences, close mother–infant attachments, and the harmful effects of repressing a child's instinctual drives emerged during this period, and these principles were applied to caregiving activities. Stendler (1950) notes that advice concerning the rearing of children advocated a mental hygiene approach. This approach emphasized (1) the dependency of emotional adjustment on the manner in which a child was treated in early childhood; (2) the acceptance of children for both their strengths and their weaknesses; and (3) the development of security in the child through tender love and care by parents, particularly during the years of infancy. Part of this attitude can be traced to the research performed by Margaret Ribble (1943), Rene Spitz (1945), and others on the effects of maternal deprivation on children (this research is discussed in Chapter 4). These individuals favored a return to the "cuddling" concept of mothering a child and stressed that such handling of infants played an extremely important part in shaping the emotional health of children. It was also during this period that Benjamin Spock (1946) gained prominence as an adviser of parents on child rearing. With the publication of *The Common Sense Book of Baby and Child Care,* Spock related concepts of Freudian psychology to parents in terms that could be easily understood.

The Twentieth Century: 1950–1970

Bigner (1972) extended the content analysis of advice-giving literature begun by Sunley (1955) and Stendler (1950) through 1970. The period from 1950 to 1970 can be described as a return to the "parents' era" in the publications, in that parents were urged to recognize their own individuality within their role in shaping a child's development. A primary proponent of this attitude was Dr. Spock. Over the twenty-year period, Dr. Spock contributed heavily to two magazines used in the analysis (*Ladies' Home Journal* and *Redbook*). Spock gave significance to the role of the parent in interacting with a child. A recurrent theme of his articles was bolstering parents' confidence in handling their relationship with their child. Time and time again, Dr. Spock emphasized the need for parents to give children consistent and firm but loving guidance.

The period between 1950 and 1970 reflected significant changes in expectations regarding the role of the father. The view appearing in 1950 was that not much could be expected from a father in participating in child rearing. In 1954 fathers were being encouraged to take a more active role in interacting with their children. By 1970 the general consensus in articles emphasized that a father was expected to participate as much as possible in sharing child-rearing responsibilities with the mother. It was thought that fathers' increased participation would result in better personality development of children.

In line with Stendler's findings, advice giving to parents of infants emphasized a great deal of handling and less rigid enforcement of schedules. Experts recommended toilet training to begin at eighteen months for girls and twenty-four months for boys, the latest age recommended in modern times.

A recurrent theme of articles appearing during the 1960s can be described as a reaction formation to all types of advice given earlier. This theme of "experts-don't-know-any-more-about-raising-children-then-I (the parent)-do" appeared in numerous articles. Articles with this theme recognized a growing sense of frustration among parents in relation to a wide range of conflicting information and opinions on child rearing. In addition, parents were perhaps beginning to recognize their own autonomy as individuals with needs and desires in relation to those of their children.

The primary approach in advice giving concerned with the topic of discipline was to urge parents not to use physical punishment. Parents were encouraged to help a child to become more self-reliant rather than using physical punishment to control behavior. The influence of modern behavioral science had its impact during these years and is found in the advice regarding the disciplining of children's behavior. Behavior modification through the positive reinforcement of desired behaviors was the most frequently recommended method of child guidance. A number of philosophies and methods emerged during this period that can be labeled humanitarian. These methods attempted to equalize the power of the parent with that of the child in social interactions. Parents were encouraged to assist children in their emotional growth by acting as counselors when children experienced problems. These methods also recognized the emotional needs of the parents in their interactions with children. For example, Dr. Haim Ginott states:

> There is a place for parental anger in child education. In fact, failure to get angry at certain moments would only convey to the child indifference, not goodness. Anger should so come out that it brings some relief to the parent, some insight to the child, and no harmful side effects to either of them. To prepare ourselves in times of peace to deal with times of stress, we should acknowledge the following truths: 1. We accept the fact that children will make us angry. 2. We are entitled to our anger without guilt or shame. 3. Except for one safeguard, we are entitled to express what we feel. We can express our angry feelings *provided* we do not attack the child's personality or character. [Ginott, 1965, pp. 57–58]

BEING A COMPETENT PARENT

Once a decision has been made to become a parent, an individual is committed to being a teacher and a caregiver. Parents have always had this function of teaching their children the skills and knowledge that they will need to function as effective adults in society. The rapid changes in society have affected family functioning in contemporary times. Other institutions in society have assumed many of the family's primary functions, so that children and their socialization are the main concerns of parents today.

Socialization has the goal of preparing children for their future. In light of the rapidly changing nature of the world, how does a parent know what his child needs to know to be an effective adult? In the past, parents knew fairly well what life in their children's future would be like, and the children were prepared accordingly. The parent of today may find it difficult to be completely sure what life will be like next year and may be much less sure of life ten years from now. It takes years of training today to be considered competent in a skilled occupation or profession. Our culture prepares people for technical jobs through education. Someone who is competent needs to refresh his skills or update his knowledge constantly. Although our society does an adequate job of preparing and maintaining the competence of individuals in the vocational aspects of life, people are prepared inadequately for the work of parenting. There is little formal education or training offered in this field. Society delegates the responsibility of socializing children to their parents but does little to prepare adults for this responsibility. Parenting, in effect, is left to trial-and-error learning by individuals who must prepare the next generation to cope emotionally and socially with the future.

There is little wonder why people may feel overwhelmed by the prospect as well as the tasks of parenting. They develop feelings of frustration and disappointment but especially the feeling of incompetence to do an adequate job of teaching their children. Pickards and Fargo (1971), in discussing the need for parent education, state that parents need to determine what values are important to transmit to children today to help them cope with changes in society in the future. These values should include a commitment to (1) personal integrity; (2) the use of one's abilities to the fullest degree in a contributive manner; (3) rationality; (4) the acquisition of abstract knowledge for its own sake; (5) effective coping with an environment that is seen as masterable; and (6) the use of self-restraint in consideration of others' needs. These values can be taught to children, but parents may wonder how this can be accomplished.

The childhood experiences of today's parents are different from what children experience today. The parents who raised those people who are parents today also were affected by this time lag in preparing children for their future. The isolated, nuclear family of today has few supports from outside itself to assist in child rearing. Modern behavioral science has made many attempts to fill the void created in the modern nuclear family by proposing methods of child guidance that can be conflicting in philosophy, content, and expected results. Parents have been and continue to be bombarded by articles in magazines and books on parenting that describe approaches suggested by academic advice-givers on how to raise children.

The competent parent of today is one who develops a variety of approaches for guiding children. Although there are a number of strategies for child rearing available, each usually focuses on fostering the emotional needs of both parents and children. Some of these strategies are therapeutic in nature, others attempt to resolve or prevent conflicts between parents and children, and others propose a more humanitarian approach for conducting parent–child interaction. These approaches and strategies for parenting are eagerly embraced by adults who need the information because they may have found the models of parenting learned from their own parents inadequate for guiding their behavior as contemporary parents.

STRATEGIES OF CONTEMPORARY PARENTING

The discussion of changes in caregiving over time showed the rise and fall of a number of strategies for caregiving. What was appropriate for one generation became inappropriate for the next. The increasing knowledge of human development and behavior contributed to much of this vacillation in advice giving. In exploring these philosophies in their interactions with children, the public have come to realize that there is no one adequate recipe for being an effective, competent parent. There continues, however, to be a large number of publications each year on how to achieve this status, and they sell well to the public.

Four contemporary strategies for parenting are distinct from others that have appeared within the last fifteen years. The popularity of these strategies lies in their being effective but not absolute methods for guiding parent–child interactions. These strategies include (1) the democratic approach of Rudolph Driekurs (1958); (2) the humanistic approach represented by Haim Ginott (1965); (3) the parent-effectiveness strategy of Thomas Gordon (1975); and (4) the transactional analysis approach of Eric Berne (1961, 1964). Each of these strategies should be considered representative of applied modern behavioral science. None of them gives a guarantee of consistent results in its applications to parenting. Each of these approaches is briefly described here.

General Characteristics of the Four Strategies

The four approaches discussed here have common characteristics. For the most part, each strategy attempts to achieve certain goals in the interactions between parents and children.

1. *Reduction of parental power.* Most strategies attempt to lessen the degree of power of the parent in controlling children's behavior. These strategies can be considered child-oriented methods of child rearing that recognize the children's needs in relation to those of the parent. Interactions between parents and children have the inherent quality of accentuating the power of parents. The greater physical size and strength of the parent contributes to his greater power over the child.

Power in itself is not seen by the advocates of these strategies as being the cause of difficulties in parent–child interactions. Rather it is the way power is used by the parent that causes difficulties, and children are usually pictured as the victims of parental power. Power assertion by parents has not received a good report by investigators when they have examined the effects of such methods on child behavior. Power-assertive methods of controlling child behavior include physical punishment, such as spanking, and psychological punishment, such as shaming or making derogatory remarks about a child's character. These methods have been found to produce a variety of reactions in children that range from high anxiety levels to inhibition of creative abilities. The contemporary strategies of parent–child relations recognize the tendency of adults to adopt such power-assertive methods in interactions based on their past exposure to the model presented by their own parents. These contemporary strategies act to educate adults in new patterns of egalitarian interaction with children.

2. *Improving children's self-control.* These patterns focus on democratic interactions that attempt to teach children self-control as they progress through the more advanced levels of development. The parents transfer some portion of their power to the child by teaching him to take greater responsibility for his own actions. In achieving this goal, parents hope to spend less time and emotional energy in policing their child's behavior so that interactions can concentrate on building emotional bonds and meeting emotional needs within the family.

3. *Accentuating nurturance in caregiving.* Each strategy attempts to accentuate the aspects of teaching and caring for children within the parental role. Several strategies encourage parents to adopt a counselor role by listening to children's problems in an understanding and helpful manner (see Figure 1-3). Certain interactions with children call for a parent to respond to feelings and emotions expressed by children in a manner that is both appropriate and encouraging of their emotional growth. Although it may not seem the case to parents who are unfamiliar with these strategies, controlling children's behavior does not or should not occupy the majority of their attention in interactions with children, according to the advocates of these strategies. There are times when a parent takes a therapeutic role in interactions with children and caregiving is generated through empathetic understanding of a child's problem. Parents are taught by these strategies to counsel their child but not preach to him or attempt to solve his problem for him.

4. *Understanding children's behavior.* Most strategies teach parents to learn the causes of children's behavior. Principles of child growth and de-

Figure 1-3.

velopment are included in the instructions parents are given for particular patterns of interaction. Parents are taught to recognize how differing levels of development cause differing problems and changes in children's needs.

Driekurs's Democratic Child-Training Strategy

The writings of Rudolph Driekurs and his colleague (Dinkmeyer and Driekurs, 1963; Driekurs, 1958) represent a strategy of parenting based on a number of assumptions:

1. Behavior is purposive or caused; it does not merely happen.
2. It is necessary to understand behavior in its social context.
3. Goals of behavior explain actions.
4. To understand a child's behavior, one needs to understand the child's interpretation of the events he experiences.
5. Belonging to social groups is a basic need of people, both young and old.
6. People, including children, develop a life plan that guides their behavioral decisions even though these decisions may be based on faulty assumptions.

These assumptions form the basis for the manner that should guide a parent's interactions with a child, according to Driekurs. The starting point for developing an effective, loving relationship with a child is for the adult to learn the impact of the family unit in shaping a child's emerging patterns of behavior. The family is seen by Driekurs as the child's model for social interaction. The life plan—that is, the consistent pattern of decision making that guides behavior—is encouraged and developed first within the family. The life plan is based on decisions about behavior that relate to how goals are reached. It is a plan of behavior that a child discovers to be effective in solving particular problems. As children grow older, logic is developed to justify actions constituting the life plan.

Driekurs believes that there are four basic goals of misbehavior that occur from flaws in the logic of the life plan. These include (1) *attention getting* that is either positive or negative and makes others notice the child ("showing off" or crying, for example); (2) social *power* that the child uses to control others by doing what he or she wants and refusing to cooperate with others; (3) *revenge* is antagonistic behavior by which a child makes a niche in a group by making others hate him; and (4) *displaying inadequacy,* in which failure in all endeavors is expected and is used by the child to escape participation with others.

A child's order of birth and position among siblings act to shape the life plan that is adopted. Competition for parents' attention, alliances that emerge between siblings, and different parental expectations for behavior among siblings account for differences in life plans and personalities of children from the same family, according to Driekurs. The firstborn child, for example, may learn to adopt behavior patterns that work toward the goal of power or power with revenge first in interaction with siblings and parents and later with those from outside the family group. Being the oldest child carries responsibilities and higher behavioral expectations from parents. Competition for parental attention and affection may be intense with the next child, who is seen as an adversary who usurped the former position of the firstborn in receiving the majority of attention from parents.

The second child is made to feel inferior to the older through their interactions. The older child makes the younger child feel that he has to catch up with or be better than the older sibling, according to Driekurs. This child may learn patterns of behavior that display inadequacy or power with revenge in interactions with others.

The middle child may learn power-oriented or attention-getting styles of behavior to make himself noticed among the other siblings. The baby of the family may learn patterns that achieve getting others' attention or that display inadequacy.

Driekurs's approach is well known for a particular method of child training that features teaching the child the *logical consequences* of his behavior. The democratic aspect of his philosophy of guidance emphasizes the equality of all family members in working together for the efficient functioning of the group. Social groups function well when the individuals understand and follow rules that govern the behavior of all, according to Driekurs. Parents as well as children are encouraged to discuss family rules and the reasons underlying the rules. For example, a mother may wish to serve family meals at certain times. It is unfair treatment of her and other family members to be late and delay a meal. Stragglers to mealtime interrupt the gathering, make the server angry, and upset one of the few times that the family can interact as a group during the day. The rule is established, then, that meals are served at a particular time. The logical consequences of breaking the rule are established by the family. For example, if anyone arrives late for a meal, the logical consequences may be eating alone, eating cold food, cleaning up his or her own dishes, and so on.

When parents use logical consequences to teach the effect or results of behavior, Driekurs believes that children quickly learn to control and take greater responsibility for their actions. The most difficult aspect of this method is for parents to enforce the logical consequences of the rules. It takes courage to allow a child to learn, sometimes quite harshly, the effects of his behavior on himself and on others. By experiencing the consequences of his behavior, a child is thought to learn to conform to expected standards that ensure the fair treatment of all family members. Parents, through methods such as these, encourage children to learn effective ways of interpersonal interaction.

Ginott's Humanistic Strategy

Haim Ginott's text *Between Parent and Child* (1965) represents one of the early contemporary strategies aimed at improving communications between parents and children. Ginott's philosophy of parent–child relations focuses on the avoidance of conflicts by showing parents how to listen to children and how to get children's full attention. Parents are shown as well how to look for the "hidden meanings" of children's communications. Ginott's strategy educates parents in taking a therapeutic, counselor role with children and in communicating their feelings to their children.

Much of what Ginott advocates for effective communications with children derives from the methods that were developed in progressive nursery schools during the 1940s and 1950s. These methods were formalized by Ginott into a more readable and understandable format for the average parent. The major points of his strategy for facilitating interaction and communication between parents and children include the following:

1. *Communications with children are based on respect and skill.* Parents are advised not to attack or criticize a child's personality or character but to focus on the offensive behavior. For example, Ginott suggests that parents not say, "It's not nice of you to call other children bad names," or "If I have to ask you once more to stop doing that, you're going to be in BIG trouble!" Rather parents are taught to look for the reasons that motivate children to misbehave, be angry, and so on. A typical Ginott-type response would be, "I'm angry and very irritated at what you've done; not at you." The adult is shown that he can help a child learn how to express his emotions, how to label these for future recognition, and how to react in the future in similar situations. Parents reinforce more positive self-concepts of their children, in Ginott's opinion, if the behavior of the child is distinguished from the child who performs it.

2. *Praise and positive reinforcement should not be overused by parents.* When these are used, they should be directed to reinforcing a child's realistic attempts and accomplishments rather than to communicating how "good" he is.

3. *In dealing with conflicts or stress in interactions with children,* Ginott advises: (1) that some children's behavior makes adults angry; (2) that adults are entitled to feel angry at children's behavior without feeling guilty or ashamed; and (3) that adults should express their feelings without attacking the child's personality or character. To get children to listen to their parents, Ginott suggests that the parents use words that the children may never have heard before. These words also express feelings, such as, "I don't like it when you act so obnoxious to your sister."

4. *A number of patterns of parent–child interaction are considered by Ginott to be self-defeating.* Threats are invitations for misbehavior to occur because children are dared to repeat some forbidden act. Bribes gain only short-lived changes in children's behavior. They communicate doubt about a child's ability to change. Sarcastic comments only serve to make children feel bad about themselves, and children soon learn not to listen to parents who moralize and preach about their faults and shortcomings.

5. *Communication becomes more effective when physical differences are*

minimized between parents and children. One way to achieve this is by getting on eye level with children. One can accomplish this by squatting by them, sitting down with them, or holding them on the lap.

6. *Children can learn to take increasing responsibility for their behavior as they grow older.* Children can learn this by being offered choices between acceptable alternatives in their behavior. Instead of asking, "What do you want to wear this morning?" Ginott suggests that parents say, "Do you want to wear the blue pants or the green ones?"

7. *Discipline and responsibility are learned by children through reasonable limits that they can understand.* Comments such as "Stop doing that" identify unacceptable acts but fail to guide children into acceptable behaviors. Alternatives should be given: "If you need to hit something, Tommy, use the sofa cushion; not your sister"; or "Tell your sister how angry you are; don't use your fists to communicate."

8. *Physical punishment is less effective and more damaging to a child than verbal communication.* Children's misbehavior and conflicts can be handled more effectively by discussion of the problem. Physical punishment communicates the idea that "big people can hit little people without repercussions."

Ginott's approach to parent–child relations met with great acceptance among the public. His suggestions are a consistent recognition of a child's contributions to relations with parents in influencing their behavior toward him. These methods, although not unique to professionals, are based on sound child guidance principles that promote effective communications and the mental health of both parents and children.

Gordon's Parent Effectiveness Training

Thomas Gordon's *Parent Effectiveness Training* (1975) represents a more recent humanistic strategy in parent–child relations. The text is an outgrowth of a course developed by Gordon for teaching parents how to be more effective in their caregiving activities. The method focuses primarily on communication skills developed by the parent and a method of resolving conflicts between the parent and the child. As with other humanistic methods, this strategy teaches the parent when to act as a counselor to children and when to communicate his or her feelings and reactions to children regarding their behavior. The strategy is firmly grounded in proven counseling methods developed by other professionals and applied to parenting skills by Gordon. New words and phrases are used by Gordon to describe these techniques. As with other strategies of parenting, Parent Effectiveness Training (PET) provides a useful battery of techniques. Although there is a good possibility that these methods will work well when performed appropriately by parents, overuse may lead children to "tune out" the parents.

PET, like other strategies, has many significant features that achieve a more effective manner of communicating and interacting with children. The major features include the following:

1. *The parent acts as a counselor when a child has some particular problem.* In such situations, PET involves the use of *active listening*. This technique is commonly used in certain counseling methods. As it is applied to parent–child relations, a child may come to the parent complaining of some particular problem or difficulty. The parent sifts through the statements of the child to determine the feelings that are being covertly communicated. (This is similar to what Ginott means by determining the "hidden meaning" of children's communications.) The parent feeds back only what he or she understands the child to mean through the communications. The point here is for the parent to understand and reflect back to the child what is troubling the child. By employing active listening, the parent does not solve the child's problem. The responsibility is on the child to search for solutions through the opportunity provided by the parent as an interested but objective party. For example, a child comes to his dad complaining that nobody wants to play with him. In this interchange, notice how the father uses active listening to help the child solve his problem:

DAD: Why aren't you playing with the other kids?

BOY: Nobody wants to play with me.

DAD: You feel that you don't have any friends and that makes you feel bad, huh?

BOY: Yeah. I hate Tommy and all the others.

DAD: You just hate all of them.

BOY: Yeah. Especially Tommy.

DAD: He's the worst, huh?

BOY: That's right. He makes fun of me. I don't always throw the ball right.

DAD: It really makes you feel bad when he teases you.

BOY: You bet. It's not nice to treat anybody that way.

DAD: You feel that Tommy shouldn't be ugly to you for making mistakes.

BOY: Yeah. He calls me names.

DAD: You don't like to be called names.

BOY: No. I wouldn't do that to him.

DAD: You get along better with Tommy if he doesn't call you names, huh?

BOY: You bet. I'm his friend but I don't like to be called names.

DAD: You think you're Tommy's friend, and friends should be nice to each other.

BOY: Yeah. Friends help each other. Maybe I can ask Tommy to show me how to throw the ball better. Then he won't call me names.

This hypothetical interchange allowed the father to help his son to express feelings about the real issue that bothered him: being treated unfairly by his friend. The child's initial statement had many underlying feelings, messages, and meanings that the father helped him to identify. The father did not place himself in the position of preaching, admonishing, moralizing, or degrading his son for his feelings. He didn't offer a number of his own solutions for the child's problem. He did recognize the child's feelings of hurt and rejection. It served to teach the child that he could reach his own insights with the helpful guidance of the father.

2. *All interactions between parents and children do not call for the parent to fulfill a therapeutic role.* There are frequent occasions when the child's behavior is a problem for the parents. The child usually doesn't see his behavior as troublesome even when it is for the parent. In such situations, Gordon suggests that parents use strongly phrased "I" messages to communicate their feelings to children. This is the method that is used to get children to listen to parents and is similar to Ginott's approach. According to Gordon, "I" messages differ from the "you" messages that parents send in communications with children. Notice from the last section on active listening that the father used many sentences starting with *you.* These messages indicated that the father was listening to the child's communications. When "I" messages are used, however, the parent wants the child to listen to him. For example, "*I* can't work well if you continue to bang on the piano," or "*I* get really angry and upset when you don't come after I call you." These types of messages communicate facts and help a child to modify the behavior that is unacceptable to the parent. "I" messages are less likely to promote resistance and rebellion from children, according to Gordon, and place the responsibility for changing the child's behavior on him and not on the parent.

3. *When conflicts occur that can't be avoided, Gordon suggests that parents use the "no-lose" method of conflict resolution.* In this method, parent and child reach a compromise that is satisfactory to both. Neither parent nor child wins or loses in resolving the conflict because both come to an understanding of the mutual needs being satisfied. Gordon lists six steps for implementing this technique: (1) identify and define the conflict; (2) generate possible alternative solutions; (3) evaluate these solutions; (4) decide on the best solution for both parties; (5) work out ways to implement the solution; and (6) evaluate how well the solution worked. These steps can be illustrated as follows. "I" messages are used by a parent to identify and define a problem for the child, such as "I've been very upset lately because you've been coming home too late from school. I worry so much about you, I can't get anything done." Possible solutions are generated when the parent says something like, "What can *we* do to solve this?" Solutions are elicited at this point from the child, and both parent and child evaluate them. The child, for example, may suggest, "Well, I suppose I could keep better track of time. If you would get me a watch, I'd know when to stop playing and come home." If this solution is acceptable, the parent might respond by saying, "Let's try it out to see if this will work." The next step involves determining if the solution has worked and if improvements need to be made in the compromise.

The advantages of this technique listed by Gordon include (1) placing part of the responsibility for conflict resolution with the child; (2) encouraging the development of a child's cognitive skills in suggesting solutions; (3) increasing communications that leave nondestructive emotional effects on both parent and child; (4) eliminating the parent's need to express power; and (5) encouraging autonomous behavior from the child.

Gordon's three basic methods are similar to Ginott's approach of conversing with children, but they differ in the absence of limits being set on children's behavior by parents. His strategy is significant in recognizing the influence of children's behavior on that of parents and in showing how to teach children to recognize the rights and needs of parents. Perhaps even more importantly, ways are provided for parents to interact on a more equal basis with children instead of relying on power-assertive methods that damage children's self-concepts. Gordon recognizes that there are times when active listening, "I" messages, or the "no-lose" method are inappropriate, as when a child's safety is endangered. However, these methods are generally good and useful skills.

Berne's Transactional Analysis Strategy

Transactional analysis (TA) is a theory of psychotherapy that was originally developed by Eric Berne (1961, 1964) and has been adapted for use in understanding interpersonal relations. It had not been extensively applied to parent–child relations until recently (Babcock and Keepers, 1976; Freed, 1971, 1973, 1976). Full acquaintance with this theory requires intensive study and developing an understanding of the vocabulary and language unique to the concepts. Several publications are available, however, that have had a special appeal to the general public, such as *I'm OK—You're OK* (Harris, 1969).

The theory provides a means for individuals to analyze their interactions with others to facilitate communication. A *transaction* is a stimulus piece of communication by one person and its accompanying response by another. The response of the other becomes a new stimulus for a response by the first person and so on until the interchange ends. The purpose of analyzing transactions is to determine which part of each person's ego state generates each stimulus and response in interactions with others.

According to the theory, an individual has three ego states of his personality (see Figure 1-4). Each of these ego states is seen as being something of a separate entity within the personality that guides interactions with and reactions to others. The first ego state to be developed by an individual is the *child*. This part of the personality psychologically records the feelings and heightened emotional states of our humanity, such as "creativity, intuition, and spontaneous drive and enjoyment" (Berne, 1964). The second ego state is called the *parent*. It is developed simultaneously with the child ego state and

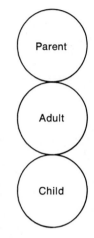

Figure 1-4. Ego states of the personality. (From *I'm OK—You're OK*, by Thomas A. Harris, M.D. Copyright © 1967, 1968, 1969 by Thomas A. Harris, M.D. By permission of Harper & Row, Publishers, Inc.)

psychologically records a number of rules, regulations, and behavior patterns that judge actions and govern behavior. The third ego state is called the *adult*. This ego state processes information from the parent and the child ego states, as well as from itself, in dealing with the reality of the moment at hand. The adult ego state takes information given it from the parent state to determine if the transaction is valid and true for that moment, and information from the child state to determine if a particular feeling is appropriate in response to a transaction. The adult state comes to a decision using this information that Harris calls, "I'm OK—you're OK" or some other combination, such as "I'm OK—you're not OK," and so on.

When individuals interact, the ego states of both are involved. Communication proceeds efficiently under a variety of circumstances but especially when transactions between ego states of individuals are parallel or complementary. For example, parent–parent transactions between two individuals' ego states smooth the flow of communication, as do child–child and parent–child transactions (see Figure 1-5). Communication ceases or conflicts are experienced when transactions between individuals are uncomplementary or crossed (see Figure 1-6). This situation occurs through a variety of combinations of transactions. In an example from Berne (1964), a transaction may begin when a husband asks his wife: "Dear, where are my cuff links?" An appropriate adult-state comment from the wife would be, "In your top left dresser drawer." However, circumstances may be that the wife has had it with lost cuff links and an inattentive husband. She replies with a parent-state comment that is directed to his child state, such as "They're where you left them!"

Transactional analysis is applied to parent–child relations by emphasizing

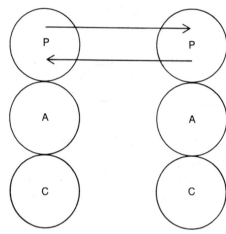

Figure 1-5. A transaction between two Parent ego states of individuals. This is a complementary transaction. (From *I'm OK—You're OK,* by Thomas A. Harris, M.D. Copyright © 1967, 1968, 1969 by Thomas A. Harris, M.D. By permission of Harper & Row, Publishers, Inc.)

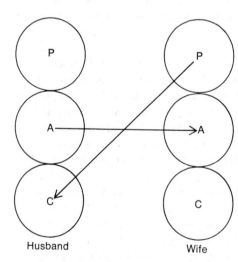

Figure 1-6. A crossed transaction between two individuals. The husband initiates an Adult state transaction aimed at the wife's Adult ego state. The wife responds instead with a response from her Parent ego state aimed at the husband's Child ego state. Crossed transactions cause conflict (From *I'm OK—You're OK,* by Thomas A. Harris, M.D. Copyright © 1967, 1968, 1969 by Thomas A. Harris, M.D. By permission of Harper & Row, Publishers, Inc.)

the parent's analysis of transactions between himself and the child (Harris, 1969). The parent learns to recognize an overuse of responses to children that are largely derived from the parent state or the child state. These are inappropriate for handling interactions effectively. Most conflicts, from the TA point of view, are produced when the parent makes an adult-state request and receives a child- or parent-state response from the child. This provokes a child-state response from the adult, and effective communication ceases. TA encourages the parent to consistently develop his adult so that that child can have an appropriate model for developing his own adult ego state. This level of interaction teaches the child appropriate methods of behavior because children are developing their adult state by using the model presented by the parent. By emphasizing what parents can achieve through adult-state responses that are nonjudgmental in nature, TA seeks to change the nature of parent–child relations so that children's behavior will change in the process. TA also has the objective of teaching children when to recognize which ego state they are using in interactions with parents and other individuals. When children learn the vocabulary of TA, it becomes possible for them to point out to parents as well as to themselves when someone is not using his adult state in interpersonal interaction.

TA emphasizes the importance of *strokes* in effecting good communications with others and in building self-confidence. Physically strokes are touching others in a nurturant, positive manner. Psychologically strokes are a recognition of others by interaction with them. They can be either positive or negative and either conditional or unconditional types of social reinforcement. For example, when someone says to another, "I like you a lot," this statement is an unconditional positive stroke. Likewise, when someone makes the statement, "I'll spank you if you don't do as I ask," the person is making a conditional negative stroke in interpersonal interaction. The position of TA theory is that people need to determine the type of strokes they need from others. The majority of strokes may be one type or another, and children learn to expect these strokes in interactions with parents. Babcock and Keepers (1976) note that children receive a heavy dose of conditional strokes in families that are achievement-oriented. These children learn to perform as expected and are reinforced by the type and frequency of the strokes used within the family. The manner that is developed within the family for providing and withholding strokes is called a *stroke economy,* according to Babcock and Keepers. By learning to recognize how strokes are used and what type are used, parents can determine the nature and frequency of strokes that children need and desire. If strokes are used in an appropriate manner to fulfill children's needs, TA theory assumes that the communication, interaction, and behavior of all family members will be maximized.

POINTS TO CONSIDER

- Young people today have greater freedom in choosing if and when to become parents.

- There are a variety of reasons for choosing to become a parent that are largely psychological and social in nature.
- The parenthood role has several cultural meanings that may act to motivate people to assume this role.
- Our current ideas of parenthood and childhood have evolved and changed over historical time. What have been considered "good" child-rearing methods have also changed over time.
- A competent parent today is one who prepares himself for this role by acquiring knowledge of child growth and development as well as a variety of methods that facilitate parent–child relations.
- A number of contemporary strategies for improving parent–child relations are available to parents. Each offers unique techniques and methods for educating adults in new patterns of interaction with children.

REFERENCES

ALLEN, A. A mother's influence. *Mother's Assistant,* 1848, *13*(5), 97–100.

ARIES, P. *Centuries of childhood.* (Translated by R. Baldick.) New York: Knopf, 1962.

BABCOCK, D., and KEEPERS, T. *Raising kids OK.* New York: Grove Press, 1976.

BERNE, E. *Transactional analysis in psychotherapy.* New York: Grove Press, 1961.

BERNE, E. *Games people play.* New York: Grove Press, 1964.

BIGNER, J. Parent education in popular literature: 1950–1970. *Family Coordinator,* 1972, *21*, 313–319.

CALHOUN, A. *A social history of the American family,* Vols. 1–3. New York: Barnes and Noble, 1945.

COOLIDGE, E. Young mother's registry. *Ladies' Home Journal,* 1920, *37*, 44.

DEWEES, W. *Treatise on the physical and medical treatment of children.* Philadelphia: Carey and Lea, 1826.

DINKMEYER, D., and DRIEKURS, R. *Encouraging children to learn.* Englewood Cliffs, N. J.: Prentice-Hall, 1963.

DRIEKURS, R. *The challenge of parenthood* (rev. ed.). New York: Duell, Sloan, & Pearce, 1958.

ERIKSON, E. *Childhood and society.* New York: Norton, 1950.

ESPENSHADE, T. *The value and cost of children.* Washington, D.C.: Population Reference Bureau, 1977.

FREED, A. *TA for kids.* Sacramento, Calif.: Jalmar Press, 1971.

FREED, A. *TA for tots.* Sacramento, Calif.: Jalmar Press, 1973.

FREED, A. *TA for teens.* Sacramento, Calif.: Jalmar Press, 1976.

GINOTT, H. *Between parent and child.* New York: Macmillan, 1965.

GORDON, T. *Parent effectiveness training: The tested way to raise responsible children* (rev. ed.). New York: Peter Wyden, 1975.

HARRIS, T. *I'm OK—You're OK* (rev. ed.). New York: Harper & Row, 1969.

HUNT, D. *Parents and children in history.* Cambridge, Mass.: Harvard University Press, 1970.

LeMasters, E. *Parents in modern America* (rev. ed.). Homewood, Ill.: Dorsey, 1974.

Locke, J. *Some thoughts concerning education* (4th ed. enlarged). London: A. & J. Churchill, 1699.

Mann, H., and Peabody, E. *Moral culture of infancy and kindergarten guide.* Boston: Burnham, 1863.

Mead, M., and Wolfenstein, M. (Eds.) *Childhood in contemporary cultures.* Chicago: University of Chicago Press, 1955.

Pickards, E., and Fargo, J. *Parent education: Toward parental competence.* New York: Appleton-Century-Crofts, 1971.

Plateris, A. Divorces: Analysis of changes. *Vital and Health Statistics,* 1973, *21,* Whole No. 22 DHEW Publication No. (HSM) 73-1900.

Rabin, A. Motivation for parenthood. *Journal of Projective Techniques,* 1965, *29,* 405–411.

Ribble, M. *The rights of infants.* New York: Columbia University Press, 1943.

Rousseau, J. *Émile, or On education.* (Translated by B. Foxley.) London: Dent, 1911. (Original French edition published, 1762.)

Silverman, A., and Silverman, A. *The case against having children.* New York: David McKay, 1971.

Spitz, R. Hospitalism. In O. Fenichel et al. (Eds.), *The psychoanalytical study of the child,* Vol. 1. New York: International Universities Press, 1945.

Spock, B. *The common sense book of baby and child care.* New York: Duell, Sloan, & Pearce, 1946.

Stendler, C. Sixty years of child training practices. *Journal of Pediatrics,* 1950, *36,* 122–134.

Sunley, R. Early nineteenth century American literature on child rearing. In M. Mead and M. Wolfenstein (Eds.), *Childhood in contemporary cultures.* Chicago: University of Chicago Press, 1955. Pp. 150–167.

U.S. Bureau of the Census. *Census of the population: General social and economic characteristics.* Washington, D.C.: The Bureau, 1970.

Veevers, J. The social meanings of parenthood. *Psychiatry,* 1973, *36,* 291–310.

Vincent, C. Trends in infant care ideas. *Child Development,* 1951, *22,* 199–209.

Watson, J. *Psychological care of infant and child.* New York: Norton, 1928.

Winch, R. *The modern family* (3rd ed.). New York: Holt, 1971.

2

Individual Parenting Roles

Most of us had occasion as children to wonder why our parents behaved in some particular manner. Sometimes the behavior in question made no sense at all to us. At other times, it was clearly in line with what we expected.

One of the lessons learned by individuals who grow up in homes where both parents are present is that a mother behaves differently from a father in many ways and also that the parents share many similar functions in caregiving. There are several factors that motivate parental behavior. One of the most significant of these is the influence of the model of parenting behavior one observes from one's own parents. Because society provides little formal education for parenting, the relation between parents and children acts as a proving ground for adults in learning the role behaviors of parents. These factors, however, do not completely explain why parents behave as they do. Why, for example, do mothers behave differently from fathers, or is there a difference in the functions of mothers and fathers in caregiving? Are mothers more important to children's development than fathers, particularly during the years of a child's infancy? These questions and others are examined in this chapter on the parenting roles of mothers and fathers.

DETERMINANTS OF PARENTING BEHAVIOR

A variety of factors contribute to the development of an individual's behavior as a parent. Several variables are known to contribute to the parent's style of interaction in relating to children. Some factors that influence parenting behavior come from our past experiences, and new ones are added as we learn how to behave as a parent. Certainly the contribution of a child to the learning of the parental role is very apparent as the child grows and de-

36

velops, causing changes in the ways adults respond to him. Certain factors, however, are brought to the parenting role by an individual as a result of his past experiences in interactions with others and from his experiences in growing up. Traditionally these predisposing factors of parenting behavior are grouped to include (1) *cultural influences,* such as social class or peer value systems; (2) *personality patterns;* (3) *attitudes toward parenting;* and (4) *role modeling,* or one's unconscious learning of parenting behavior from one's own parents (Johnson and Medinnus, 1974).

Cultural Influences

A great deal of research was conducted some twenty years ago on the assumption that social-class variations in child-rearing patterns resulted in personality and behavioral differences in children. The idea was that differences in social-class value systems caused corresponding differences in the way children were reared. Differences were found between social groups in the values taught to children and in what were considered to be the expected behaviors of children. These patterns of child rearing were thought to be perpetuated from one generation to the next.

Numerous studies at this time reported considerable differences between social groups in the way that children were reared. For example, middle-class families were found to use harshness in relating to children more than lower-class families. Middle-class families taught children to delay the immediate gratification of their needs and desires (Davis and Havighurst, 1946). These studies were refuted in later years (Miller and Swanson, 1958; Bronfenbrenner, 1958). The later studies concluded that differences in child rearing between social groups had diminished since the original studies were performed. The increase in similarity between social groups in child-rearing patterns was attributed to such factors as the increased availability of television (with many programs that featured middle-class values) and increases in lower-class families' ability to achieve upward mobility into the middle class as a result of better-paying jobs.

Although the general differences in child rearing between social groups have diminished, certain values and behavior patterns continue to appear in children's behavior. Hess and Shipman (1965, 1968) report that lower-class children's learning styles and their ability to process information differs drastically from those of middle-class children. Their findings suggest that the potential for mental growth is strongly influenced by the differences in language (teaching) styles used by mothers. Apparently the value placed on education and academic achievement in the middle-class home is demonstrated among these mothers, who interact differently with their children in teaching problem-solving behavior. A conclusion can be made that a parent's behavioral choices are guided in part by his or her social-class value system. Each group maintains essentially the same common objective in interacting with children, but differences appear in the style of interaction. Middle-class parents, for example, are known to value social achievement; acquiring abstract knowledge for its own sake; and independence and autonomous behavior early in life. Lower-class parents place greater emphasis on children's conforming to the parents' values and on gratifying needs as conveniently as possible (Hess, 1970).

The child-rearing fads in existence at the time that an individual is actively involved in parenting constitute another cultural influence. The discussion of the historical changes in conceptions of child rearing in Chapter 1 shows how trends come into style and are eventually discarded in favor of something new or different. The influence of modern behavioral science in seeking new understanding of human behavior has prompted many of these changes. In providing newer and sometimes radical advice, "experts" have probably had a greater impact on the middle-class parent than on the lower-class parent. In addition, maternal employment outside of the home has only recently occurred in great numbers among middle-class families. The presence of the full-time mother in the home, who has often been stereotyped as being preoccupied with child rearing, coupled with the accessibility to magazines and television, may account for the readiness of these women to try the recommendations of the academic experts.

Personality of the Parent

Johnson and Medinnus (1974) describe the relationship between parents and children as an emotionally charged one. Conscientious parents are aware of their role in socializing their child. They are usually acutely aware that society expects them to do as good a job as possible in raising their child. Folklore about parenting would lead us to believe that if one is a "good" parent, the result is a "good" child who grows up to be a "good" adult. In addition, a child serves as a mirror to his or her parents, reflecting the parents' own childhood and unresolved conflicts from the past, their present needs and aspirations, and their immortality in the future.

Another important contributing factor is the pervasive atmosphere generated by a parent's personality. Research findings form the idea that what parents *are* and *feel* about themselves and their role may have greater bearing on the relation with a child than the specific actions of child rearing (Sears, Maccoby, and Levin, 1957). Studies indicate that if a parent is seriously maladjusted (neurotic, for example), it is this pervading atmosphere and approach to life that is communicated to the child by the parent (Adorno et al., 1950; Behrens, 1954).

Attitudes Toward Parenting

Closely associated with parents' personalities are their attitudes toward children and child rearing in general. Such attitudes and beliefs are the result of a person's socialization and past experiences. These form the base for behavioral choices that the parent may use in interacting with his child. Diana Baumrind (1966) outlines the three basic types of child-rearing attitudes that follow.

AUTHORITARIAN ATTITUDES.   The parent who relies predominantly on authoritarian controls in child rearing places value on obtaining immediate and long-range obedience from his child. Typically the relationship is one of controlling the child's behavior. Obedience is obtained in numerous ways, often through physical punishment and other forceful methods. Little time or effort is used to explain rules and regulations. A typical response to the child's questioning of rules may be "Because I said so." Usually the parent evaluates and shapes the behavior of the child according to an established and often absolute standard of behavior. The parent's word is law for the child, who is taught to believe that the parent's actions are in the child's best interests. These parents value "keeping the child in his place, . . . restricting his autonomy, and . . . assigning household responsibilities in order to inculcate respect for work" (Baumrind, 1966, p. 890).

PERMISSIVE ATTITUDES.   Parents with permissive attitudes believe that they should respond to their children as individuals and encourage them to be autonomous. Parents who hold these attitudes typically rely on reasoning and manipulation but not on overt demonstrations of power. Parenting behaviors are expressed in ways that communicate these beliefs. For example, the parent is not interested in being viewed by the child as an authority figure or as an ideal person to be imitated so much as being seen as a resource for the child to use. There is a greater latitude permitted in children's behavior. Policies or limits to behavior are determined in consultation with the child in an attempt to allow the child to voice his or her opinion. A permissive-oriented parent "allows the child to regulate his own activities as much as possible, avoids the exercise of control, and does not encourage him to obey externally defined standards" (Baumrind, 1966, p. 889).

AUTHORITATIVE ATTITUDES.   Authoritative attitudes combine the best features of both authoritarian and permissive attitudes. Authoritative-oriented controls emphasize the development of autonomy in children within reasonable limits. Children are allowed a certain amount of latitude in their behavior but are not hemmed in by the authority of the parent. When using these controls, parents may resort to whatever lies within their grasp to achieve control over their child's behavior, such as reasoning, overt power, or psychological reinforcement. A parent who predominantly uses such controls "encourages verbal give and take, shares with the child the reasoning behind the policy, and solicits his objections when he refuses to conform" (Baumrind, 1966, p. 891).

Role Modeling

Because we come to the parental role without the assistance of instincts to guide our behavior, we rely on observation to help us to learn how to be parents. Essentially we appear to use our parents as models of our own parenting behavior. This statement, however, may be an oversimplification. The reactions, perspective, and feelings we have about how we were raised also influence how we approach our own children. Harris (1959) found that if a person who is satisfied not only with the way he or she was raised but also with how she or he "turned out" will probably replicate his or her parents' methods and attitudes. The person who is dissatisfied with his or her parents' methods because of excessive controls or interference tries to be just the opposite as a parent. Another type of response is feeling that one's parents did not give enough love or physical affection. The reaction is usually to overcompensate along these lines with one's own children.

Differences from Other Adult Roles

Parenthood is one of the major roles that an individual may assume in adulthood. In comparing the parental role with other adult roles, Alice Rossi (1968) notes four characteristics that are unique to parenthood:

1. *Women are exposed to greater cultural pressures to assume this role than men.* As children, females are oversocialized toward the parenthood role, and males are undersocialized (Winch, 1971). Girls are encouraged—if not culturally coerced—toward the role through acceptable play activities and being given toys such as dolls (see Figure 2-1). In our culture, we expect girls and boys to prefer certain sex-role-oriented play activities. Although dolls, for example, are available for boys, they are designed as action toys to encourage and stimulate aggressive, adventure-type play rather than the nurturance type of play behavior that a baby doll elicits. Boys' socialization experiences, more than girls', have been directed toward developing competency for future occupational roles outside the home. For the most part, men see the occupational role rather than the parental role as the primary focus of their adult life. Until recently, women's adult status and individual fulfillment have been expected to come from motherhood and performing the major child-rearing duties of the family.

2. *The parental role is not always voluntarily assumed, as compared with other adult roles.* Our culture allows us a certain amount of freedom in choosing occupational roles. We are able to change jobs at almost any point in adult life. People sometimes do not have the opportunity of choice about becoming a parent. Even today, when medical technology provides both men and women with reasonably successful contraceptive methods, unplanned pregnancies continue to occur because of failure to use contraceptives or because of their improper use. Despite recent judicial decisions that allow legal abortions, many women do not choose to terminate an unwanted pregnancy because of a variety of personal, religious, or moral reasons.

"You're lucky, Mommy. You get to do REAL
cleaning and ironing and cooking and..."
Figure 2-1.

3. *The parenthood roles are irrevocable.* Once the decision is made to continue a pregnancy and the birth occurs, one cannot back out of the commitment to become a parent except by placing the child for adoption. Whereas one can quit or be fired from a job, neither a parent nor a child can quit or be fired. Parenthood is a role that can be revoked only in exceptional circumstances.

4. *Preparation for parenting roles is poor as compared with preparation for other adult roles.* Rossi lists four points to illustrate this statement: (a) specific educational experiences for parenthood are lacking in our culture; (b) the experience of pregnancy involves a limited amount of preparation for parenthood; (c) the culture provides little or no guidance for successful parenting behavior; and (d) the transition to parenthood is abrupt.

There is a lack of specific preparenthood training in our educational system. When subjects are taught that deal with family life in high schools, they are usually taught as electives. Students generally receive a minimal amount of exposure (often a semester or less) to this topic. These subjects are sometimes placed in the home economics or social studies areas. Home economics, however, has the inaccurate reputation among the general public of being a feminine-oriented vocational subject. Home economics courses usually enroll larger numbers of females than males. Newly developed curricula, such as the Exploring Childhood program, have appeared in recent years. These programs concentrate on providing child development information, training for parenting skills, opportunities for peer interaction, and practical experiences in working with young children. These programs are filling a much needed gap in preparenthood training and are attracting males as well as females.

CHARACTERISTICS OF THE PARENTING ROLES

Over the past several years, the women's liberation movement has encouraged the idea that fewer distinctions should be made between the roles of men and women. In particular, a trend in the blurring of parental role functions has been occurring since World War II (LeMasters, 1974).

Sociologists describe the role of wife–mother and husband–father in sex-role-related terms (Parsons and Bales, 1955). The wife–mother role is seen as having *expressive* characteristics. This term refers to expressions of affection, warmth, and emotional support of other family members (see Figure 2-2). The functions of this role, from this traditional viewpoint, are those of being the mediator, comforter, and consoler of the family members (Zelditch,

Copyright 1977,
The Register and Tribune
Syndicate, Inc.

"Got some room left in that hug, Mommy?"

Figure 2-2.

1955). The husband–father role is characterized by *instrumental* functions and qualities. These are described as being managerial and administrative in nature, from the traditional point of view. The father is seen as being the final judge and executor of punishment, discipline, and control of the children's behavior (Zelditch, 1955; see Figure 2-3).

Changes in social attitudes have stimulated people to think in terms of *androgynous* parenting roles, that is, roles that have similar functions. This line of thought stresses that parenting roles, whether performed by mothers or fathers, should have qualities that are similar rather than distinct from one another. The introduction of increasing numbers of women into the labor force may have stimulated this redirection in thinking about the nature of the parenting roles. Women have probably incorporated both instrumental and expressive aspects into their mothering behavior since the Industrial Revolution because of the less direct involvement of the father in child rear-

" THEN HOW 'BOUT 'GET TO *HEAVEN* OUTA MY ROOM'? IS *THAT* OKAY?"

Figure 2-3.

ing. The emphasis today, however, takes the form of encouraging men to incorporate a balance of expressive aspects in addition to the instrumental qualities already expected of them as fathers.

Robert Winch (1971) discusses two functions of parenting behavior that may be shared by both mothers and fathers. The *nurturance* function has been traditionally or culturally assigned to the wife–mother (expressive) role. *Nurturance* may be defined in both narrow and broad terms. A narrow interpretation of this function refers to the daily maintainance aspects of child care, such as feeding, bathing, and dressing children. Defined more broadly, nurturance is seen as the psychological process of emotional gratification and meeting emotional needs through words, actions, and physical touch. In other words, the emotional tone of interactions associated with nurturance, whether performed by a mother or a father, is warmth. *Control* is the second parental function which has traditionally been placed within the instrumental role of the husband–father. Control is based on the parent's exercise of authority and responsibility for the child's welfare (see Figure 2-4). In this

"THEY **LIKE** TO PUNISH ME. MAKES 'EM FEEL **BIG!**"

Figure 2-4.

sense, the exercise of control is seen as the mechanism underlying the socialization of children into behavior patterns, values, and attitudes that are believed to be appropriate and important.

Wesley Becker (1964) describes a model of parenting behavior that shows the operation of the control function of parenting behavior. The model is based on a sophisticated statistical analysis of previous research on parental discipline. This analysis suggests that three broad dimensions can be used to describe the control function of parenting behavior. Becker's model is shown in Figure 2-5. An adequate understanding of the presentation requires that the graph be pictured in a three-dimensional manner.

Behavior on all three dimensions is shown to occur in graduated degrees that range from one extreme type on a continuum to the opposite. The restrictiveness–permissiveness dimension is shown on the horizontal plane. Becker defines parental restrictiveness as the parent's strict enforcement of demands on the child's behavior, including obedience, not showing aggression, developing good table manners, taking care of property, and so on. The warmth–hostility dimension is shown on the vertical plane. At the warmth end this dimension includes parental behavior that shows tenderness and affection, the giving of reasons and explanations for discipline, low use of physical punishment, and so on. Hostile parent behavior is the opposite extreme of warm behavior. The anxious emotional involvement–calm detachment dimension should be visualized as projecting out on the page, perpendicular to the other dimensions in space. The anxious dimension is characterized by behavior such as babying the child and showing highly emotional responses to the child's behavior. Calm, detached behavior is the opposite.

The graph includes a number of parenting types, such as the indulgent parent, the authoritarian, and the overprotective parent. The authoritarian type of parenting behavior is rated high in hostility, restrictiveness, and anxious emotional involvement. An overprotective parent's behavior would be interpreted on the graph as being high in warmth, anxious emotional involvement, and restrictiveness. The democratic parent's behavior would be rated high in permissiveness, warmth, and calm detachment.

THE MOTHERING ROLE

The mothering role is a conspicuous role in our society. It has been and continues to be the primary role to which girls are socialized. For years, motherhood stood as the ultimate proof of a woman's femininity and the core of her adult life. Her identity as a person and the reason for her existence were equated with her role as a mother. The division of labor within the family increasingly emphasized the woman's responsibilities in child rearing over the years. No doubt has existed, until recently, that motherhood should be the primary occupation of women in society. With other changes in family functions, the importance and value of mothering as conceived of in the past

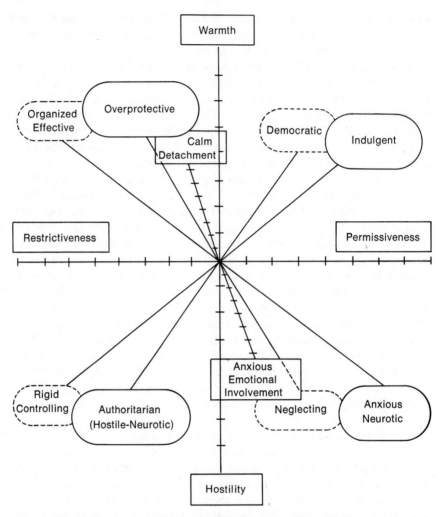

Figure 2-5. Becker's (1964) hypothetical model of parental behavior. (Source: From "Consequences of Different Kinds of Parental Discipline," by Wesley C. Becker, in *Review of Child Development Research*, Volume 1, edited by Martin L. Hoffman and Lois Wladis Hoffman, © 1964 Russell Sage Foundation, New York.)

have been reassessed. Influences from outside the family, such as television, the school, and other agencies, have tended to undermine the formerly important education functions of mothering. Child rearing is now viewed as only one of the many functions that women perform in the family.

Society has yet to find another institution or agency that can completely replace the mother or the father in the socialization and emotional functions of the family. The mother continues in many families to be the primary agent in carrying out the expressive role with her children. The expressive qualities of mothering can be seen in the concepts used to describe a "good" mother. Evelyn Duvall (1946) compared the responses of 433 mothers to the question, "What are five things a good mother does?" The responses were classified into two categories, as either traditional or developmental concepts. Traditional concepts of mothering were interpreted by Duvall as relating to what a mother does for her home and her children (see Table 2-1). These concepts have an all-or-nothing quality. A good mother in the traditional sense is rather rigid, but it should be noted that incorporated into these descriptions are both nurturant and control functions. Developmental concepts differ from the traditional in emphasizing a change from rigidity to flexibility in how the role is performed. The stress is placed on encouraging the development of the individual within the role rather than on the specifics of how to make the role function. These concepts focus on the expressiveness of mothering, but instrumental qualities also exist that are tempered into more humanistic terms.

Table 2-1. Traditional and Developmental Concepts of a Good Mother

Traditional Concepts	*Developmental Concepts*
1. Performs domestic duties (cooks, cleans, washes, etc.).	1. Trains child for self-reliance and autonomy.
2. Meets child's physical needs.	2. Provides for child's emotional needs.
3. Performs training of child (e.g., regular habits).	3. Encourages social development of child.
4. Performs moral education and training.	4. Stimulates child's mental growth.
5. Disciplines child.	5. Provides a nurturant environment for child.
	6. Attends to individual developmental needs.
	7. Disciplines with understanding.

Source: From *Marriage and Family Development* by Evelyn M. Duvall. Reprinted by permission of the publisher, J. B. Lippincott Company. Copyright © 1977.

The mothering role is perceived by children somewhat differently than by adults (see Figure 2-6). Schvaneveldt, Freyer, and Ostler (1970) interviewed eighty-six middle-class preschool children about their perceptions of what constituted "goodness" and "badness" in both mother and father roles. The majority of the children described a good mother in terms of functions relating to the home, nurturance, discipline, and social behavior. According to these young children, a good mother is one who doesn't spank children and keeps them from doing things they shouldn't; she cooks food; she is

Copyright 1977,
The Register and Tribune
Syndicate, Inc.

"Mommies cook, talk on the phone, and hug you."

Figure 2-6.

happy; she helps little babies; she gives kisses; and she takes care of children. A bad mother is described as one who hits, doesn't kiss children, and doesn't straighten the house.

LeMasters (1974) feels that the wife–mother role is characterized not only by its dual nature but also by its expansion into a multitude of different but related subroles. Women's roles today are not simply confined to child care or to the relationship with the father. The role extends into areas that were once more the responsibility of the husband–father role. Mothers have become more involved in the management of the home, including supervising family budgets, performing maintenance work, and shopping for major family purchases. Mothering involves acting as a connecting link between the family and the community. Mothers maintain the communications between the family and the schools, the church, and other community groups. Some mothers are very actively involved in volunteer work with community service agencies, such as hospitals, crisis centers, and charitable organizations. The most noticeable addition to the mother–wife role today, however, is that

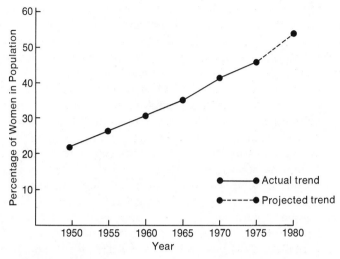

Figure 2-7. Married women in the labor force from 1950 to 1980. [Source: U.S. Bureau of the Census. *Statistical abstract of the United States: 1976.* (97th ed.) Washington, D.C.: 1976.]

of being a wage-earner. Labor statistics show the dramatic increase in women who are employed outside the home, as shown in Figure 2-7. This particular role function has numerous implications for changes in the husband–father role and in how the family functions as a whole.

RESEARCH ON MOTHERING

The majority of research on parenting has actually focused on mothering behavior. The intensive study of fathering has only occurred within the last ten years. This state of affairs in the research literature is an indication of the view that Western society is characterized as being "mother-centered" in its child-rearing approaches and that the rearing of children is regarded as largely a female responsibility (Nash, 1965).

The research that has been conducted on mothering in the past shows a concentration on the nurturant and control functions of the role. For the most part, these studies were conducted during the 1940s and 1950s, when the thrust of research was directed at testing the validity of theories of personality development and social learning in children.

Maternal Nurturance

Freud's theory of personality development contains a number of concepts that have generated research on maternal nurturance and its effects on children's development. Freud's theory contains a strong implication that a child's personality is formed during the first several years after birth. The experiences of the child during the years of early childhood were thought to be crucially important in determining his or her adult personality.

Research performed by three individuals—Margaret Ribble, Rene Spitz, and William Goldfarb—is usually mentioned in studies of the hypothesis that maternal nurturance has a profound effect on personality development in infancy and early childhood. These studies represent the clinical approach to human behavioral research that uses case studies of individuals who are seen by a professional because of something that has gone "wrong" in their development or behavior. Essentially the studies represent a deficit model of human development because the subjects' experiences are considered abnormal or lacking in some way when compared with others. In this regard, these investigators were interested in studying what occurred in a child's personality development when he or she was deprived of the normal experiences of mothering (nurturance) in infancy and early childhood.

Margaret Ribble (1943) was very much concerned with how infants were cared for immediately after birth. Her observations of these practices led her to believe that infants were mishandled and actually experienced psychological harm. She was specifically concerned with the procedures used in hospitals and advocated by child-rearing experts that seemed to work against the infant's receiving adequate mothering. These included separating the infant from the mother in a special, sterile room (the hospital nursery) for long periods of time; keeping him on a stable, flat surface that provided little tactile (touch) or kinesthetic (movement) stimulation; and providing inadequate amounts of physical handling either by nurses or by the mothers. Ribble reported that almost 30 per cent of six hundred newborns she studied showed patterns of intense muscular tension. Her observations of these infants indicated that the tension was removed or relieved when the baby was sucking, placed in close contact with the mother, rocked, given a warm bath, stroked or cuddled, or held in a secure position. Dr. Ribble believed that the results of her study showed that infants who lacked such mothering experiences in sufficient quantity developed a condition called *marasmus*. The symptoms of this condition are poor muscle tone, a protruding belly, poor skin color, and sometimes liver congestion. Ribble concluded that if babies were deprived of mothering during this important time of their life, marasmus could result, leading to the early death of the child if the lack of mothering experiences continued.

The effects of institutionalization on emotional development in infants and young children were studied by Rene Spitz (1945) and William Goldfarb (1945). In a prison nursery, Spitz observed the development of infants whose mothers were serving sentences for various crimes. These infants were compared with those who had been placed in a foundling home (a charitable agency that cared for abandoned and illegitimate babies). The infants in the prison nursery were cared for by their mothers and were adequately super-

vised by members of a professional staff. The adult–child ratio in the foundling home, however, was about 1:8. This meant that because of the small
number of adults available, the babies in this environment failed to receive
sufficient attention and handling. The lack of mothering among the foundling
home babies resulted in what Spitz called *anaclitic depression.* This condition
was characterized by loss of appetite, little interest in the environment, developmental retardation, poor weight gains, and sleeping problems.

Goldfarb's study centered on children ranging in age from three to twelve
years who had lived primarily in institutions since birth. Goldfarb observed
that the institutionalized children were emotionally apathetic and passive in
their behavior. He concluded that deprivation in interacting with mother
figures produced lasting effects on the children's personality development.

These studies pointed a condemning finger at institutions and their de-
humanizing effects on infants and children, who experienced emotional
trauma because they failed to be adequately nurtured. The studies were pub-
licized widely among professionals and the general public.

The effects of maternal deprivation received even greater attention through
the writings of John Bowlby (1952). He concluded that physical, intellectual,
and social development are usually retarded when children are deprived of
nurturance and maternal care. Symptoms of physical as well as mental illness
appear from this deprivation. Bowlby's observations served to alert society to
the conditions that institutionalized children experienced and to arouse interest in preventing these experiences. The public may have jumped to the
hasty conclusion that the same conditions could develop in children in the
typical home or day-care center if the baby failed to receive full-time care
from its own mother.

Research with animals also provides insights into the effects of maternal
deprivation and the importance of nurturance. A well-known series of studies
by Harry Harlow (1958) and his associates examined the effects of maternal
deprivation in rhesus monkeys. Harlow used monkeys in these experiments
rather than human infants because of the obvious ethical problems. In the
early studies, Harlow discovered that severe emotional trauma resulted in the
mother and especially in the infant monkeys when the infants were separated
from their mothers following birth. Absence of direct physical contact with
the mother produced disturbed behavioral patterns (staring into space, stereotyped rocking patterns, inability to mate, poor social interactions with other
monkeys, and so on) in these infants after they had grown up.

Later studies examined maternal deprivation in more detail. Two groups
of infant monkeys were separated from their natural mothers and were reared
by two artificial (surrogate) mothers. One of the mother surrogates was built
of wood that was covered with soft terrycloth, and the other was built of
bare wire mesh. The difference in texture stressed the importance of the infant
monkeys' need for what Harlow termed *contact comfort;* the terrycloth
mother provided a softer, more comfortable sensation for the baby monkeys.

Both mothers were equipped with bottles so that the infant monkeys could be nursed (see Figures 2-8 and 2-9).

The results of these studies showed that the infant monkeys spent more time clinging to the terrycloth mother surrogate, regardless of which mother fed them. The group of infants raised with the cloth mother were definitely more curious and more interested in exploring a strange new environment. This mother was also preferred to the wire mesh mother when the infants were exposed to fear-producing stimuli.

The effects of poor or inadequate caregiving among these monkeys were found to be overcome in their later years of life. Another study by Harlow and his associates (1963) suggests that interaction between infant monkeys who were raised by natural mothers and those "reared" by artificial mothers compensated for the lack of adequate mothering in early infancy.

The studies on human infants and children supporting the contention in Freudian theory that early mothering experiences are significant in determining later adult personality have received critical attention from other investigators. Studies by Neilon (1948) and Sewell (1952) and comments by Pinneau (1950) have served to challenge the idea that a child's personality is fixed or determined by the presence or absence of maternal nurturance.

Figure 2-8. Surrogate mothers used in Harlow's experiments. (Courtesy of the University of Wisconsin Primate Laboratory.)

Figure 2-9. The cloth surrogate mother provided the infant monkey with contact comfort. (Courtesy of the University of Wisconsin Primate Laboratory.)

At issue in all these studies is a question regarding the effects of nurturant, expressive functions in interaction with infants and the degree of nurturance that should be provided by the caregiver. Clearly a baby's helplessness and its very survival require that someone within the family act as an agent of care. What is debatable is whether there are biological differences between mothers and fathers that may make one or the other more capable of or suited to these functions.

Maternal Control of Child Behavior

Research dealing with the control of children's behavior by mothers reflects the increased involvement of traditional instrumental qualities in the mothering role over the years. A thorough review of the research literature on mothering gives the impression that this aspect of mothering has received an extreme amount of attention. The picture of the mother in popular magazine articles, television programs, and research studies is the picture of a woman who clearly cannot cope with her children and who is confused about the "right" way to discipline them. This is the stereotype of the typical middle-class housewife who vainly tries to hold the family together, getting little if any support in the tasks of child rearing from the father.

However misleading and erroneous this stereotype of the full-time mother, little doubt exists that mothers have a legitimate concern about how to direct the behavior of their children into manageable patterns. Their nurturance and love are seen as unconditional and always present, serving as the base of their relationship with their children. Support and advice in matters of child rearing may come from the father, from friends who may or may not share a similar life-style, and from books and magazine articles on child rearing.

The exercise of controls on children's behavior by a mother requires the expression of assertiveness in making certain decisions about what controls to use. The decision-making process may or may not be a conscious effort and is determined by numerous situational and background variables.

When mothers use controls to make children's behavior more manageable or acceptable, many research studies (Emmerich, 1959a,b; Gardner, 1947; Hawkes, Burchinal, and Gardner, 1957; Kagan, 1956; Sears, Maccoby, and Levin, 1957) have demonstrated that psychological rather than physical methods of control are used frequently by mothers. These studies, based largely on children's reports of their mothers' behavior, also show that (1) an opposite-sex parent grants more independence to a child than the same-sex parent; (2) the same-sex parent is seen as more benevolent but more frustrating than the opposite-sex parent; and (3) boys feel that they are more frequently punished than girls.

Researchers have termed the most predominant type of psychological controls used by mothers *love-oriented* methods. These techniques focus on positive methods of control, such as praise and reshaping of children's behavior. Negative methods include expressions of disappointment at the child's behavior, isolating him from others, threatening to leave him, or threatening to withdraw love from the child. When mothers use love-oriented methods consistently, research shows that the children tend to develop a strong sense of responsibility for their behavior and to have feelings of guilt and sorrow when they've done something wrong. Conflicting results of other studies, however, make it unclear whether the use of these methods helps a child to learn to resist temptation (Becker, 1964).

Although nurturance-oriented methods of control are commonly used by mothers, power-assertive methods may be used as a last resort to control children's behavior when love-oriented methods fail. These methods usually involve physical punishments and include verbal behaviors such as yelling, making threats, and commanding a child. These controls are examples of hostility and frustration on the part of the mother in response to the child's behavior.

When power-assertive methods are used consistently by mothers over love-oriented techniques, the research reported by Becker points to specific reactions by children. Increased aggression toward other children, resistance to cooperation with authority figures, and hostile acting-out behaviors are the usual finding. In the long run, the continuous use of power-assertive methods may result in children who withdraw from social interaction with others, quarrel extensively among each other, and openly express aggression when provoked.

THE FATHERING ROLE

There was little intensive research on fathering until ten years ago. The past decade has seen an increase in the discovery of the contributions of fathering to child development. The fathering role, which has been taken for granted, ignored, or simply misunderstood in the past, is being examined more carefully today. The findings of research are helping to change many of our misconceptions about the nature of this role (see Figure 2-10).

Social scientists have produced several explanations of why the family unit even contains the fathering role. This role is seen as the weak link in the family organization as compared with the mothering role. Kleinberg (1954)

"But, Mommy! DADDY'S don't get sick!"

Figure 2-10.

states that the father's duties in family life were imposed on the male as the price for having sexual rights to the adult female. Margaret Mead (1949) states that fatherhood is a social invention, implying that the family group had to find some reason to keep the father within the family. A social role was invented that made him responsible for providing protection, shelter, food, and support for his mate and children.

Leonard Benson (1968) agrees with Mead that fatherhood was an important social invention in the evolution of the organization of the human family. His discussion emphasizes the origins of the instrumental qualities associated with fatherhood. These include providing economic support, exercising greater social power by virtue of strength, and providing security and protection.

Fathers today may choose to remain with their families through social convention. In describing the development of the fatherhood role, however, Benson quotes from an article by Hockett and Ascher (1964). These researchers point to the increased need for having the father's help in child rearing because of the evolutionary enlargement of the human brain over time. Hockett and Ascher explain that in the course of evolution, the development of language and the ability to invent and use tools were associated with the enlargement of the brain in size and weight. Having a larger brain meant that babies had to be born long before the brain matured, so that they would survive the birth and not damage the mother in the process. Because of being born with a small, immature brain, the human baby is dependent for a longer period than babies of lower animal species. In turn, the human baby develops a stronger and deeper attachment to the mother as the primary caregiver. The authors explain the invention of fatherhood by the family's need for the adult male's strength and ability to provide economic and material support. This function has not changed much over time (see Figure 2-11). The fact that such explanations of the fathering role are made is an indication of the contrast between our social understanding of the importance of mothering versus fathering in influencing child development.

Rachael Elder's (1949) research, similar to that of Duvall's (1946) on concepts of motherhood, provides information on how the fathering role is conceptualized in both traditional and developmental frameworks. The descriptions in Table 2-2 define a traditional type of "good" father within the provider framework. This concept holds that the father serves as the head of the family group. These descriptions give substance to the instrumental qualities of the role as defined by Parsons and Bales (1955) in their socialization theory of the family.

The concept of a good father from a developmental point of view loses little of the instrumental qualities as compared with the traditional concepts. The developmental concept differs from the other, however, in that the father is concerned with the development of self-control and autonomy of his children as well as in himself as a developing individual. What is noticeably lack-

Table 2-2. Traditional and Developmental Concepts of a Good Father

Traditional Concepts	Developmental Concepts
1. Sets goals for child.	1. Emphasizes autonomous child behavior.
2. Emphasizes doing things for child and giving things to child.	
3. "Knows" what is good for child.	2. Tries to understand child and himself.
4. Is a strong individual who is always right.	3. Recognizes individuality of child and self.
5. Expects obedience from child.	4. Promotes mature behavior of child.
6. Becomes a parent out of a sense of duty.	5. Chooses to become a parent.

Source: From *Marriage and Family Development* by Evelyn M. Duvall. Reprinted by permission of the publisher, J. B. Lippincott Company. Copyright © 1977.

"Our Daddy got a raise!"

Figure 2-11.

ing from the developmental description is the focus on discipline and power of the father that is evident in the traditional descriptions.

The study, quoted earlier, by Schvaneveldt, Freyer, and Ostler (1970) also includes reports of preschool children's perceptions of "goodness" and "badness" in the fathering role. The children's concept of a good father was of a man who did good things for children and physically showed his affection with hugs and kisses. A good father played with children, read them stories, and sang songs to them. Another prominent feature of a good father was that he "worked." A bad father to these children was seen as the opposite of a good father. The bad father was one who wasn't nice or one who left the mother and the children; who smoked; and who read the newspaper. The discipline issue was part of the concept of a bad father, as he sent children to bed and used physical punishment. Most unexpectedly, a bad father was seen also as someone who allowed children to misbehave and did not discipline them.

Components of the Fathering Role

The instrumental nature of the fathering role, as presented by Parsons and Bales (1955), implies that the father serves as a master teacher of children. The mother acts as a master teacher in the ways of living on a daily basis and serves as the humanizing agent in the socialization process. The father, however, is described as a representative of society and the connecting link between the family and the culture that pervades every aspect of family life. By teaching his children appropriate skills, the father ensures that each child will be able to assume responsibility for his or her behavior and actions as an effective member of society. According to the theory, the father acts as the final judge in decision making by relating the values of society to the functioning of the family. The mother, in enacting her expressive role, is primarily concerned with making the family function as smoothly as possible as a unit within the larger society.

Zelditch (1955) states that the father bases his position as teacher, decision maker, and problem solver on his ability to deal with the larger society. His life is clearly based outside the family so that he can provide for their existence and survival. This position results in a different perspective on life when compared with that of the mother. It may also reflect his own experiences both in being socialized as a child for his eventual role as an adult male and in his preparation to provide support for a family.

Aberle and Naegele (1952) argue that middle-class fathers develop a set of values and attitudes for evaluating children's behavior, based on the fathers' occupational role-learnings, which serve to shape their expectations of children's behavior. These fathers, in evaluating their sons' behavior, tend to focus primarily on the general character traits that will facilitate the sons' success in a middle-class occupational role. The fathers' emphasis here is on the sons' learning to set goals, to show initiative, and to act aggressively when necessary.

In our industrialized society, however, fathers have few opportunities to instruct their children directly in the skills needed in the larger society because these are no longer performed in the home. What fathers do teach children today are skills that indirectly relate to effective living in the larger society. Such skills are more appropriately labeled as values and behavior patterns that children learn through modeling by the father. These may include how to react toward and solve problems and crises, how to establish and work toward goals, what society expects from individuals in daily interactions, and how to function in an occupational role outside of the family. More specifically, the father represents maleness and manhood to his children, providing them with a concept of this particular sex role as the father himself interprets it through his behavior, values, and attitudes. A father teaches his children—but the process is more likely to be by example than by direct instruction.

LeMasters (1974) presents a role analysis of the modern father. Several issues raised in this analysis are given brief discussion here.

1. *Parenting is a peripheral role for the male in our society.* Our mother-centered society does not place emphasis on the parenting skills of men. Success and competence for men come primarily through their involvement in an occupation. The male is regarded as the head of the household and the chief wage-earner despite the fact that his wife may also be earning a living. The father's focus on the children and their rearing differs from the mother's. She confronts these challenges daily if she is a full-time mother. A man usually considers his occupational role to be an integral part of his paternal behavior, however. In his working role, he transmits many examples of appropriate behavior and values to children while fulfilling the instrumental nature of fatherhood.

2. *There is no attachment process or bonding between father and child equivalent to that between mother and child.* The psychological and physical process of attachment between mothers and their children occurs in a manner that fathers rarely, if ever, can achieve, according to LeMasters. The extensive amount of research on this topic has focused on mothers rather than fathers in interaction with babies.

Cultural ideas about fatherhood, maleness, and the father's absence from the home due to occupational commitments tend to exclude men from developing close emotional bonds with children as easily as does the full-time mother. The biological events of pregnancy and birth are very real experiences for the mother. There is time for her to identify with her new role by carrying a baby within her body and physically experiencing its birth. The bonding of the father to his child lacks these benefits. Fathers have to work harder at developing the attachment than mothers.

Although an increasing number of physicians and hospitals encourage the involvement of fathers in their wives' pregnancies and the birth of their children, society generally works to exclude the father from what is considered to be a woman's concerns. The father is not expected to show any great interest in these events and processes. He is not usually encouraged to witness or participate in the birth of his child. He is usually treated as unsterile and dirty in the eyes of medical personnel. Hospital policies allow him only limited access to his wife and usually none at all to his child until it is allowed to go home. How can we fail to wonder why most men feel that their initial fathering behavior is confined to simply working hard in order to pay all the bills involved in having a new baby? This treatment is fully in line with the way boys are socialized into manhood. The shock that is sometimes experienced by being around a new baby leads men to avoid handling their babies because they have usually had limited experiences with infants while growing up. Nurturant behavior, so closely identified with femininity in our culture, is threatening to males, and a man may consider the demonstration of this kind of loving behavior unmanly or inappropriate. Only with time, experience, and a great deal of encouragement from the mother will the father become comfortable with his role.

3. *The fathering role is closely tied to the success of the marriage relationship.* Unlike many societies, the father in our culture is allowed to function successfully in his role only on the condition that the marriage also succeeds. In other words, according to LeMasters, it is difficult to be a good father if the male is not also a good husband. It is still customary in most divorce proceedings for the mother to be granted custody of the children while the husband continues to provide for their support. This may further confine the man's fathering behavior to its elemental economic function.

RESEARCH ON FATHERING

There has been a proliferation of research studies on fathering behavior within the last few years. Leonard Benson's (1968) authoritative writings on the fatherhood role provide an extensive listing of the material available through 1964. A recently published bibliography (Price-Bonham, 1976) lists the literature relating to fathering after this date.

The majority of studies that focus on fathers are not based on actual observation of men interacting with their children. This is unfortunate because direct observation of behavior as it occurs either naturally or within the laboratory provides advantages to the researcher over other methods of investigation. Getting fathers to cooperate in research studies has presented difficulties because they are away from home during the day, and when at home they want to relax. Fathers as a group are suspicious of researchers and look at behavioral research with a jaundiced eye. The research literature relating to fathering will be reviewed under the categories of nurturance and control functions, as these are role characteristics shared with the mother in child rearing.

Paternal Nurturance

PREPARATION FOR FATHERING. The current trends in reexamining the role definitions of men and women encourage women to look beyond their parenting role in life and men to become more involved in parenting (Price-Bonham, 1976). The present state of knowledge provides little information on the types of experiences that are necessary to prepare men to become fathers. The most probable answer is to look at the socialization of girls to prepare them for parenthood. Girls are literally pushed into preparation for parenting by being given dolls as toys and having experiences with children by babysitting, for example. Society ensures to some degree that most girls will be somewhat acquainted with children and how they behave before reaching adulthood. For most men, fatherhood is the first exposure to caregiving responsibilities. Research confirms that it may be a crisis experience that can result in a difficult adjustment period (this matter is discussed in Chapter 4).

An indication that some improvement is being made in the socialization of boys for fatherhood is the introduction of children's books that have a nonsexist theme. *William's Doll* (Zolotow, 1972) is an excellent example of this type of book. The story is about a little boy who wants a doll more than anything else. Other boys tease him, and his father gets him boy-type toys, such as a basketball and an electric train. William enjoys these toys but still wants a doll as well. His grandmother, who comes to visit, understands William's need to have a doll and buys one for him. When his father protests that a boy doesn't need a doll, the grandmother explains that "he needs it to hug and to cradle and to take to the park so that when he's a father like you, he'll know how to take care of his baby . . . and bring him the things he wants, like a doll so he can practice being a father" (Zolotow, 1972, p. 12).

The experience of the first pregnancy is the most common time when men confront the reality of their lack of familiarity with children. Childbirth preparation classes offer an opportunity for an increasing number of men to become involved in the birth of their children. These classes offer training to both the mother and father in what to expect throughout the pregnancy and also may provide training in various methods of prepared childbirth. One popular method (Lamaze) features the father as an active participant who coaches his wife in the methods she will use in labor and delivery. The assumption is that the active involvement and participation of the father provides emotional support to the mother and that adjustment to his new role will be easier after the birth. Evidence from research suggests conflicting opinions about this assumption. One study (Russell, 1974) reports that men who prepared for parenthood by attending classes, reading books on child development, and caring for other people's children experienced greater satisfaction in or adjustment to the fathering role.

Another study (Wente and Crockenberg, 1976) found that there was no difference in adjustment to the new fathering role between men who did and men who did not have training in the Lamaze method of childbirth. The validity of the results of this study is questionable, however, because men from both groups were present during the labor and delivery of their child. Ordinarily only men who have had the training are interested and encouraged to be present at the birth. The authors of this study noted, however, that many of the fathers who were questioned remarked that although Lamaze training was helpful in preparing them for the birth, nothing completely prepared them for what followed in their home life after the baby's birth. We can conclude, then, that too much has been expected of childbirth preparation classes in aiding men in their fathering behavior. Such training is, after all, just what it claims to be: training for childbirth, not for parenthood. The value of Lamaze preparation may be in acting as a stimulus to interest fathers in their children and to allow the expression of nurturance toward children as an approved and appropriate behavior for males. The training and experience serve as a valid attempt to include, not exclude, fathers in what is a major life event.

FATHERING IN INFANCY.   Our traditional stereotype of maleness does not include the expression of nurturant qualities or behaviors. Emotional expressiveness is culturally associated with the female role rather than with the male role. We have the idea that because males generally don't show behaviors that are expressive, they are not as capable as females of expressing emotions. To deny that males can experience and demonstrate these types of behavior is to deny their basic humanity.

Life presents two opportunities for the male to show expressive, nurturant behavior: in the marriage relationship with the wife and through fathering behavior with his children. The nature of family life today generally emphasizes expressiveness of all family members, including the father. When our society changed from a rural way of life to one based on technology and industrialization, the focus of the family shifted from instrumental to expressive activities. The time that was once devoted to survival and to the production of goods centers now on interpersonal relationships within the family. The more compacted size of the nuclear family produces more frequent interactions that are more intense in nature.

Problems are certain to result when a father approaches his role within the traditional, instrumental concept to the exclusion of most expressive behaviors. When fathering behavior is conducted in a manner that places the man at an emotional distance from his family, the children may come to view their home, and their father in particular, as lacking in warmth. The father image may be one of stability and strength in a demanding world, but these qualities are more effectively communicated to children in a nurturant manner. Emotional aloofness of males, as Benson (1968) states, is out of place in contemporary society and fails to provide growing children with the security they need from the emotionally cold, bureaucratic world of urbanized society.

Most writers and researchers have ignored or discounted the interest, importance, and competence of fathers during their child's years of infancy. Erikson and others have set the mother up as the individual who is responsible for developing a sense of security and trust in the infant. The significance of the father has, until recently, been seen as influential in a child's development during the years that follow infancy. Research that has been performed in the past substantiates this position regarding fathering behavior. As an illustration, Rebelsky and Hanks (1971) studied father–infant interaction by attaching a microphone to infants' clothing and tape-recording the interactions with the baby and its parents for a twenty-four-hour period every two weeks for three consecutive months. The babies were two weeks old when the study began. The results were rather startling regarding the amount of time the fathers spent in talking with their babies. The fathers interacted verbally with the babies an average of 2.7 times each day, and the average amount of time spent in talking with the infant was 37.7 seconds. As the study progressed through the three-month period, fathers were found to spend even less time talking with their babies, especially the fathers of girl babies.

New discoveries about fathering during infancy are appearing more frequently. A series of investigations by Ross Parke and his associates studies the behaviors of fathers with their newborn infants. The first investigation (Parke, O'Leary, and West, 1972) examined the behaviors of new, first-time fathers in the mother's hospital room shortly after the child's birth. The fathers were found to be just as involved as the mothers in smiling at, looking at, touching, feeding, and holding the baby. Questions could be raised, however, as to whether these fathers were typical of all fathers. They were from the middle class, they were well educated, over half had attended childbirth preparation classes, and all but one attended the baby's delivery. Another investigation was conducted (Parke and O'Leary, 1976) that studied a group of lower-class fathers who had not attended childbirth preparation classes and were not present at their baby's delivery. These fathers were observed both alone with the baby and with the baby and the mother. The same results were found in the degree of involvement with the babies as in the study of middle-class fathers. The conclusion could be made that fathers are interested and become involved with their babies at the earliest stages in infancy (Parke and Sawin, 1976). The investigators also report that the fathers in both studies were just as nurturant as the mothers but played a less active role in caregiving activities.

When Parke and O'Leary (1976) measured the sensitivity of both the mother and the father to infant cues, they found that the father was as sensitive to the baby as the mother. This was intended to be a measure of parents' competence in caregiving activities. Feeding an infant requires that the parent shape or modify his own behavior in response to cues provided by a baby while he is feeding. Such cues include coughing, burping, and so on. This finding serves as an additional illustration of the feedback that occurs within the parent–child interaction system. Fathers are just as capable as mothers of responding to the behavioral cues that infants give.

Redina and Dickerscheid (1976) studied the fathering behavior of forty middle-class fathers with their firstborn infants, who averaged 5.8 months of age. The evidence suggests that the type of involvement of the fathers changed with these older infants. These fathers spent the majority of their time in socializing activities and in watching the infant. Routine caregiving activities received the least amount of their attention. One of the implications drawn from this study was the point stressed earlier in this chapter: that fathers offer a unique socializing experience to children through their presence in the family. The authors of this study mention that when mothers are primarily involved in meeting the physical needs of their baby, they probably have little time or energy to engage the baby in as many social activities as they would like. Because fathers can fulfill this important aspect of interaction, children who live in homes where the father is relatively inactive or absent lack the socialization experiences that the father can offer.

The results of these and other studies on fathering in infancy should not come as any great surprise. Theorists and researchers have pointed to the early months of infancy as a critical period in the development of the relationship between the mother and the baby, mentioning numerous variables that assist in this process. Why, then, should fathers be so radically different? Why should they be so inconsequential to the baby that it comes to prefer its mother over its father? Lamb and Lamb (1976) explored this issue in a study in which infants seven to thirteen months old were observed in interaction with both the mother and the father. The investigators were specifically interested in whether there were differences in the types of interaction with either parent. In the course of the baby's development, such differences in parenting styles might influence the personality development of the child. Mothers in this study were found to socialize with the baby by playing games like pat-a-cake and by playing with toys. Fathers were found to engage the baby in vigorous, physically stimulating games or in play activities that involved unpredictable behaviors of the father. Fathers differed from mothers in their reasons for holding the baby. The mothers more frequently held the baby to control its behavior and exploration of the environment, whereas fathers more typically held the baby because it wanted to be held or in order to play with it. These types of behavior by the father were interpreted as being psychologically stimulating for the baby. The authors mention an important point about the value of this type of fathering in shaping children's social competence.

Suomi (1974), in reviewing evidence on the development of social competence in infant monkeys, states that more socially competent and sophisticated social behaviors were developed when the social environment was more complex in nature. If we can translate this finding to relate to humans, the value of the father may emerge in assisting the mother to make the baby's social environment more complex in nature. This may lead the baby to develop greater social competence in later years.

Another investigation reported by these researchers provides evidence of how the nature of the father's behavior as a sex-role model emerges during his child's infancy. Fathers were observed to be twice as active in social interaction with their sons as with their daughters throughout the second year of the baby's life. Whereas the fathers showed active social involvement with both boys and girls before the first birthday, interaction concentrated on the boy after the first birthday. A related finding was that girls became more dependent on or sought social contact with their mothers, whereas boys showed more dependency on their fathers during this age period. This finding led the authors to speculate that the emerging relationship with the father helped boys to adopt sex-appropriate behavior by using the father as a model and instructor in the male sex-role.

The studies that have been discussed here represent only a small portion of the numerous, complex issues concerning the contributions of parents, and especially fathers, to the growth and development of children during infancy.

FATHERING AND THE SEX-ROLE DEVELOPMENT OF CHILDREN.   One of the first and more intensely studied aspects of fathering is the father's contribution to his children's sex-role development. Many of these studies are the by-product of researchers' interest in validating theories of personality development. The studies represent an overwhelming preoccupation with how boys develop a masculine sex-role orientation. A number of investigations of this nature were designed to test the idea that children learn to pattern their sex-role behavior on the model presented by the same-sex parent. Another explanation of the interest in male sex-role development is that our culture is more tolerant of girls who show masculine personality traits than of males with feminine traits (Lynn, 1974).

A sex role is thought to be acquired by children in three stages (Biller and Borstelmann, 1967). Sex-role *orientation* refers to a child's cognitively based evaluation of his or her masculinity or femininity. This evaluation is based on a child's recognition that his or her behavior should match what she or he is physically. The recognition that boys and girls are expected to behave in certain ways orients the child to evaluate his or her own behavior according to cultural standards.

Biller (1971) believes that the process of sex-role orientation begins during the first few years of a child's life. Orientation to sex-role behavior is associated with sex-role *preference* or the desire of a child to adopt the behaviors of the sex-role that he or she prefers or admires (Brown, 1957). Sex-role *adoption* occurs when children actively participate in rehearsing and practicing the behaviors that are characteristic of the preferred sex-role

"HELLO, DARLING! WHAT'S FOR DINNER?"
Figure 2-12.

(Lynn, 1974; see Figure 2-12). These processes serve as components of sex-role *identification* or the automatic and nondeliberate behavior patterns that are seen by society as appropriate to a particular sex role.

The research on fathering behavior and sex-role development in children is helping to revise some aspects of theoretical explanations of the identification process, according to Lynn (1974). A long-standing belief about how children gain their sex-role identification is that boys pattern themselves after a masculine father and girls acquire femininity by imitating a feminine mother. Lynn offers a convincing argument that this assumption is very inaccurate in describing how children acquire sex-role behaviors. He states that although parents are still available to children as models of appropriate sex-role behaviors, girls have fewer obstacles in acquiring the correct role orientation than boys because of the greater availability of the mother as a model. Boys, however, have a more difficult time in using the father as a sex-role model because his involvement in work away from the home places the child with the mother for a considerable period of time. Lynn believes that boys may use other boys, heroes of television shows and books, and instructions from mothers and teachers in acquiring a masculine orientation. Fathers, then, perhaps serve as a general outline of a masculine model that lacks details, whereas mothers serve as a detailed map of feminine behavior, according to Lynn.

Maccoby and Jacklin (1974), however, contend that parents serve as a model of general behavior patterns for children but not as models of sex-typed behaviors. They believe that children adopt their particular sex role because of the more broadly experienced cultural pressures to conform to standards of behavior considered appropriate to a particular sex role.

Kagan (1958) lists three conditions that are necessary for a boy to establish an optimally strong masculine identification: (1) the model (the father) must be perceived as being in command of desired goals, such as social power, and as being competent in tasks that the boy regards as important; (2) the model must be perceived as being nurturant; and (3) the boy must perceive some basis of similarity between himself and the father.

Research shows that sex-role development in boys is facilitated by a warm, rewarding, nurturant father who openly expresses interest in his son's development of aggressiveness and other culturally prescribed masculine traits (Biller and Borstelmann, 1967; Mussen and Distler, 1959). Many other studies associate nurturance of the father with sex-role development of the son. Mussen and Rutherford (1963) have found that nurturance of the father is related more directly with the sex-role development of boys than with that of girls. Henry Biller (1969) reports that kindergarten boys' perceptions of the nurturant qualities of the father are related to the sons' masculine orientation.

Other researchers have examined the first two points mentioned by Kagan in investigating masculine preferences of college-aged males. Moulton and his associates (1966) state that the young men of their study had high masculine preferences on a questionnaire when they perceived the father in strong, disciplinarian, but affectionate terms. If the father was seen as demonstrating his power without affection, the son was more likely to have less masculine preferences. When the mother was reported as being the dominant parent in the family, the son was more likely to report preferences that were feminine in nature.

Evidence on fathers and their role in the sex-role development of their children suggests that it is the father who is most concerned about whether boys and girls adopt different sex-appropriate behaviors (Lynn, 1974). For many individuals, the matter of concern is not so much that boys become masculine as that they not be feminine in their behavior. This is the hidden and unexpressed fear of the father in the story of *William's Doll* (Zolotow, 1972). There are fewer pressures on girls not to show masculine traits in their emerging sex-role behaviors. Perhaps this explains why there is a relative wealth of material on the father's impact on the sex-role development of boys and so little is currently known about his impact on the sex-role development of girls.

Mussen and Rutherford (1963) studied the efforts of parents who actively encouraged traditional sex-role behaviors in first-grade children. Girls who were rated as feminine in orientation had fathers who reinforced their feminine behaviors. The father was the important figure in the girls' acquiring sex-typed behaviors, as neither the mothers' encouragement nor ratings of femininity were related to the sex-role orientation of boys or girls.

As fathers may enhance the masculinity of boys, the femininity of daughters may also be strengthened by a nurturant, expressive father. Al Heilbrun (1976) explored the paradoxical issue of how a daughter uses a masculine father as a model for adopting a feminine sex-role orientation. Heilbrun proposes that the father shows behaviors that have a "double standard." To the world at large, he presents the image and behaviors that characterize him as masculine. When he interacts with his daughter, however, his behavior has a warmer, more nurturant quality. Heilbrun presents evidence from an earlier study (Heilbrun, 1965) to illustrate this hypothesis. College students were asked to rate their fathers on scales that measured nurturant, expressive behaviors such as showing physical affection, giving encouragement, and generating trust. These ratings allowed Heilbrun to judge the fathers as being masculine or feminine according to the degree of nurturant, expressive behaviors reported by the students. Fathers rated as feminine showed a higher degree of these behaviors than fathers rated as masculine. The fathers who were rated as masculine by their sons were less nurturant than fathers who were rated as feminine. Females, however, rated masculine fathers very similarly to feminine fathers. Heilbrun interpreted this to mean that masculine fathers were seen by daughters as just as expressive and nurturant as the fathers rated as feminine.

EFFECT OF FATHER'S ABSENCE ON CHILD DEVELOPMENT.   Much of the current interest in discovering how fathers contribute to children's development was stimulated by studies of what occurred in children's development when the father was absent from the home environment. This initial approach to studying fatherhood is based on the deficit model of development and is similar to the approach used when researchers first became interested in mothering.

Fathers may be absent from families for a variety of reasons. Divorce, separation, desertion, or death are the frequent causes for extended permanent absence. Absence of the father may result also from an occupation that involves lengthy absence from the home. An increasing number of single women also establish one-parent families.

Absence of the father occurs more frequently among lower-class families and among black families in all social classes (Biller, 1968, 1971; Deutsch and Brown, 1964; Mischel, 1961). In these families, however, it may be difficult to connect the problems in the family unit with the father's absence alone. Many of the emotional and psychological problems found in father-absent homes are complicated by the loss of his economic support, which has almost as many implications for children's development (Herzog and Sudia, 1970).

Studies of children who lack the fathering experience indicate that (1) adjustment is difficult in the areas of personality and social development, and (2) the father's absence may have a greater effect on a boy than on a girl. Research on father-absence effects have centered extensively on boys' sex-role development. One of the findings from several studies indicates that boys experience a critical period for masculine development during the early years of childhood (Biller, 1969; Hampson, 1965; Hetherington, 1965; Money, 1965). Girls are affected by their fathers' extended absence in ways that may appear in the later years of childhood, in adolescence, and in adulthood. The adolescent girl's ability to relate satisfactorily to male peers may be adversely affected as well (Hetherington, 1972). Father absence has been related to adult women's involvement with addictive drugs, alcoholism, and frequency of suicide attempts (Lynn and Sawry, 1959; Rathod and Thomson, 1971; Tiller, 1961). During the years of early childhood, girls with absent fathers are reported to be overly dependent on their mother, who is seen as being overprotective of her.

Lack of access to fathering experiences generalizes to areas of development that we least expect. Cognitive or thought skills are adversely affected, for example, in children from father-absent homes (Blanchard and Biller, 1971; Landy, Sutton-Smith, and Rosenberg, 1969; Santrock, 1972; Santrock and Wohlford, 1970). The results point to a part of instrumental fatherhood that children, especially boys, may incorporate into their own behavior through the identification process. Adult males have consistently performed better than females on tests that measure quantitative skills. When the father is absent from the home, children may fail to receive the modeling necessary for their learning of these skills. A recent study (Hillenbrand, 1976) reports that father absence in military families is associated with enhanced quantitative ability in fifth-grade boys who are firstborn children. The oldest son shows an adaptive reaction to the father's absence by assuming the father's instrumental role in the family. This enhances his cognitive skills to a greater degree than it does his younger siblings.

The effects of the father's absence for an extended period of time or permanently appear in another way that influences family life. Several researchers report that absence of the father leads mothers to change to more authoritarian child-rearing patterns in compensating for the father's lack of help in controlling children's behavior (Lynn and Sawry, 1959; Sears, Pintler, and Sears, 1946; Stolz et al., 1954).

Much has been learned from studies of the influence of father absence on children's development and of the style or quality of family life without a father's presence. Researchers are beginning to realize that additional work needs to be done on the actual interactions and specific behavioral components of nurturant fathering. Such research designs will provide a more accurate understanding of the significance of fathering experiences in child development and will show that the relationship between father and child is as important as that between mother and child.

Paternal Control of Child Behavior

Western culture still clings to a fragmented idea of a patriarchal family system. The discussion in Chapter 1 on changes in ideas about family roles within our culture showed how the father's authority has become diluted and deemphasized over the years. Expressiveness, however, has gained in importance in his role behavior.

Despite the fact that fathers spend the majority of their time away from their families, they are expected to participate in child-rearing responsibilities as much as possible. The control function of fathering has received more attention from researchers than the nurturant function because social control is considered to be an integral by-product of the power and authority associated with fatherhood.

When fathers insist on playing the traditional, instrumental-type, authoritarian role, the effects on children are largely negative. Common sense tells us that consistent restrictive behavior of parents in controlling children will inhibit much of their socially competent behavior. Research generally supports this contention. When restrictive child rearing is conducted in a warm manner, research shows that children become submissive, dependent, polite, and obedient; lack creativity; and show reduced autonomous and aggressive behavior. On the other hand, when child rearing is performed in both a restrictive and a hostile manner, the results are neurotic problems, increased quarreling with peers, social withdrawal, shyness, and exaggerated aggression, particularly among boys (Becker, 1964).

Diana Baumrind's (1971) study of patterns of parental authority essentially substantiates these general findings and adds a few insights into paternal control of children's behavior. Baumrind uses the terms *authoritarianism, permissiveness,* and *authoritativeness* to classify control patterns and to define the type and degree of control parents exercise in relating to their child. Her study of parents of preschool-aged children shows that fathers are more rejecting and authoritarian and are more likely to value conformity in boys than in girls. Fathers who were judged to be authoritative and whose wives emphasized nonconformity in their child rearing approach preferred children to be autonomous and motivated by ideals. The children of these parents were found to be socially dominant and goal-directed in their behavior.

When a child is described as dependent as opposed to independent, research generally indicates that the father rather than the mother is responsible for reinforcing the dependent nature of the child's behavior. This effect may be more visible in a girl than in a boy. Robert Sears and his colleagues (1965) have found that a number of dependent-type behaviors are shown by children whose fathers place intense pressures on them to be neat and orderly, punish or fail to reward independent behavior, reward traditional sex-typed behaviors of both boys and girls, and discourage children from expressing their affection for them physically.

Other researchers (Osofsky and Oldfield, 1971) have discovered that fathers reward dependence rather than independence in preschool-aged children. Fathers were observed interacting with their children in a laboratory setting and were later interviewed about their attitudes toward and use of child-rearing methods. The results of this study strongly suggest that mothers more than fathers encourage children toward self-control.

Many studies indicate that fathers, as opposed to mothers, rely on power-assertive techniques to control children's behavior (Becker, 1964). These techniques typically include physical punishments and hostile verbal methods to show authority. Power assertion may be subdivided into high and low degrees. Verbal threats and nonviolent physical punishments comprise the low-assertive methods, and spanking, yelling, and physical abuse constitute high power-assertive methods.

One of the more consistent findings about power assertion by a father is that children show a higher level of aggression toward others (Becker, 1964). Aggression toward the child by the parent is thought to breed aggression of the child toward others. In this sense, the parent may act as a model of aggression for the child, who, in seeing the father behave in this manner, transfers the aggression to his or her relationships with siblings and peers. In other words, the school bully is created in the home, not on the playground. Children raised in the emotional environment of parental hostility are seen as frustrated children who learn to express their rage and angered emotions outside the home with others rather than exposing themselves to punishment within the home for expressing these same emotions.

POINTS TO CONSIDER

- A variety of factors influence an individual's behavior as a parent. These include social class or peer value systems, personality patterns, attitudes toward parenting, and role modeling of parenting behavior.
- Both mothers and fathers share similar role functions in caregiving. These roles are enacted in different ways with different effects on child behavior.
- Two functions that may be shared by mothers and fathers are nurturance and control in caregiving activities.
- The parenting roles differ from other adult social roles.

- The majority of research on parenting has studied mothers' caregiving behavior more than fathers'.
- Much research on mothering has centered on the effects of lack of maternal nurturance on the early development of children.
- Research shows that mothers use psychological rather than physical controls to manage and shape children's behavior. These psychological controls are termed *love-oriented methods,* such as praise and withdrawal of love.
- The nature of men's roles as fathers is changing to include a greater emphasis on expressiveness in balance with instrumental qualities.
- Research on fathering is increasing. Recent work indicates that fathers' expressions of nurturance have a positive influence on children's development, especially during infancy and early childhood.
- The consensus of many research studies is that fathers, as opposed to mothers, rely on power-assertive techniques to control children's behavior.

REFERENCES

ABERLE, D., and NAEGELE, K. Middle class fathers' occupational role and attitudes toward children. *American Journal of Orthopsychiatry,* 1952, *22,* 366–378.

ADORNO, T., FRENKEL-BRUNSWIK, E., LEVINSON, D., and SANFORD, R. *The authoritarian personality.* New York: Harper, 1950.

BAUMRIND, D. Effects of authoritative parental control on child behavior. *Child Development,* 1966, *37,* 887–907.

BAUMRIND, D. Harmonious parents and their preschool children. *Developmental Psychology,* 1971, *4,* 99–102.

BECKER, W. Consequences of different kinds of parental discipline. In M. Hoffman and L. Hoffman (Eds.), *Review of child development research,* Vol. 1. New York: Russell Sage, 1964. Pp. 169–208.

BEHRENS, M. Child rearing and the character structure of the mother. *Child Development,* 1954, *25,* 225–238.

BENSON, L. *Fatherhood: A sociological perspective.* New York: Random House, 1968.

BILLER, H. A note on father-absence and masculine development in lower-class Negro and white boys. *Child Development,* 1968, *39,* 1003–1006.

BILLER, H. Father absence, maternal encouragement, and sex role development in kindergarten age boys. *Child Development,* 1969, *40,* 539–546.

BILLER, H. *Father, child and sex role.* Lexington, Mass.: D. C. Heath, 1971.

BILLER, H., and BORSTELMANN, L. Masculine development: An integrated review. *Merrill-Palmer Quarterly,* 1967, *13,* 253–294.

BLANCHARD, R., and BILLER, H. Father availability and academic performance among third-grade boys. *Developmental Psychology,* 1971, *4,* 301–305.

BOWLBY, J. *Maternal care and mental health.* Monograph Series No. 2. Geneva: World Health Organization, 1952.

BRONFENBRENNER, U. Socialization and social class through time and space. In

E. Maccoby, T. Newcomb, and E. Hartley (Eds.), *Readings in social psychology*. New York: Holt, 1958. Pp. 400–425.

BROWN, D. Masculinity–femininity development in children. *Journal of Consulting Psychology*, 1957, *21*, 197–202.

DAVIS, A., and HAVIGHURST, R. Social class and color differences in child rearing. *American Sociological Review*, 1946, *11*, 698–710.

DEUTSCH, M., and BROWN, B. Social influences in Negro–white intelligence differences. *Journal of Social Issues*, 1964, *18*, 24–35.

DUVALL, E. Conceptions of parenthood. *American Journal of Sociology*, 1946, *52*, 193–203.

ELDER, R. Traditional and developmental characteristics of fatherhood. *Marriage and Family Living*, 1949, *11*, 98–100, 106.

EMMERICH, W. Parental identification in young children. *Genetic Psychology Monographs*, 1959, *60*, 257–308. (a)

EMMERICH, W. Young children's discriminations of parent and child roles. *Child Development*, 1959, *30*, 403–419. (b)

GARDNER, L. An analysis of children's attitudes toward fathers. *Journal of Genetic Psychology*, 1947, *70*, 3–28.

GOLDFARB, W. Effects of psychological deprivation in infancy and subsequent adjustment. *American Journal of Psychiatry*, 1945, *102*, 18–33.

HAMPSON, J. Determinants of psychosexual orientation. In F. Beach (Ed.), *Sex and behavior*. New York: Wiley, 1965.

HARLOW, H. The nature of love. *American Psychologist*, 1958, *13*, 673–685.

HARLOW, H., HARLOW, M., and HANSEN, E. The maternal affectional system of rhesus monkeys. In H. Rheingold (Ed.), *Maternal behavior in mammals*. New York: Wiley, 1963.

HARRIS, I. *Normal children and mothers*. New York: Free Press, 1959.

HAWKES, G., BURCHINAL, L., and GARDNER, B. Pre-adolescents' view of some of their relations with their parents. *Child Development*, 1957, *28*, 393–399.

HEILBRUN, A. An empirical test of the modeling theory of sex-role learning. *Child Development*, 1965, *36*, 789–799.

HEILBRUN, A. Identification with the father and sex-role development of the daughter. *The Family Coordinator*, 1976, *25*, 411–416.

HERZOG, E., and SUDIA, C. *Boys in fatherless families*. Washington, D.C.: Department of Health, Education, & Welfare, 1970.

HESS, R. Social class and ethnic influences on socialization. In P. Mussen (Ed.), *Carmichael's manual of child psychology*, Vol. 2 (3rd ed.). New York: Wiley, 1970. Pp. 457–558.

HESS, R., and SHIPMAN, V. Early experience and socialization of cognitive modes in children. *Child Development*, 1965, *36*, 869–886.

HESS, R., and SHIPMAN, V. Maternal influences on early learning: The cognitive environments of urban preschool children. In R. Hess and R. Bear (Eds.), *Early learning*. Chicago: Aldine, 1968. Pp. 91–104.

HETHERINGTON, E. A developmental study of the effects of sex of the dominant parent on sex-role preference, identification, and imitation in children. *Journal of Personality and Social Psychology*, 1965, *2*, 188–194.

HETHERINGTON, E. Effects of father absence on personality development in adolescent daughters. *Developmental Psychology*, 1972, *7*, 313–326.

HILLENBRAND, E. Father absence in military families. *Family Coordinator*, 1976, *25*, 451–458.

HOCKETT, C., and ASCHER, P. The human revolution. *Current Anthropology*, 1964, *5*, 135–147.

JOHNSON, R., and MEDINNUS, G. *Child psychology: Behavior and development* (3rd ed.). New York: Wiley, 1974.

KAGAN, J. The child's perception of the parent. *Journal of Abnormal and Social Psychology*, 1956, *53*, 257–258.

KAGAN, J. The concept of identification. *Psychological Review*, 1958, *65*, 296–305.

KLEINBERG, O. *Social psychology* (rev. ed.). New York: Holt, 1954.

LAMB, M., and LAMB, J. The nature and importance of the father–infant relationship. *Family Coordinator*, 1976, *25*, 379–386.

LANDY, F., SUTTON-SMITH, B., and ROSENBERG, B. The effect of limited father absence on cognitive development. *Child Development*, 1969, *40*, 941–944.

LEMASTERS, E. *Parents in modern America* (rev. ed.). Homewood, Ill.: Dorsey, 1974.

LYNN, D. *The father: His role in child development*. Monterey, Calif.: Brooks/Cole, 1974.

LYNN, D., and SAWRY, W. The effects of father-absence on Norwegian boys and girls. *Journal of Abnormal and Social Psychology*, 1959, *59*, 258–262.

MACCOBY, E., and JACKLIN, C. *The psychology of sex differences*. Stanford, Calif.: Stanford University Press, 1974.

MEAD, M. *Male and female*. New York: Morrow, 1949.

MILLER, D., and SWANSON, G. *The changing American parent*. New York: Wiley, 1958.

MISCHEL, W. Father-absence and delay of gratification: A cross-cultural comparison. *Journal of Abnormal and Social Psychology*, 1961, *63*, 116–124.

MONEY, J. Psychosexual identification. In J. Money (Ed.), *Sex research: New developments*. New York: Holt, 1965. Pp. 3–23.

MOULTON, R., BURNSTEIN, E., LIBERTY, P., and ALTUCHER, N. Patterning of parental affection and disciplinary dominance as a determinant of guilt and sex typing. *Journal of Personality and Social Psychology*, 1966, *4*, 356–363.

MUSSEN, P., and DISTLER, L. Masculinity, identification, and father–son relationships. *Journal of Abnormal and Social Psychology*, 1959, *59*, 350–356.

MUSSEN, P., and RUTHERFORD, E. Parent–child relations and parental personality in relation to young children's sex-role preferences. *Child Development*, 1963, *34*, 589–607.

NASH, J. The father in contemporary culture and current psychological literature. *Child Development*, 1965, *36*, 261–297.

NEILON, P. Shirley's babies after fifteen years: A personality study. *Journal of Genetic Psychology*, 1948, *73*, 175–186.

OSOFSKY, J., and OLDFIELD, S. Children's effects on parental behavior: Mothers' and fathers' responses to dependent and independent children. *Proceedings of the Annual Convention of the American Psychological Association*, 1971, *6*(Part 1), 143–144.

PARKE, R., and O'LEARY, S. Father–mother–infant interaction in the newborn period: Some findings, some observations, and some unresolved issues. In K.

Riegel and J. Meacham (Eds.), *The developing individual in a changing world,* Vol. 2. The Hague: Mouton, 1976.

PARKE, R., O'LEARY, S., and WEST, S. Mother–father–infant interaction: Effects of maternal medication, labor, and sex of infant. *Proceedings of the American Psychological Association,* 1972, *7,* 85–86.

PARKE, R., and SAWIN, D. The father's role in infancy: A re-evaluation. *Family Coordinator,* 1976, *25,* 365–371.

PARSONS, T., and BALES, R. *Family, socialization, and interaction process.* New York: Free Press, 1955.

PINNEAU, S. A critique on the articles by Margaret Ribble. *Child Development,* 1950, *21,* 203–228.

PRICE-BONHAM, S. Bibliography of literature related to roles of fathers. *Family Coordinator,* 1976, *25,* 489–512.

RATHOD, N., and THOMSON, I. Women alcoholics. *Quarterly Journal of Studies on Alcohol,* 1971, *32,* 45–52.

REBELSKY, F., and HANKS, C. Fathers' verbal interaction with infants in the first three months of life. *Child Development,* 1971, *42,* 63–68.

REDINA, I., and DICKERSCHEID, J. Father involvement with first-born infants. *Family Coordinator,* 1976, *25,* 373–378.

RIBBLE, M. *The rights of infants.* New York: Columbia University Press, 1943.

ROSSI, A. Transition to parenthood. *Journal of Marriage and the Family,* 1968, *30,* 26–39.

RUSSELL, C. Transition to parenthood: Problems and gratifications. *Journal of Marriage and the Family,* 1974, *36,* 294–302.

SANTROCK, J. The relation of type and onset of father absence to cognitive development. *Child Development,* 1972, *43,* 455–469.

SANTROCK, J., and WOHLFORD, P. Effects of father absence: Influence of the reason for the onset of the absence. *Proceedings of the American Psychological Association,* 1970, *5,* 44–45.

SCHVANEVELDT, J., FREYER, M., and OSTLER, R. Concepts of "goodness" and "badness" of parents as perceived by nursery school children. *Family Coordinator,* 1970, *19,* 98–103.

SEARS, R., MACCOBY, E., and LEVIN, H. *Patterns of child rearing.* New York: Harper & Row, 1957.

SEARS, R., PINTLER, M., and SEARS, P. The effect of father separation on preschool children's doll-play aggression. *Child Development,* 1946, *17,* 219–243.

SEARS, R., RAU, L., and ALPERT, R. *Identification and child rearing.* Stanford, Calif.: Stanford University Press, 1965.

SEWELL, W. Infant training and the personality of the child. *American Journal of Sociology,* 1952, *58,* 150–159.

SPITZ, R. Hospitalism. In O. Fenichel et al. (Eds.), *The psychoanalytical study of the child,* Vol. 1. New York: International Universities Press, 1945.

SUOMI, S. Social interactions of monkeys raised in a nuclear family environment versus monkeys reared with mothers and peers. *Primates,* 1974, *15,* 311–320.

STOLZ, L., et al. *Father relations of war-born children.* Stanford, Calif.: Stanford University Press, 1954.

TILLER, P. *Father separation and adolescence.* Oslo, Norway: Institute of Social Research, 1961.

WENTE, A., and CROCKENBERG, S. Transition to parenthood: Lamaze preparation, adjustment difficulty, and the husband–wife relationship. *Family Coordinator,* 1976, *25,* 351–358.

WINCH, R. *The modern family* (3rd ed.). New York: Holt, 1971.

ZELDITCH, M., JR. Role differentiation in the nuclear family. A comparative study. In T. Parsons and R. Bales (Eds.), *Family, socialization, and interaction process.* New York: Free Press, 1955. Pp. 307–351.

ZOLOTOW, C. *William's doll.* New York: Harper & Row, 1972.

3

Parenthood:
A Developmental Role

A central idea is evident in the historical cultural concepts of childhood and parenthood that were discussed in Chapter 1. This idea is that a parent is an agent of socialization and the child is the object of the parent's socialization efforts. This idea of parent–child relations is called a *unidirectional model of socialization*. Simply stated, this model features the parent's behavior as a stimulus that produces some particular response by the child. More broadly interpreted, this model implies that if a parent is "good" (that is, if he behaves properly as a parent, says and does the "right" things, and meets the necessary material and psychological needs of his child through caregiving activities), then the child will also be "good." Following this logic, if the formula of good parental performance is consistent over the years of child rearing, then it is assumed that the child will become a "good" adult. The child's socialization by the parent can then be judged successful.

Researchers in human development have come to view the unidirectional explanation or model of parent–child relations as being too simplistic and imprecise for several reasons (Bell, 1968, 1971). First, there is no real recognition of the interaction between parents and children. The flow of information is seen in this model as going only in one direction: from parent to child. Second, this model disregards the contribution of the child to the exchange of information that occurs between two or more dynamic people. Third, new information gained from research on humans and animals, as discussed by Bell, tends to invalidate this model as an adequate explanation of reality in the everyday world of parents and children.

This chapter discusses the relationship between parents and children that provides a primary opportunity for the psychosocial development of both individuals, especially the adults. Our culture promotes the idea that the development of an individual ceases after physical maturity is reached in adulthood. The psychosocial development of individuals within the family is dependent on interactions with others. Adults are socialized into their roles as parents through interactions with children, and children are socialized into adulthood by parents. The interaction between parents and children produces the healthy psychosocial development of each.

This chapter also presents Erikson's (1950) theory of psychosocial development through the life cycle as a frame of reference for understanding the interactional relationship between parents and children. The relationship between parents and children occurs within the context of family settings, and the family itself experiences changes in its development. Socialization is explained as an interactional process within the context of parent–child relations that changes as the individuals change throughout the course of life.

A FRAMEWORK: ERIKSON'S EIGHT AGES OF MAN

The majority of modern developmental theories focus on the development of the individual child. Extensive, abstract explanations have been formulated about the interaction between heredity and environment in influencing individual development. Whereas the growing years of childhood and adolescence have received the greatest attention, few developmental theorists use basic concepts to explain or interpret development beyond these age periods and into the years of adulthood and aging.

The theory of Erik Erikson (1950) is a notable exception to this cultural belief and to the notion that the development of an individual occurs only within the context of psychological and biological forces. Erikson's theory features development as a continuous process throughout life—not just as a primary process during the growing years. His explanation of the psychosocial development of the individual throughout the life cycle is a modern reinterpretation of Freudian psychology. It differs from earlier theories in the explanation of the developmental and social tasks that a person should accomplish at each stage of his or her development.

Erikson's concept of development emphasizes that the individual experiences a series of "childhoods" throughout life. Development is viewed as an evolutional process based on a universally experienced sequence of biological, social, and psychological events that take place between birth and death. Because an individual enters each stage of psychosocial development with the goal of developing the specific skills and competencies appropriate to this particular time, an individual never has *a* personality; rather she or he is always in the process of reshaping and revising his or her personality (Maier, 1975).

Each stage of development throughout life has its own theme, which Erikson terms a *psychosocial crisis*. Development is enhanced or retarded by an individual's experiences in confronting and handling each psychosocial crisis.

The person must confront a central problem (a specific psychosocial crisis) at each stage of development. The individual is given the opportunity to develop strengths and skills at each stage. Provided with an environment, both social and psychological, that is conducive to development, an individual faces each problem at each stage with the potential result of healthy, "normal" accomplishment. If the person experiences overwhelming difficulty in accomplishing what is expected, the result is subsequent difficulty in dealing with the psychosocial crises at future stages of development.

Development, however, does not occur in a vacuum. The process of development is not structured so that a person is forced to face the trials of life alone. Development usually occurs first within the context of a family and then within an increasingly wider social radius (friends, the school environment, and so on). "Significant others," or those who are singularly important to an individual, assist or inhibit his or her development at each stage. An individual proceeds to the next stage when she or he has met the particular requirements of biological, social, and psychological *readiness*. This readiness to progress further in development is significantly influenced by others in the environment and especially by the parents of a developing child.

The psychosocial crises at each stage of development present the individual with the challenge of developing what Erikson calls *psychosocial senses*. These senses correspond to the various stages that the individual experiences through the life cycle. The senses are attitudes or general feelings that result from how adequately the individual meets the psychosocial crisis at any particular stage of development. Eight stages of development are presented by Erikson in his theory. Each stage has its own particular psychosocial sense. Erikson describes the eight senses in an either/or manner. An individual develops either one or the other as a result of his experiences. In the early years of childhood, for example, children are thought to experience a psychosocial stage where they develop either a sense of autonomy or a sense of shame and doubt. Healthy development is represented by the child's achievement of the first sense: a sense of autonomy. At each of the eight stages, healthy development of the individual is believed to occur when the first of the two opposing senses is developed. Future difficulty is believed to be experienced if the individual develops the alternate sense.

The establishment of each of the eight senses at the corresponding stages of the life cycle implies that an individual develops the competencies required for healthy psychological and social functioning in society. An individual, for example, is faced with the challenge of developing what Erikson terms a sense of basic trust during infancy. Through his parents, the infant is provided with numerous experiences to interact with his physical and social environments. Consistency in care provided by parents and gentle handling, for example, help a baby to place its trust in those who care for it and in its surroundings. However, a series of experiences such as rough handling, being neglected, and severe inconsistency in caregiving can make the baby mistrust the social environment. The establishment of either of these senses has a bearing on the subsequent development of the child.

The optimistic nature of Erikson's theory provides the possibility of redemption at each stage of an individual's development. Although success in meeting the developmental tasks at any stage implies readiness to move to the next, failure or difficulty in establishing what is required at one stage does not condemn him or her to complete failure in the next, although development can be slowed or progress made more difficult.

Erikson uses a timetable to illustrate his eight stages of psychosocial development (see Table 3-1). Although the ages listed by Erikson are flexible guidelines for when the stages are experienced, the first five occur during the growing years of childhood and adolescence, and the remaining three occur during adulthood:

1. Sense of basic trust versus mistrust (birth to 18 months)
2. Sense of autonomy versus shame and doubt (18 months to 3 years)
3. Sense of initiative versus guilt (3 to 6 years)
4. Sense of industry versus inferiority (6 to 12 years)
5. Sense of identity versus role confusion (12 to 18 years)
6. Sense of intimacy versus isolation (18 to 24 years)
7. Sense of generativity versus self-absorption (24 to 54 years)
8. Sense of integrity versus despair (54 years to death)

Basic Trust Versus Mistrust (Stage I)

The primary developmental task of an infant from the time it is born until approximately 18 months of age is developing a *sense of basic trust* in his environment and in those who populate it. In our culture, the mother is the person within the family who is charged with providing the primary care of an infant and assisting it to develop a trusting attitude. The caregiving procedures and the forms of handling a baby receives determine if it is to develop a sense of basic trust or a sense of mistrust. Erikson believes that the process by which the baby achieves basic trust is by "getting and by giving in return" (see Table 3-1). An infant "gets" the attention and stimulation it needs from its parents and "gives" social stimulation to its parents in return.

One of the most significant factors that helps an infant to establish the sense of basic trust is the consistency of care provided by the parent. The quality of the interaction process between the mother and the baby is seen by Erikson to be of special importance. Anyone, from his point of view, can simply feed a baby. The establishment of a consistent pattern of holding, cuddling, speaking to, smiling at, and expressing love to a baby is best performed by the nurturant mother figure.

Learning to trust the environment occurs when a baby experiences consistency in his interactions with the physical world as well. The baby learns

Table 3-1. Erikson's Timetable of Developmental Stages

Stage	Psychosocial Crisis	Radius of Significant Others	Theme	Period of Life Cycle
I.	Trust vs. mistrust	Maternal person	To get; to give in return	Birth to 18 months
II.	Autonomy vs. shame/doubt	Paternal person	To hold on; to let go	18 months to 3 years
III.	Initiative vs. guilt	Family	To make; to make like	3 to 6 years
IV.	Industry vs. inferiority	"Neighborhood," school	To make things; to make together	6 to 12 years
V.	Identity vs. role confusion	Peer groups	To be oneself; to share being oneself	12 to 18 years
VI.	Intimacy vs. isolation	Partners in friendship, sex, competition	To lose and find oneself in another	18 to 24 years
VII.	Generativity vs. self-absorption	Partner	To make be; to take care of	24 to 54 years
VIII.	Integrity vs. despair	Mankind	To be, through having been; to face not being	54 years to death

(Adapted from Erikson, E., Identity and the life cycle: Selected papers. *Psychological Issues*, 1959, *1*, No. 1.)

that the day proceeds in a routine, its body experiences rhythms of wakefulness and rest, and it demands and receives food at certain intervals. Consistency in the environment is also learned when objects are released and the
baby notices that they always fall, making sounds and curious movements.
The factor of predictability cannot be underestimated, for the sense of mistrust is derived from unpredictability and inconsistency in caregiving experiences as well as in interactions with the environment.

Autonomy Versus Shame and Doubt (Stage II)

As a baby approaches the second birthday, many different events have occurred in his or her development. He or she is beginning to talk and to communicate with others, is able to walk, and eagerly explores the environment.
Many of the events experienced during the period from 18 months to three
years lead the young child toward greater independence and autonomy. For
the most part, a child is trying to communicate to the world-at-large the atti-

"DID YOU *HEAR* ME? AT *ONCE!* ...."

Figure 3-1.

tude, "I am BIG! I'm as strong as you are! I can do *anything*—BY MY-SELF!" This can be a somewhat bewildering experience not only for a child but also for the parents. The toddler discovers that she or he has a strong drive to attempt to stand alone and assert himself or herself. Most parents eventually learn that the "terrible two-year-old" maintains this strong-willed attitude through the third year. It is a period of tension and conflict not only between parents and child but also within the child. Having learned to be dependent on others, she or he discovers that this is no longer a satisfying experience. Negativism becomes a way of life for children at this time, and it is expressed by the proverbial "NO!" to almost every adult request.

Erikson believes that children become concerned at this stage of development with "holding on and letting go." They have a basic conflict of wanting and wishing for the aid and assistance of others but are also motivated toward mastering their ability to function independently. Tasks are learned that en-

" JIMMY, IT'S TIME TO GET UP, IF YOU STILL WANT TO GO FISHING WITH ME "

Figure 3-2.

sure their autonomy, such as toilet training, self-dressing, self-feeding, and so on. The father takes on additional importance in helping the child and the mother to relax the close emotional bonds that were established between them in the child's infancy. The ways that this is accomplished are discussed in Chapter 4.

Initiative Versus Guilt (Stage III)

The third through the sixth years of a child's life are a time for aggressive exploration of the social and physical worlds. At this time, a child devotes much attention to discovering what he or she can accomplish. Erikson calls this stage the time for developing a *sense of initiative:* an attitude of "I can" (see Table 3-1). Behavior during this stage is characterized by the theme of "making and making like." Children attempt many acts and are concerned with developing an awareness of the variety of social roles that are present in their environment. The basic social framework during this period is the child's family, and the value of siblings, grandparents, cousins, and other relatives as significant others increases.

The *sense of guilt* may be established if children of this age are penalized too severely or too frequently for their attempts to establish initiative behavior. Rather than learning that it is a positive matter to try new and different things, they may learn that it is far safer not to try too much. A pattern of passivity may be set for future behavior. Adults are challenged to reinforce initiative behaviors that are acceptable as the child explores and discovers his or her environment and capabilities. The problem for the child basically becomes a matter of learning to be responsible for his or her own behavior (see Figure 3-3).

Industry Versus Inferiority (Stage IV)

The middle childhood years are designated by Erikson to be the period when children are challenged to develop a *sense of industry* (see Table 3-1). The major theme of this period of psychosocial development is the child's determination to master what he is doing. Great efforts are placed on producing not only material things but things of a social nature. The conflict of this period is a fear of not being able to do enough, to be enough, or to be as good as others the same age. School-aged children become more involved in learning to relate and communicate with the individuals who are most significant to them at this time in their life: their peers. There is a striving to accomplish, to do something well, to be the first, or to be the best in some endeavor. Play activities and personal feelings reflect a competitive rather than an autonomous or a cooperative striving. Self-imposed segregation of the sexes is common and may promote the mastery of sex-role identification.

A child's fear of inferiority is founded on the knowledge that he or she is

"Jeffy opened all the cans of tennis balls just to hear them go 'ssss'!"

Figure 3-3.

still a child and an incomplete person who lacks the abilities to compete successfully in the adult-oriented world. As a consequence of these feelings, there is an ambivalence about growing up. On the one hand, the child aspires to have the responsibilities and privileges of the adult world, yet she or he wishes to retain the prerogatives of childhood.

The *sense of inferiority* becomes reinforced during the school-aged years when children come to believe that they cannot succeed or accomplish as much as they expect of themselves or as much as is expected of them by the school, their family, or their peers. A child's basic identity as a member of a peer group and status within that group becomes endangered when he or she perceives his or her abilities or "tools" (academic skills, athletic skills, and so on) to be inferior to those of others of the same age.

Identity Versus Role Confusion (Stage V)

The fifth stage of psychosocial development begins with puberty and lasts through the adolescent years (see Table 3-1). The challenge presented by this stage involves one of the major questions an individual confronts during life: "Who am I?" By experiencing a wide variety of roles and relationships

"Mommy, when other kids are around could you
call me Bill instead of Billy?"

Figure 3-4.

during the years of childhood and adolescence, the individual comes to form idealistic impressions and concepts about how things should be in the family, among friends, with himself or herself, and in social relationships. The resolution of the primary task of this stage represents an integrative process of assimilating and resolving the issues that emerged in all of the previous stages of psychosocial development. A clear identity of who one is, what is valued, what types of attitudes are important, and how to become involved in occupational roles becomes more focused during this time of the life cycle. Parents have almost completely been replaced by the peer group as the essential element of social support. The adolescent continues to utilize the family to assess her or his place in society and the values that the family have supported during the growing years of childhood.

The *sense of role confusion* results from failing to reach a certain degree of clarity about the primary role that the teenager will assume in adult life. This attitude reflects uncertainty about one's worth as a contributor in some way to society, not knowing where one belongs in life's work, and what values are important or how to go about achieving a vocational role or objective.

The support of parents during these years is important to help the adolescent sift through the questioning of life's purpose and how he or she fits into the environment called society.

Intimacy Versus Isolation (Stage VI)

By establishing an idea of who one is and where one is going in life, an individual is prepared for the next stage of development where he or she is concerned with "losing and finding himself or herself in another," according to Erikson. During this time of the life cycle, an individual is presented with the challenge of developing a close, warm, and intimate relationship with another person. The effectiveness of the sense of trust, learned and acquired long ago and reinforced over the years of childhood and adolescence, assists the individual in sharing his or her identity as a unique, worthwhile human being with another.

If a *sense of intimacy* is not acquired during this optimal time of life, a *sense of isolation* may develop. This attitude is reflected in a growing degree of self-devaluation. Experiences of the individual that reinforce the development of a sense of isolation are those in which she or he learns that others cannot be trusted in a close, intimate manner. It becomes too painful psychologically to be intimate and much safer for the individual's ego to stand alone and try to face life alone.

Generativity Versus Self-absorption (Stage VII)

The productive years of adulthood comprise the longest stage of psychosocial development (see Table 3-1). During this period, productivity may be seen in the establishment of a family, in achievements in one's occupation, or in an individual's creative involvements. Erikson describes the sense of generativity as the "interest in establishing and guiding the next generation or . . . the absorbing object of a parental kind of responsibility" (1950, p. 222). The person who fails to establish this sense of caring for others or of becoming involved with creative production becomes preoccupied with his or her own personal needs and interests above those of others. He or she comes to treat himself or herself as what Erikson calls "his own infant and pet" and acquires a *sense of self-absorption*.

Integrity Versus Despair (Stage VIII)

The last stage of psychosocial development is the fulfillment, result, and culmination of the preceding seven stages. The achievement of a *sense of integrity* is produced by an identification with mankind. The individual comes to understand and accept the meaning of his or her life and the uniqueness of his or her existence during a particular period of historical time in a particular culture (see Table 3-1). It is the time when one learns to accept the temporal limits of life.

The emergence of a *sense of despair* is derived from a feeling of loss in the way one's life was lived. This attitude is one of apology, regret, and fear of the end of life. The individual experiences a pervasive sense of "if only," that is, "*If only* I had gone to college, I might have had a better job," or "*If only* I had married someone else I might have been happier," and so on.

Erikson ends this description of psychosocial development through the life cycle by noting that trust is defined as reliance on another's integrity. Erikson makes the connection between adult ego integrity and infantile trust in concluding that "healthy children will not fear life if their elders have integrity enough not to fear death" (1950, p. 233).

DUVALL'S CONCEPT OF FAMILY DEVELOPMENT THROUGH THE LIFE CYCLE

The family as we know it today is called a *nuclear* family. This unit usually is composed of two adults and their children, although there may be variations in the composition. Burgess (1926) is widely quoted among family sociologists in describing the family as a *"unity of interacting personalities."* A unity in this sense describes the family as a whole focusing on the entire group as a functioning unit. Social interaction serves a vital purpose in the functioning of the family by promoting the psychological well-being and survival of each member.

The family plays an expressive role in social interaction. This means that within the family each member is nurtured and assisted by others as a developing individual and is provided with the means for meeting his or her emotional needs. The idea of a unity of interacting personalities implies that the family is a dynamic system that responds to change. The very fact that its members are dynamic, developing individuals ensures that families change as well.

Just as individuals follow predictable stages in their personal psychosocial development, families are thought to experience stages that follow a similarly predictable course of development. The family life cycle is a concept that explains the course of development that a family follows from its establishment to its demise.

Evelyn Duvall (1977) describes the family life cycle as progressing in two broad categories: (1) the *expanding family stage* consists of the development of the family from its establishment until the time when the children are grown; (2) the *contracting family stage* includes the time when the children are launched into family lives of their own and through the later years when the original couple is left at home. These broad categories are refined by Duvall into eight separate stages that trace the development of the family from its inception through the ending point in the life cycle of its original members. The developmental progress of the firstborn child is used to distinguish each stage during the years when children are being produced and raised to maturity. The stages and the length of time they are experienced are as follows (see Figure 3-5):

Stage 1. Married couples (without children)
Stage 2. Childbearing families (birth of oldest child to 30 months of age)
Stage 3. Families with preschool-aged children (oldest child 2½ to 6 years)
Stage 4. Families with school-aged children (oldest child 6 to 13 years)
Stage 5. Families with teenagers (oldest child 13 to 20 years)

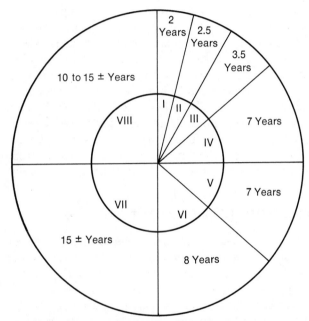

I. Married couples (without children).

II. Childbearing families (oldest child, birth–30 months).

III. Families with preschool children (oldest child 30 months–6 years).

IV. Families with schoolchildren (oldest child 6–13 years).

V. Families with teenagers (oldest child 13–20 years).

VI. Families as launching centers (first child gone to last leaving home).

VII. Middle-aged parents (empty nest to retirement).

VIII. Aging family members (retirement to death of both spouses).

Stage 6. Families as launching centers (first child gone to last child's leaving home)

Stage 7. Middle-aged parents ("empty nest" to retirement of couple)

Stage 8. Aging family members (retirement to death of both spouses)

Each stage of the family life cycle is thought to have its own characteristic events and developmental tasks, which affect not only each member of the family but the entire family unit as well. These tasks are similar to Erikson's psychosocial crises because each member of the family continues to develop as an individual within the context of the family setting. The life cycle of the family is punctuated by the stages that are experienced as a group and include the landmarks of marriage, the birth of children, the "empty nest" (when all children have left the home), and the death of a spouse in older age. The changes that are experienced by the family through the life cycle come from the development of the individuals who constitute the unit. Although parts of the cycle (Stages 1, 7, and 8) involve the married couple only and their development at these particular times in life, the others (Stages 2 through 6) center on producing and socializing children until they reach maturity. It is these portions of the family life cycle that are addressed in several of the following chapters of this book. Each stage of the family life cycle, then, draws its existence, its success, and its problems or challenges from the particular stage of personal development of its members *acting in unity*.

THE CONCEPT OF DEVELOPMENTAL INTERACTION

Erikson's description of psychosocial development through the individual's life cycle provides the basic framework for an understanding of the process of individual psychology. A family, however, is composed of several individuals of various ages who are involved in developing the tasks of different psychosocial stages simultaneously. The parents are usually at the stage of psychosocial development termed *generativity* versus *self-absorption*. If several children have been produced by the couple, it is possible that one child is involved in the tasks of industry versus inferiority, another is developing the tasks of the initiative versus guilt stage, and the baby is learning to accomplish the tasks of basic trust versus mistrust.

Erikson feels that development throughout life does not occur in a vacuum of social isolation from others. Although the individual is guided by basic biological laws in the overall process of development, he or she is assisted in his or her development first by the family and later by other agents, including individuals, groups, and institutions.

When examining the socialization processes within the family, noting that this group is composed of individuals who are each involved in a dynamic state of development, we are introduced to the concept of *developmental interaction* between parents and children. The intertwining nature of an individual's own present stage of development with those being experienced by others within the family is the basis of developmental interaction. Erikson illustrates this concept by stating that:

> man's psychosocial survival is safeguarded by vital virtues which develop in the interplay of successive and overlapping generations living together in organized settings. Here, living together means more than incidental proximity. It means that the individual's life-stages are "inter-living," cogwheeling with the stages of others which move him along as he moves them. [Erikson, 1964, p. 114]

Developmental interaction is apparent in the mesh of ongoing developmental stages of parents with those of their children. This concept depicts the family as a system of interacting personalities (Burgess, 1926), with each member affecting the others in the process of development. It features the parent–child relationship as a dyadic or triadic interactional system involving sequences of behavior in which there is mutual stimulation, reinforcement, and responses so that each individual is the recipient as well as the initiator of behavior.

Focusing more closely on this concept, there is a correspondence of developmental stages between parents and children that lies primarily at a point in developmental time when the adults approach the psychosocial stage of generativity versus self-absorption. The focal point of parents at this time is the investment of their interest in the care and nurturance of the next generation: their children. The psychosocial need of parents at this time in life is "to give and to take care of." The infant, for example, is at a point in developmental time when it confronts a problem of learning to trust others, and its psychosocial response is to receive, "to get and to give in return." There is a direct correspondence and reciprocity between the needs of the parents and the needs of the child. Erikson illustrates developmental interaction in infancy, for example, by stating that:

> newborn man (a baby) is endowed with an appearance and with responses which appeal to the tending adults' tenderness and make them wish to attend to his needs; which arouse concern in those who are concerned with his well-being; and which in making adults care, stimulate their active caretaking. [Erikson, 1964, p. 113]

The correspondence of developmental stages and needs between parents and children does not end with infancy but continues throughout the lives of the individuals involved in this mutual relationship. As a child moves up the developmental ladder, his or her needs and responses to these needs change and affect a corresponding shift in the parents' methods of child rearing. Parents learn, from their interactions with a growing, developing child, that they must change their approach according to the child's developmental level. This shift on the part of parents is affected in numerous ways by their child. The striving for autonomy, for example, during the early years of childhood prompts entirely different patterns of parental caregiving than are called for in aiding children to develop a sense of basic trust or a sense of initiative. Life, for both parents and children, proceeds according to these interactional sequences, with the child assisting or inhibiting the parents in their feelings of developing a sense of generativity and with the parents assisting or inhibiting the child in meeting the challenges of each developmental stage.

A study by Clifford (1959) on the types, time, and frequency of discipline used by mothers of three-, six-, and nine-year-old children provides evidence on how a child's development affects changes in parenting behavior. As the children grew older, their ability to communicate verbally, to respond to reasoning, to use logic, and to develop control of their own behavior was shown in the shift from the mothers' use of physical punishments to verbal methods of control (see Figure 3-6). The change in the children's behavior effected a corresponding change in the responses of the mothers to control unacceptable behavior.

SOCIALIZATION THROUGH DEVELOPMENTAL INTERACTION

The process of socialization involves the learning of the various attitudes, values, and expectations of appropriate behavior, social roles, and so on that are considered important for effective social functioning. The learning process may occur through a variety of methods, such as observation learning, imitation, and behavioral conditioning.

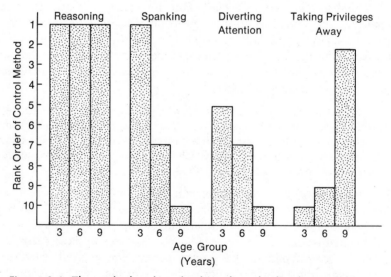

Figure 3-6. The ranked order of selected methods of parental controls of children's behavior in three age groups. (Source: Clifford, E. Discipline in the home: A controlled observational study of parental practices. *Journal of Genetic Psychology*, 1959, 95, 45–82.)

Placed within the context of developmental interaction are the changes that occur within the parent–child system as a result of the dynamic maturational process occurring in both individuals, but especially within the child. A growing, developing child does not present the parent with a stable, continually consistent behavior pattern over time. The changes that occur within children force them to organize their behavior into more complex patterns and effect corresponding changes in the parents' behavior.

Socialization has been viewed by researchers until recently as lying within the domain of the parent who actively or covertly teaches children many of the things they need to know to function later in life as adults. The contribution of children to the socialization of parents has been ignored or minimized for the most part.

Johnson and Medinnus (1974) present this unidirectional process of socialization as a one-way, cause-and-effect relationship between parent and child:

Parent   ——————————→   Child
Characteristics   Characteristics

The concept of developmental interaction, however, implies that the varying nature of children's developmental demands induces a comparable variety and change in the caregiving responses of parents. Parents become significantly affected by their children in their own development as adults, just as they are influential in the development of their children. This interaction between parents and children is shown by Johnson and Medinnus as:

Parent ←————————— Child

Parent	Child
Characteristics ————————→	Characteristics
Individual traits	Individual traits
Behavior	Behavior
Attitudes	Personality
Personality	Sex of individual
Sex of individual	Developmental stage

This relationship recognizes the child as affecting how the parent reacts to him or her and features the mutual influence of both participants on the behavior of the other in social interaction (see Figure 3-7).

The very nature of a developing child assists parents in meeting their psychological need to "take care of" in developing their sense of generativity. The constancy of this challenge to parents' development of a sense of generativity, however, is tempered by the ever-changing, dynamic stages of development that the child experiences throughout the growing years. In the process of developmental interaction between parents and children, all the participants are involved in meeting the parents' need to be needed and a child's accomplishment of his or her own developmental tasks. For example,

"THE LITTLE NEIGHBOR BOY MUST BE BEHAVING BETTER.
YOUR BLOOD PRESSURE IS."

Figure 3-7.

in the first stage of a child's psychosocial development, parents convey to their child through the quality of their caregiving a philosophical attitude concerning the trustworthiness of society and of themselves in particular. Parents encourage their child to achieve autonomy in the second stage, and as a result the child learns the value of individuality within acceptable limits and a respect for the authority of those who are in charge of his or her well-being. During the third stage, after learning the value of social autonomy, a child discovers the notion of parental domesticity and sex-role identification: models by which to pattern his or her own future roles in life. By enacting their need to be needed, parents provide a child with a concept of initiative that is accompanied by a host of life lessons in learning the cultural expectations of appropriate social functioning for the future.

The actual child-rearing methods employed by parents become modified in part by the changing nature of the child as development takes place (see

Figure 3-8.

Figure 3-8). Differences in the individual predispositions of both parents and children influence the nature and quality of the interaction that occurs. The inherent nature of a child has an inescapable influence on modifying a parent's approach toward specific child-rearing practices. Researchers have recognized that every child, like every adult, seems to have a unique style of behavior, which is believed to have partially genetic origins and to become modified through environmental experiences (Bell, 1968; McClearn, 1970). When parents have preconceived notions of how they intend to conduct the socialization of their child, it is very likely that they will find their responses being modified and changed by the child's individual style of response. Attempts to change or shape a child's behavioral style are often determined by the resistance or compliance of a child in responding to parenting efforts.

The correspondence of the psychosocial stages of the parents with those being experienced by a child constitutes the basis of developmental interaction. Families, however, typically include more than one child, each of whom progresses through the stages outlined by Erikson. The stages being experienced by the children overlap one another by several years (Duvall, 1977). Conflicts and pressures are placed on parents to respond simultaneously to the different developmental needs of children of different ages. Differing needs and developmental demands of children may clash with the different needs of the parents.

The oldest child may have the greatest socializing effect on the parents and the family as a whole in that she or he is the one who first "teaches" the parents their roles as caregivers and who acts as a pace setter for the children who follow. The oldest child provides the parents with their first experiences in child rearing and presents them with all of the problems and challenges that a changing, developing child experiences while growing older. The younger children experience an entirely different type of parenting experience than the firstborn child (Lasko, 1954), although each child has his or her own unique style and rate of development.

POINTS TO CONSIDER

- Erikson (1950) provides a theory of eight stages describing the psychosocial development of individuals through the life cycle.
- The theory provides a frame of reference for an understanding of the interaction between parents and children.
- Families are thought to experience stages of development that follow a predictable pattern.
- The concept of developmental interaction is derived from Erikson's description of the psychosocial development of individuals through the life cycle.
- Developmental interaction implies that children, who in presenting their own developmental needs and tasks, serve as a stimulus for the psychosocial development of their parents.
- The concept functions throughout the course of family development and is seen primarily in the context of parent–child relations.
- The concept conveys the notion that (1) the parent–child relationship is neither a one-sided nor causal relationship; and (2) interaction throughout the child-rearing years between parents and children affects the healthy development of each.

REFERENCES

BELL, R. A reinterpretation of the direction of effects in studies of socialization. *Psychological Review*, 1968, *75*, 81–95.

BELL, R. Stimulus control of parent or caretaker behavior by offspring. *Developmental Psychology*, 1971, *4*, 63–72.

BURGESS, E. The family as a unity of interacting personalities. *Family*, 1926, *7*, 3–9.

CLIFFORD, E. Discipline in the home: A controlled observational study of parental practices. *Journal of Genetic Psychology*, 1959, *95*, 45–82.

DUVALL, E. *Marriage and family development* (5th ed.). Philadelphia: J. B. Lippincott, 1977.

ERIKSON, E. *Childhood and society*. New York: Norton, 1950.

ERIKSON, E. *Insight and responsibility*. New York: Norton, 1964.

JOHNSON, R., and MEDINNUS, G. *Child psychology: Behavior and development* (3rd ed.). New York: Wiley, 1974.

LASKO, J. Parent behavior toward first and second children. *Genetic Psychology Monographs*, 1954, *49*, 99–137.

MAIER, H. *Three theories of child development* (rev. ed.). New York: Harper & Row, 1975.

McCLEARN, G. Genetic influences on behavior and development. In P. Mussen (Ed.)., *Carmichael's manual of child psychology* (3rd ed). New York: Wiley, 1970. Pp. 39–76.

TWO

Developmental Interaction in the Child-Rearing Years

The family unit is concerned with producing children and socializing them for an estimated 20-year period. During this time, the oldest child progresses through five psychosocial stages in developing the sense of basic trust, autonomy, initiative, industry, and identity. The parents, during these years, are involved in developing their sense of generativity.

Developmental interaction between parents and children during these years assists the individuals in the family to achieve the developmental tasks that are unique to each stage. Parents assist children in meeting the demands and challenges of their progress through the stages outlined by Erikson (see Chapter 3). Their style of interacting with their children changes as a response to the changing nature and goals of the children's developmental stages. The shifts and refinements that occur in interaction between parents and children are evident in many ways that are discussed in the following chapters. Parents learn, for example, that as a child matures they must change from being physical helpers to being psychological helpers in assisting the child to cope with cultural expectations of appropriate behavior. Other expressions of caregiving change as well. When children are young, parents' physical expressions of nurturance predominate, whereas verbal methods such as encouragement, reassurance, and listening to problems appear more frequently as children grow older. Parents also change in their methods of control. Physical means of control are used more frequently when children are young and shift to psychological and verbal methods as children enter the school-age and teenage years. Isolating a child may be more effective and appropriate, for example, during the preschool years than in the teenage years. Denying privileges may be more successful in controlling inappropriate behavior of adolescents.

This part of the text examines the changes that occur in the interaction between parents and children during the child-rearing years of the family life cycle. A discussion of what parents confront in their development as adults is included as a part of several chapters. The concept of developmental interaction recognizes that adults in the family are developing individuals who have needs that are unique to their stage of the life cycle. Adults are challenged in their own personal development to meet certain tasks. Throughout the child-rearing years, the challenge for the family unit as a whole involves each individual's meeting his or her own personal developmental tasks while being supportive of the others in meeting their developmental needs.

4

Developmental Interaction in Infancy

THE TRANSITION TO PARENTHOOD

The achievement of a sense of intimacy during early adulthood serves as a foundation for preparing individuals to face the challenges of the next stage of psychosocial development, termed the *sense of generativity*. When individuals are involved in establishing the sense of intimacy, their ego involvement is focused on what Erikson calls "losing and finding oneself in another" (see Chapter 3). This is accomplished in our culture in a variety of ways.

Perhaps the most common experience in establishing the sense of intimacy occurs through dating and engagement, which usually result in marriage. By the time an individual has reached the level of maturation that leads to this stage of psychosocial development, he or she has had numerous dating experiences with a variety of individuals, in most cases. These experiences allow the person the opportunity to discover those qualities in another that she or he considers to be important, necessary, and desirable in a mate.

The sense of intimacy generally emerges in a close, warm, and trusting relationship that is established over a period of time with another individual. Patterns of interaction are developed; each partner learns the likes and dislikes of the other; actions of the other are learned and eventually come to be anticipated; and routines are established. Living together aids the couple in developing this psychosocial attitude of closeness. The ritual of marriage, whether formally or informally performed, acts as a symbol of the emotional commitment of one individual to another.

The new roles of husband and wife are usually well known to us as children. We generally grow up knowing what is expected as appropriate role behaviors of a husband and wife. Our culture prepares us in numerous ways throughout the childhood years to assume these roles. We are generally reared in a family unit that has these roles occupied by a man and a woman, and these roles become familiar to us through books, movies, and television shows. The parenting roles of father and mother are familiar to us as well, but preparation for these roles is quite lacking for most people.

The biological event of a couple's having their first child serves as the stimulus for a variety of changes that occur not only in their relationship but also in each individual. What was formerly a fairly manageable relationship and interactional pattern between husband and wife is now transformed into a more complicated situation that involves a six-way interactional pattern (see Figure 4-1). A family has been established with the birth of the first child; one that gives meaning to the phrase "a unity of interacting personalities."

The transition to the parenting roles is not as easy, comfortable, or successful as we may wish. Family researchers have studied the changes and adjustments that occur after the birth of the first child. Pregnancy forces the couple to confront the impending change in their life styles and interaction patterns, but the confrontation is more like the preparations that are made for a trip to a foreign country never visited before by the couple. Certain arrangements must be made for the new baby, such as preparing and equipping a nursery and seeing that the mother is provided with adequate nutrition and medical supervision. Once the birth has occurred, however, most people know little about what to expect from the baby itself, how parenting behavior should be conducted, and even how to perform the most essential parenting skills, such as breast-feeding, bathing the baby, and other caregiving practices.

Pregnancy has come to be viewed as a medical concern rather than a normal aspect of family life. Our increased control of conception has resulted in fewer births per family unit, to the point where pregnancy is almost a phenomenon rather than an expected result of marital sexual encounters. Young people grow up knowing very little about babies. This is particularly the case for males, who usually lack the extensive experiences of baby-sitting or caring for younger siblings. The increasing popularity and acceptance of child-

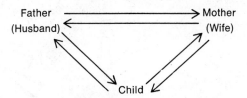

Figure 4-1. The addition of the baby into the interactional pattern already established between the father and mother increases the possible number of interactional bonds from two to six.

birth preparation classes aids couples to gain a rudimentary idea of what to expect during the birth itself. Couples are still left, however, to trial-and-error learning of parenting skills after the baby is born.

One point made by Rossi (1968) in the last chapter concerned the abruptness of the transition from being a childless couple to being parents. The birth of the baby brings immediate caregiving responsibilities. There is the overwhelming realization that these responsibilities are a twenty-four-hour, every-day-of-the-week, year-long reality. As compared with other adult roles, there is no gradual assumption of the duties and responsibilities of parenting; there is no beginning and no quitting time; there are few vacations; and there is no provision for resigning from the role (see Figure 4-2).

The "Parenthood as Crisis" Studies

The point discussed by Rossi, the abruptness of change into new roles, was the basis of E. E. LeMasters' (1957) proposal that the birth of the first child is a crisis event in a couple's marital relationship. LeMasters believes that our culture supports a "romantic complex" about parenthood. This complex

"I said, DO YOU HAVE ANY CHILDREN?"

Figure 4-2.

involves an extensive folklore about the joys of parenthood that create un-realistic expectations about the nature of child rearing. LeMasters thought that people had feelings of disenchantment after having their first child. He collected interview data on forty-six middle-class couples who had their first child five years previous to the interview. Of these couples 83 per cent re-ported an extensive or severe crisis in adjusting to the baby's presence. Mothers reported feelings or experiences such as losing sleep, worrying about their appearance and housekeeping standards, being chronically tired, and giving up social contacts and the income from employment outside the home. Fathers reported similar feelings and also mentioned a decline in the sexual responsiveness of the wife.

Although the LeMasters study brought attention to the effects of the first baby on the parents' marital relationship, other researchers questioned the validity of his findings. Everett Dyer (1963) performed a subsequent investi-gation to replicate the results of LeMasters's study. Dyer's results confirmed the prediction that the first baby forced the couple to reorganize many pat-terns of interaction. Dyer also found that the severity of the crisis was de-pendent on (1) the degree of the marital and family organization at the time of the baby's birth; (2) the degree of the couple's preparation for parent-hood and marriage; (3) the degree of adjustment in the marital relationship after the birth; and (4) other variables, such as the number of years married prior to the child's birth, whether the child was planned, and the age of the child. Most couples who reported severe crisis in Dyer's study were able to recover and reorganize their relationship several months after the baby's birth.

One researcher remained unconvinced that these studies truly represented the experiences and reactions of most married couples to the birth of their first child. Dan Hobbs (1965) performed additional studies that focus on the reports of a more representative group of parents than those interviewed by LeMasters or Dyer. In his study 86 per cent of the couples reported slight crisis reactions, a finding that was diametrically different than what LeMasters and Dyer had found. Other studies have confirmed Hobb's findings (Cole and Hobbs, 1975; Maynard and Hobbs, 1975).

The results of these studies lead to various conclusions and take on addi-tional meaning when one is examining the changes in satisfaction within the marriage relationship over the family life cycle. Boyd Rollins and Harold Feldman (1970) used a large sample of middle-class couples much like those surveyed in the crisis studies to investigate marital satisfaction through the family life cycle. From the reports of the husbands and wives, as shown in Figure 4-3, it becomes apparent that evaluations of marital happiness are lowest during the years when children are in the home, beginning with the birth of the first child.

Whether the birth of the first child is termed a crisis or a transitional event, changes *do* occur in the marriage relationship, adjustments occur in the life

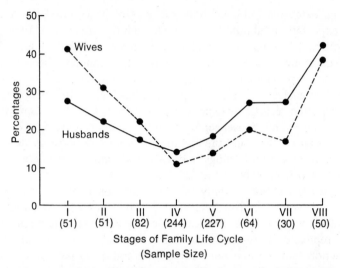

Figure 4-3. The percentage of individuals at each stage of the family life cycle who reported their marriage was going well "all the time." A reanalysis of scores on a 6-point scale with 1 equaling "never" and 6 equaling "all the time" indicated that only 4 per cent of the variance of marital satisfaction scores was associated with family life cycle stages. This is because a large percentage of those in the middle stages are satisfied "most of the time." (Source: Rollins, B., & Feldman, H. Marital satisfaction over the family life cycle. *Journal of Marriage and the Family,* 1970, *32,* 20–28. Copyright 1970 by the National Council on Family Relations. Reprinted by permission.)

styles of both husband and wife, and reorganization of interactions takes place. The parents are launched by the birth of the child toward the challenges of the sense of generativity in their own particular and unique ways.

THE INFANT: AN ACTOR/REACTOR

There are two principal views concerning the nature of an infant. One concept of infancy is a legacy of Freudian psychology. This is the *psychoanalytical* view, which places importance on the early experiences of the infant as determinants of characteristics in later life. The second view is termed the *developmental* concept of infancy. The infant is seen as an adaptable individual who is able to initiate behaviors and make responses in interacting with the environment. Early experiences are important in this framework as well but lack finality in their impact on the child's future development, unlike the psychoanalytical viewpoint.

The Psychoanalytical View of Infancy

The discussion in Chapter 1 presented the evolution of the unidirectional effects model of socialization from parent to child. This behavioral model, which has been accepted for generations, was reinforced and gained support from the writings of Sigmund Freud, the founder of psychoanalytical psychology.

Stated in general terms, the psychoanalytical view holds that the early experiences of children, especially in their infancy, have a profound effect on the determination of their adult personalities. These early experiences are provided primarily through the caregiving activities of the parents and especially of the mother during the infant's first months and years. Proponents of this viewpoint place an immense amount of psychological pressure on parents to perform the "right" actions in their caregiving. Whether a child develops a healthy personality or is handicapped with personality and behavior problems is thought to be solely dependent on how well the parents conduct their child-rearing activities. This viewpoint makes parenting and the experiences of growing up an all-or-nothing affair. Stated in another way, the human personality is believed to be permanently formed in infancy and early childhood and cannot be changed later in life except through a long and involved examination of the personality through psychoanalysis.

Many studies have been performed to investigate the validity of this view. The results of these studies influenced what were considered the "appropriate" caregiving methods during the 1940s and 1950s. The writings of Margaret Ribble (1943, 1944), John Bowlby (1952), William Goldfarb (1945), and Rene Spitz (1945) emphasized the influence of mothering on the physical and psychological well-being of the baby. Psychologists who supported this view of the infant felt that the nature and degree of a mother's intervention with the infant's "natural" drives determined its reactions and subsequent personality development. Freudian psychology, for example, emphasizes that an infant could be exposed to psychological dangers if it is frustrated in satisfying the inborn drive to suck. The source of this frustration lies in the way the baby is fed and later weaned. These concepts in Freudian psychology led to controversy among professionals as to whether it was psychologically better for the baby to be fed on a regular, fixed schedule (whether it was hungry or not) or to be fed by self-demand (only when it indicated that it was hungry). There was controversy also regarding breast versus bottle feeding, how long the baby should be fed before weaning, if he should be allowed to suck his thumb, when the best time was for weaning, when toilet training should begin and what the best methods were, and so on. The recommended "good" child-rearing practices of this period were considered important in preventing the infant from developing fixations. These fixations were thought to retard the baby's normal psychological development.

The Developmental Point of View

The developmental view holds that the infant is an actor in as well as a re-actor to the physical and social environment. Developmentalists believe that a baby can initiate as well as react to a large number of stimulations. Unlike in the psychoanalytical view, a single traumatic event is not thought to be devastating to the baby's future psychological development. Difficulty occurs when a traumatic event is repeated or continually reinforced during the course of a child's developing years. An example would be of a baby who is frightened by a large dog, is continually reminded of the traumatic episode by his parents each time a dog approaches him, and is not allowed to touch or play with dogs or to have a dog.

The baby, from the developmental point of view, is not like a human sponge that simply absorbs each and every stimulation that it perceives. Anderson (1948) expresses the developmental view by stating that the baby is an integrated psychological system capable of selectively choosing those stimuli from the environment to which to respond. The infant is believed to be an interactor with that environment and those who populate it but on a selective basis. As Anderson states, "The infant does not respond passively to all the stimulations to which he is exposed without action or selection on his part" (1948, p. 412).

The developmental view of the infant is supported by empirical evidence and incorporates the model of parent–child relations presented in the last chapter. The effects of the baby are seen as interacting with those of the parents in influencing the behavior of both individuals.

The evidence that shows a child's behavior influencing that of an adult is especially pertinent when a baby is the central figure. Harriet Rheingold (1966, p. 7) states that, "The amount of attention and the number of responses directed to an infant (by adults) are enormous—all out of proportion to his age, size, and accomplishments" (see Figure 4-4).

What motivates an adult to behave as she or he does toward an infant? Although we don't yet have all the answers to this question, one explanation may be that it is the baby's appearance, its helpless and dependent nature, and certainly its cries of distress or discomfort, which serve as powerful stimuli in eliciting caregiving from adults. The crying of a baby may serve as a particularly effective stimulus for caregiving. Rheingold (1966, p. 11) states, for example, that "So aversive, especially to humans, is the crying of an infant that there is almost no effort we will not expend, no device we will not employ, to change a crying baby to a smiling one—or just a quiet one." The appearance and nature of an infant may have an equally strong impact.

"IT DIDN'T SOUND LIKE 'DADDY' TO ME. HECK, I'VE HEARD *PARAKEETS* TALK PLAINER'N *THAT!*"

Figure 4-4.

Although there is little empirical evidence to support this view, Erikson (1964, p. 115) believes that, "Newborn man (an infant) is endowed with an appearance and with responses that appeal to the tending adults' tenderness and make them wish to attend to his needs . . . and which in making adults care, stimulate their active caretaking."

Richard Bell (1968) proposes that children are born with congenital determinants of their behavior. These congenital determinants may be influential in eliciting certain types of parenting behavior. Barry Brazelton (1969) discusses the effects on parenting behavior of these different types of dispositions of babies. He believes that all infants can be classified into three general groups on the basis of their behavior: (1) average; (2) quiet; and (3) active babies. These different types of dispositions, which are present at birth, may elicit different reactions and styles of parenting behavior. For

Table 4-1. Caregiving Sequence Between Mother and Infant

Recorded Time	Baby's Behavior	Mother's Behavior
Minute 1 to 13	Is awake, but lies quietly in crib.	—
Minute 13 to 16	Begins to fuss.	Orients to baby; no caregiving behavior is shown.
Minute 16 to 17	a. Begins to cry loudly; grimaces; thrashes around in crib.	b. Comes over and stands by crib; talks to baby.
	c. Continues crying.	d. Picks up baby; cradles him in arms.
	e. Reduces movements, but continues crying.	f. Talks again to baby.
	g. Crying continues.	h. Shifts baby about.
	i. Crying continues.	j. Holds baby up in air and in front of her.
	k. Crying continues.	l. Holds baby against shoulder and bubbles him; rubs and pats him.
	m. Crying is reduced to fussing but begins crying again, then becomes quiet.	n. Talks to baby.
	*o. Remains quiet; makes a small sound.	p. Talks again to baby; places him in infant seat.
	*q. Continues to be quiet; smiles.	r. Leaves baby and returns to her work.

* These acts denote behaviors by the baby that reinforce parenting behavior.

Source: R. Q. Bell. Stimulus control of parent or caretaker behavior by offspring. *Developmental Psychology*, 1971, *4*, 63–72. Copyright 1971 by the American Psychological Association. Reprinted by permission.

example, babies who would be classified as the quiet type may be slower to respond to adult stimulation. Such a disposition may make adults work harder to stimulate any type of response.

The behavior of a baby influences the parenting responses of the adults and constitutes an important part of the sequence of developmental interac-

Table 4-2. Interaction Sequence Between Mother and Infant *

Recorded Time	Baby's Behavior	Mother's Behavior
Minute 1 to 3½	Vocalizes 8 times.	Responds by talking to baby 8 times.
Minute 4	a. Smiles at mother.	b. Talking to baby increases to one utterance every 3 seconds.
	c. Vocalizing increases to once each 4 seconds.	
Minute 5 to 7½	Vocalizes 6 times.	Responds by talking to baby 6 times.
Minute 8		a. Picks baby up and holds him; tickles him; turns attention to something else.
	b. Baby fusses, then cries.	c. Picks baby up.
	d. Continues to cry	e. Leaves baby.

* This interaction shows what Bell (1971) considers to be a "game" between the mother and the baby, in which each participant alternates in providing a response that serves as a stimulus for the other's response. The vocalizations of the baby and the talking of the mother are especially pertinent to this "game" of developmental interaction.
Source: R. Bell. Stimulus control of parent or caretaker behavior by offspring. *Developmental Psychology*, 1971, *4*, 63–72. Copyright 1977 by the American Psychological Association. Reprinted by permission.

tion between parents and child. The two roles are reciprocal in action and in effect, however. There is an interchange during social interactions between the adult and the baby in which a unit of behavior is at the same time a response for one individual and a stimulus for the other. In developmental interaction between a parent and a baby, each caregiving response of the parent affects the child, and the behavior of the child stimulates and modifies the caregiving behavior of the adult.

Richard Bell (1971) suggests that certain classes or types of behavior of a baby elicit a variety of responses from the adult caregiver and vice versa. Bell describes two sequences of behavior that involve a three-month-old baby and his mother. The first example illustrates the effects of the baby's behavior in influencing the caregiving activities of the mother. The second example shows the interaction of the baby and the mother influencing the behavior of each (see Tables 4-1 and 4-2).

The sequences of behavior that Bell describes may seem to be very mundane or commonplace and lack significance to the untrained observer. Exchanges of these types of interaction occur daily between mothers and babies. The important point about these descriptions is that researchers are just beginning to investigate the enormous complexity of behavior that occurs in behavioral sequences like these. The examples are significant in helping us to understand that although the behavior of the adult does influence the behavior of the child, numerous cues and stimuli come also from the child to influence, control, and determine a wide variety of alternatives in parenting behavior. The changes in a baby's behavior are not necessarily the result only of the stimulations by the adult because the baby is both an actor and a reactor in influencing parenting behavior.

LANDMARKS OF INTERACTION IN INFANCY

An Infant's Developmental Needs

The period of life that includes infancy is defined by Erikson as occurring from birth to eighteen months of age. Many complex changes and events occur in a child's development that are unique to this time of the life cycle. We are aware of the fact that many developmental events occurring in the stage of infancy are the product of maturational changes within the baby. Under adequate conditions, these developmental and maturational changes include (1) appropriate growth in size and weight; (2) changes in physiological structures and their functions; (3) changes in body proportions; and (4) the development of certain physical skills, including walking and speech. Other developmental events occurring in infancy are more psychological in nature and are more sensitive to environmental influences. These events include (5) the emergence of critical periods in the developmental scheme of the infant's psychological development; and (6) the effects of early experience with an environment that is both physical and social in nature.

Babies come into their world with the capacity for experiencing certain developmental events that have been "programmed" to occur and others that are subject to modification by the environment in their impact on the child. Because we believe that infants are active participants in influencing their social environment and the responses of their caregivers to their behavior, the caregiver needs to be aware that the baby will provide certain behavioral cues. These will be of assistance to the caregiver in guiding the kinds of stimulation the baby needs for healthy development. To recognize these cues, caregivers need to be observant of the baby's behavior and know what is occurring appropriately at different times during this stage of development and those that follow.

Age-specific characteristics are often used as guides to assist observers in being alert to expected behavioral and developmental events in children's lives. These descriptions of normative characteristics are rather general and somewhat idealistic. They should be used only as guides to landmarks that punctuate the different developmental stages of the life cycle. No particular child will fit the characteristics perfectly, but their value lies in showing the organization and trends in development that are typical of the human species as a whole.

DEVELOPMENTAL EVENTS OF INFANCY

During the time from birth to eighteen months of age, there are four major developmental events that an infant experiences:

1. Adjusting physically to the birth.
2. Learning self-regulated behaviors.
3. Establishing a sense of basic trust.
4. Learning self-differentiation.

Physical Adjustments to Birth

The first year after birth is characterized by (1) the multitude of adjustments that must be made to a new environment outside of the uterus following birth; and (2) a resumption of the developmental and growth processes, begun prior to the birth, that follow the adjustment period.

The birth of the baby can be considered an interruption of the processes that were begun at conception, according to Hurlock (1975). The change brought about by the birth is rather abrupt and calls for several major adjustments for the baby's survival. They include (1) the initiation of respiration; (2) stabilization of body temperature; and (3) the initiation of certain organ functions.

The event of the birth itself is hazardous, but additional problems can arise from breech or Caesarean presentations; the amount of medication given to the mother during labor; the length of labor; the health status and age of the mother during pregnancy; the ease of establishing respiration following the birth; the length of the pregnancy (full-term or premature); the weight of the baby at birth; the presence of congenital disease or malformations; and multiple or singleton birth.

Immaturity of the baby at birth is a major factor in inhibiting the baby's adjustment following birth (Williams, 1975). Developmental immaturity is recognized by a short gestation period; weak or poorly organized reflexes; and a low birth weight (under 5½ pounds). These conditions result in difficulty in establishing and maintaining respiration, in feeding, and in initiating other organ functions. This situation is difficult not only for the baby but also for the parents. The parents may develop attitudes of overprotection, anxiety, and overconcern, which in turn, may produce subsequent problems in establishing the emotional bonds between the parents and child. The prolonged hospitalization that is usually required under these conditions may cause a similar problem.

Self-regulated Behaviors

The maturational processes that a baby experiences following birth lead to an increased ability to regulate certain behaviors and body functions. The types of self-regulated behaviors that emerge and come under control during the next eighteen months include feeding, sleeping, and basic motor skills.

FEEDING.   The sucking reflex is one of the earliest to appear during prenatal development and is exceptionally well developed at birth in full-term infants. This necessary reflex—which is easily elicited by almost any stimulation to the lips, cheeks, and mouth area—ensures that the infant can be nourished.

Most normal infants require a feeding once every three or four hours for the first few months after birth. After the introduction of solid foods into the baby's diet (usually during the second month), the number of feedings is reduced throughout the day as the baby grows older.

Self-feeding is generally accomplished by babies when they are able to

Figure 4-5.

hold a cup and drink from it as well as coordinate their hands to bring food to the mouth and chew it adequately. These events largely emerge as a result of maturational processes and cultural expectations or experiences (see Figure 4-5). Developmental norms have been established that show the times at which these events can be expected to occur (see Table 4-3).

Feeding behavior is closely associated with other developmental events. It also acts as a vehicle for promoting development in other areas affecting the baby's psychological well-being.

SLEEPING.   It has been said that babies and old dogs have much in common: they both spend most of their time sleeping. Sleeping patterns in infancy are subject to wide individual differences. Some infants may require long periods of sleep, and others may sleep for only short, restless periods. Sleep

Table 4-3. Development of Self-feeding Skills in Infancy

Age	Developmental Landmark	Associated Behavior of Infant
Birth	Rooting reflex Sucking reflex	Orients head and mouth to nipple or toward source of stimulation; begins sucking motions that involve lips, tongue, and throat muscles.
2 Months	Extrusion reflex	Food pushed out of mouth.
4–6 Months	Beginning hand-to-mouth coordination	Extrusion reflex weakens. Appearance of finger sucking. Palmar grasp present when reaching for objects. Begins to drink from cup.
6–9 Months	Improvement of hand–eye coordination Begins to sit erect without support Thumb and forefinger grasp develops	Can chew on objects. Bangs objects on floor, table, and so on. Can hold a cup or bottle. Explores food with fingers
12–18 Months	Increased hand–eye coordination	Begins to use spoon for self-feeding. Feeds self messily with frequent spills. Holds cup or bottle with both hands.

Source: E. Getchell, and R. Howard. Nutrition in development. In G. Scipien et al. (Eds.), *Comprehensive pediatric nursing.* New York: McGraw-Hill, 1975.

during the first several months after birth is interrupted only long enough for the baby to be fed. This round-the-clock pattern of alternating periods of sleep with feedings changes to longer intervals of wakefulness after the third month. During the remainder of the time until eighteen months of age, sleep needs decrease to ten to fourteen hours daily. The morning and afternoon nap is usually needed by most toddlers and is definitely welcomed by the caregiver!

As most children approach their eighteenth month after birth, a pattern of negativism may appear in their willingness either to take a nap or to go to bed at night. Many parents learn that their child comes to resist bedtime perhaps as a means of expressing a growing sense of autonomy. Children may also develop a fear of the darkness or of being left alone. They may express their difficulty in developing self-regulated sleeping behavior by resisting the development of bedtime routines. Parents should respond to these behavioral cues by staying with the child to reassure him or her and by not asking the child if he or she is ready for bed. The child's response will most likely be in the negative. Americans are perhaps the only major Western society that expects children to develop this self-regulated behavior early in life with little guidance from parents. Children are placed in their cribs and the door is shut shortly thereafter in the belief that children should learn to develop their character along these lines of self-regulated behavior. Parents in other cultures typically sing their children a short, soft lullaby or rock the child to sleep.

There are no simple answers or approaches for parents to use in interacting with a resistant, uncooperative child who obviously needs to sleep. The establishment of bedtime routines usually helps the child to get the rest she or he needs without exasperating the parents beyond their limits of endurance or patience.

BASIC MOTOR SKILLS.   The acquisition of motor skills follows the inherent laws of developmental direction. Control over the muscles of the body appears first in the head region and proceeds to the legs (cephalocaudal) and from the trunk region out to the extremities (proximodistal). Voluntary control appears earlier in the head than in the leg region.

During the first months of infancy, the baby's movements are random and global in nature. His bodily movements become better coordinated and under voluntary control through the interaction of maturation of his muscles and nerves and the opportunity to experience bodily movements.

According to Hurlock (1975), motor skills in infancy fall into two major categories: (1) those involving the hands; and (2) those involving the legs. The major hand skills of infancy are listed by Hurlock as self-feeding (holding a bottle, cup, spoon, and so on), self-dressing (pulling off socks, putting on coats, and so on), self-cleaning (using a wash cloth, attempting to brush the hair, and so on), and play skills (scribbling with crayons or pencils, opening boxes, throwing objects, turning book pages, and so on). Leg skills that emerge during this developmental period are involved in climbing, walking, running, and swimming.

Establishing Basic Trust and Self-differentiation

The processes and events that promote the establishment of the first psychosocial stage of development were discussed in Chapter 3. Another developmental event of infancy that is closely allied to this major developmental task is learning self-differentiation.

Our impressions of the infant, gained from both informal observation and empirical research, suggest that the sense of trust emerges through numerous interactional activities between the mother and baby. The feeding situation provides ample opportunity for the infant to explore the caregiver both by vision and by touch. This activity is considered to be a significant opportunity for the infant to identify the caregiver as the primary source of physical and psychological nurturance. A consistent caregiver who holds the infant in a consistent manner, who has a consistent pattern of behavior in the feeding situation, and so on, leads the child to learn to trust: a synonym for predictability in the environment. This early learning of a consistent pattern of life helps the infant to predict that certain events or sensations will occur if it behaves in particular ways. For example, the infant learns that a lusty cry will produce the appearance of the caregiver to attend to its needs.

Other interactions with the physical environment contribute to the infant's learning of predictability or consistency in the environment. The baby discovers that movements in the crib make a mobile also move in response. As babies gain more motor control, they learn that fingers and feet move according to their will. Their behavior becomes instrumental or goal-oriented. As maturation of the body occurs, babies learn that objects can be manipulated and that they can move their bodies from one location to another. In essence, they can experience and explore their physical setting and actively reach out to interact with their environment.

The learning of predictability is established during the last half of the first year. By this time, the infant has the idea that the caregiver is a significant, predictable person. The baby's mental image of the environment is probably one that is characterized by permanence, that is, objects and events are perceived in concrete terms. If something or someone is within the baby's visual or tactile fields, it is there because it can be experienced (seen, touched, tasted, smelled, and so on). If the object or person goes out of the baby's range of experience, it is gone forever—it has disappeared, vanished—and the baby must feel that there is no guarantee that it will ever return to be experienced again (see Figure 4-6).

Self-differentiation begins when the infant learns that objects can be manipulated and that he or she is a separate entity from significant others. Sep-

**"What do you mean, 'where's PJ?'
he's RIGHT THERE!"**

Figure 4-6.

aration anxiety, or distress experienced by the baby when the caregiver is gone or is out of his or her reach psychologically, appears around the sixth or seventh month. When the caregiver leaves, the baby "understands" that the adult has permanently disappeared. This is a frightening and anxiety-producing perception for the baby. The situation is corrected by experience. The return of the caregiver or object reinforces the baby's learning that it has not gone away forever and assists the child in developing a sense of trust.

CRITICAL PERIODS AND EARLY EXPERIENCE IN INFANT DEVELOPMENT

It would be intellectually dishonest to dodge the issues promoted by the Freudian psychoanalytical concept of the infant. One of the central issues of this viewpoint is that critical periods exist in the developmental stages of the life cycle.

The *critical periods hypothesis* suggests that there are periods at each stage of an individual's life that are optimal times for learning to occur. During these times, the individual is especially sensitive or responsive to environmental events that pertain to that particular stage. These same environmental events would have relatively little influence if they occurred before or after the critical period of readiness to learn.

The first, and by far the most crucial in terms of physical development, occurs during the prenatal stage. The first forty-five days following conception seem to be the critical period that is most sensitive to environmental influence, for better or worse, in determining the physical development of an embryo. Proper nutrition of the mother and avoidance of exposure to infectious diseases (such as rubella, or German measles), excessive radiation, and harmful or excessive doses of drugs help to ensure that the embryo will develop in a normal manner. These first forty-five days are the time when the major organ systems and functional anatomical parts of the body are formed.

Critical periods are also thought to be present during the socialization process. Most of the studies that have investigated this type of critical period have used animals as subjects for obvious ethical and moral reasons.

Some studies of critical periods performed with animals (mostly birds and dogs) focus on the phenomenon of *imprinting*. Imprinting is the development of a particularly strong attachment between the young of a species and their caregiver shortly after their hatching or birth. Researchers have found that the process of imprinting is influenced by genetic factors and that the apparent purpose of the process is to ensure the survival of the young animals. Although the length of the critical period of imprinting varies among species, its presence has been demonstrated, and identification with the adult animal will not be accomplished by the offspring either before the optimal time for learning or after it has ended.

The presence of critical periods in the socialization process of humans is speculative, but the possibility of their occurrence can be inferred from two developmental events that occur in infancy. These two landmark developmental events suggest the time when a baby is sensitive to identifying with and making an optimal attachment to his caregiver. The beginning of this period is thought to begin with the consistent appearance of the first true social smiles of the infant (at about six weeks after birth) in response to stimulation from its caregiver. The attachment is considered to be established and the critical period may be ended when the infant begins to show stranger or separation anxiety (sometime during the seventh month after birth).

The studies on imprinting performed with animals and those conducted by Harlow on maternal deprivation in monkeys (discussed in Chapter 2) have implications that can be applied to the human situation. One speculation is that early experiences with a consistently nurturant caregiver who handles the baby and provides body contact encourage the development of a healthy attachment to the caregiver. Studies performed with infants who have been placed in institutions that were inadequately staffed by adults report marked differences in infants' development of sensory and perceptual–motor skills (Dennis, 1960; Dennis and Najarani, 1957).

Generalizations from another study (Schaffer and Emerson, 1964), however, suggest that not every human infant responds to body contact or tactile stimulation in the same way. Of the group that these authors studied, about half of the infants responded well to cuddling and enjoyed the experience. The other half showed variations in response to cuddling that shifted from acceptance to rejection of the experience.

This study by Schaffer and Emerson brings us back again to the effect of the infant's behavior in shaping parenting behavior and responses. An infant who accepts and responds well to cuddling reinforces the parents' desire to nurture it. The infant who vacillates between accepting and rejecting the parents' nurturing behavior can frustrate the parents' desire and frequency of showing this type of behavior. This situation could possibly result also in feelings of resentment or hostility toward the baby.

SUPPORTS FOR CAREGIVING IN INFANCY

An ideal situation for many families is having the mother conduct the full-time caregiving. This is not always possible or even desirable in some families for a number of reasons. The increasing number of women who enter the work force, ill health of the mother, and the absence of the mother from the family may account for the more common reasons for families to use substitute child care.

The majority of people who are consumers of child-care services are families in which the woman is employed. The need for such services by these families is obviously based on the need for child care while the mother is working or in training for an occupation. A number of arrangements are made by these families for infant and child care. Mothers, for example, who were enrolled in Work Incentive Programs (work-training programs for mothers receiving welfare assistance) in large midwestern cities used friends, neighbors, sitters, relatives, an older child, or child-care centers to provide care while in occupational training (Smith and Reid, 1973).

Families with an infant are less likely to use group-care arrangements provided by either commercial or nonprofit centers (Rutman and Chommie, 1973). Group care for infants has a negative reputation in our society. The research on maternal deprivation has raised serious questions about the disruption of the baby's ability to form an attachment to its mother when deprived of her consistent caregiving. Women who placed their older children and especially their infant in a child-care agency have been seen in the past as "bad" mothers. Most of these agencies have provided meager custodial care and have had the reputation of neglecting children's developmental needs. Because of these negative implications for an infant's developmental progress, there have been few institutionalized full-day care services offered in communities for infants. The costs of operating such centers are also very high because of the large number of adults needed to supervise infants. These costs usually preclude the wider availability of such programs for infants. Home-based or family day-care services are available to families in communities but may lack the experiential component that stimulates enhanced development that is found in group care settings.

Researchers have only recently begun to investigate the influence of group care on infant development. The results of these studies suggest several conclusions that feature both positive and less desirable effects on infants' and toddlers' behavior and development.

1. *Attachment patterns between child and mother are not adversely affected by long-term group care.* Caldwell, Wright, Honig, and Tannenbaum (1970) describe the findings of an innovative program of group care for disadvantaged infants that featured a stimulating, enriched environment and caregiving experiences. These researchers compared a group of home-reared infants and toddlers with a group who had participated in an infant day-care center. The groups were compared in terms of the quality of mother–infant attachment, the level of development, and the amount of stimulation received in the home or the day-care center. At thirty months of age, no significant differences were noted in the groups in degree of attachment of the mothers to their children or the children to their mothers. A study reported by Fowler (1972) confirms the findings of Caldwell and her associates regarding no differences in emotional security or attachment behavior of group-care versus home-reared infants. Fowler also states that the day-care children in his study were more comfortable in entering a new group-care setting than children who had not been exposed to day-care arrangements. Schwarz, Krolick, and Strickland (1973) also report failure to find differences in the emotional security of group-care and home-reared infants at three and four years of age.

2. *Infant group-care provides an enriching experience that enhances or stimulates development.* The study by Caldwell and her associates (1970) showed the beneficial impact of group care within a stimulating environment on enhancing the level of children's development. At twelve months of age, home-reared infants in the study were much more advanced than the day-care infants. However, by thirty months of age, there were few differences between the groups. Over this period of time, the home-reared group showed a decline in developmental level, which is expected of disadvantaged children. The day-care group improved over this period in their developmental level, which produced the lack of difference between the groups at thirty months of age (see Figure 4-7). The group experience acted to prevent further declines in development that were concurrently experienced by the home-reared group. One of the primary conclusions of Fowler's (1972) study is

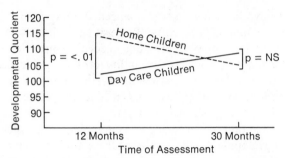

Figure 4-7. Time trends in developmental quotients for home and day care children at 12 and 30 months. (Source: Caldwell, B., Wright, C., Honig, A., and Tannenbaum, J. Infant day care and attachment. *American Journal of Orthopsychiatry*, 1970, *40*, 397–412. Copyright 1970 the American Orthopsychiatric Association, Inc. Reproduced by permission.)

that a consistent infant care program that features cognitive stimulation, nurturance, and social stimulation produces enhanced intellectual development, whether in the home or in a group setting.

The beneficial effects of an enriched, stimulating group-care environment on infant development are also described by Robinson and Robinson (1971). Comparisons were made between children who had participated as infants for 2½ years in a stimulating day-care program and children who did not have these experiences. The results show that the group-care experiences enhanced cognitive development and verbal abilities in children.

3. *A few less desirable behavior traits may be observed in early group-care children at later ages.* Several studies corroborate the finding that children who have been enrolled in infant-care centers may show some less desirable behavior traits in later years. These group-care children have been rated as less cooperative with adults, more verbally and physically aggressive with peers and adults, and more physically active at four years of age than children who are relatively new to day-care settings at this same age (Macrae and Herbert-Jackson, 1976; Schwarz, Krolick, and Strickland, 1973; Schwarz, Strickland, and Krolick, 1974). It is difficult, however, to say that this may be the result of long-term group care for all children because the samples were small and the types of centers were different in each of these studies.

4. *The greatest impact of quality infant care may be on disadvantaged families.* Despite the high costs of such services to families or to the nonprofit agencies who operate them, such programs, whether conducted in the home (Weikart and Lambie, 1970) or in group settings, serve to compensate for the adverse effects of an impoverished environment on infants' development.

POINTS TO CONSIDER

- Most couples are poorly prepared for the new role of parenthood and the changes that are initiated by the introduction of the first child into established adult routines, roles, and relationships.
- Two principal concepts may be considered regarding the nature of an infant: (1) the *psychoanalytical* view, which stresses the primacy of early experiences in determining later development; and (2) the *developmental* view, which emphasizes the adaptable nature of the baby in manipulating and responding to the environment.
- Recent research shows that children's behavior is a significant factor in shaping adults' behavior in interaction with them.
- Babies are capable of influencing the quality and nature of a caregiver's behavior by virtue of their own nature and the achievement of their developmental tasks and needs.
- Landmarks of developmental interaction between parents and infants serve as cues for recognizing developmental events and the shaping of adult caregiving behavior by the baby.
- Research shows that group care of infants (1) does not adversely affect attachment patterns between infants and caregivers; (2) enhances or stimulates development of the infant; and (3) may have the greatest impact for disadvantaged families.

REFERENCES

ANDERSON, J. Personality organization in children. *American Psychologist,* 1948, *3*, 409–416.

BELL, R. A reinterpretation of the direction of effects in studies of socialization. *Psychological Review,* 1968, *75*, 81–95.

BELL, R. Stimulus control of parent or caretaker behavior by offspring. *Developmental Psychology,* 1971, *1*, 63–72.

BOWLBY, J. *Maternal care and mental health.* Geneva: World Health Organization, 1952.

BRAZELTON, T. *Infants and mothers: Differences in development.* New York: Delacorte, 1969.

CALDWELL, B., WRIGHT, C., HONIG, A., and TANNENBAUM, J. Infant day care and attachment. *American Journal of Orthopsychiatry,* 1970, *40*, 397–412.

COLE, S., and HOBBS, D. Transition to parenthood: A decade replication. Paper presented at the Research Section of the National Council on Family Relations, Salt Lake City, 1975.

DENNIS, W. Causes of retardation among institutionalized children: Iran. *Journal of Genetic Psychology,* 1960, *96*, 47–59.

DENNIS, W., and NAJARANI, D. Infant development under environmental handicap. *Psychological Monographs,* 1957, *71*, Whole No. 436.

DYER, E. Parenthood as crisis: A restudy. *Journal of Marriage and the Family,* 1963, *25*, 196–201.

ERIKSON, E. *Insight and responsibility.* New York: Norton, 1964.

FOWLER, W. A developmental learning approach to infant care in a group setting. *Merrill-Palmer Quarterly,* 1972, *18,* 145–175.

GOLDFARB, W. Effects of psychological deprivation in infancy and subsequent stimulation. *American Journal of Psychology,* 1945, *102,* 18–33.

HOBBS, D. Parenthood as crisis: A third study. *Journal of Marriage and the Family,* 1965, *27,* 367–372.

HURLOCK, E. *Developmental psychology* (4th ed.). New York: McGraw-Hill, 1975.

LeMASTERS, E. Parenthood as crisis. *Marriage and Family Living,* 1957, *19,* 352–355.

MACRAE, J., and HERBERT-JACKSON, E. Are behavioral effects of infant day care program specific? *Developmental Psychology,* 1976, *12,* 269–270.

MAYNARD, N., and HOBBS, D. Transition to parenthood by black couples. Paper presented at the Research Section of the National Council on Family Relations, Salt Lake City, 1975.

RHEINGOLD, H. Development of social behavior in human infants. In H. Stevenson (Ed.), The concept of development. *Monographs of the Society for Research in Child Development,* 1966, *31,* Whole No. 107. Pp. 1–17.

RIBBLE, M. *The rights of infants.* New York: Columbia University Press, 1943.

RIBBLE, M. Infantile experience in relation to personality development. In J. McV. Hunt (Ed.), *Personality and behavior disorders.* New York: Ronald, 1944. Pp. 621–651.

ROBINSON, H., and ROBINSON, N. Longitudinal development of very young children in a comprehensive day care program: The first two years. *Child Development,* 1971, *42,* 1673–1683.

ROLLINS, B., and FELDMAN, H. Marital satisfaction over the family life cycle. *Journal of Marriage and the Family,* 1970, *32,* 20–28.

ROSSI, A. Transition to parenthood. *Journal of Marriage and the Family,* 1968, *30,* 26–39.

RUTMAN, L., and CHOMMIE, P. A comparison of families using commercial and subsidized day care services. *Child Welfare,* 1973, *52,* 287–297.

SCHAFFER, H., and EMERSON, D. Patterns of response to physical contact in early human development. *Journal of Consulting Psychology and Psychiatry,* 1964, *5,* 1–13.

SCHWARZ, J., KROLICK, G., and STRICKLAND, R. Effects of early day care experience on adjustment to a new environment. *American Journal of Orthopsychiatry,* 1973, *43,* 340–346.

SCHWARZ, J., STRICKLAND, R., and KROLICK, G. Infant day care: Behavioral effects at preschool age. *Developmental Psychology,* 1974, *10,* 502–506.

SMITH, A., and REID, W. Child care arrangements of AFDC mothers in the Work Incentive program. *Child Welfare,* 1973, *52,* 651–661.

SPITZ, R. Hospitalism. In O. Fenichel et al. (Eds.), *The psychoanalytical study of the child,* Vol. 1. New York: International Universities Press, 1945.

WEIKART, D., and LAMBIE, D. Early enrichment in infants. In V. Denenberg (Ed.), *Education of the infant and young child.* New York: Academic Press, 1970. Pp. 85–107.

WILLIAMS, D. The neonate: Birth to 1 month. In G. Scipien et al. (Eds.), *Comprehensive pediatric nursing.* New York: McGraw-Hill, 1975. Pp. 100–114.

5

Developmental Interaction in Early Childhood

The time of a child's life between eighteen months and six years of age comprises the early childhood period. Two stages of psychosocial development are experienced by children during this period, according to Erikson (see Chapter 3). The establishment of the sense of autonomy versus shame and doubt occurs between eighteen months and three years of age. This is followed by the stage of developing the sense of initiative versus guilt between the third and sixth birthdays. The parents remain involved with developing a sense of generativity during this time of the child's life. The challenges of interaction in the family change, however, to reflect an increasing involvement of the growing child in his or her role as a member of the family. Adjusting to the challenges of a developing child whose behavior and general personality traits are rapidly emerging presents the greatest concern to parents at this time.

The early childhood period has received the most attention from developmental theorists and researchers of all the stages in the life cycle. The views of Freud, especially, have had a profound influence on the importance we attach to these years of a child's life. Although our opinions have been adapted in light of research findings, we continue to believe that the experiences of a young child have great bearing on the establishment of many patterns of behavior, attitudes, and values in later life.

THE DYNAMICS OF BECOMING: EIGHTEEN MONTHS TO THREE YEARS

The first stage of psychosocial development in the early childhood years is the establishment of a sense of autonomy versus shame and doubt. Parents

125

may view this time as a series of troublesome encounters with their child because so much of his or her behavior is directed toward establishing an identity as a person independent of the parents. *Discovery* is a good word to characterize the child's nature at this time in life: discovery of himself or herself as a person, discovery of the ability to do things and make things happen; discovery of the family and what they are like; discovery of the ability to communicate with others; and beginnings of the discovery that there is a big, wide world beyond his or her doorstep. This is the nature of a child who is in the process of becoming a total person.

What amazes and confounds parents of a child at these ages is not so much the changes in development but the rapid nature and the intensity of these changes. Stubborn insistence on having their own way in interaction with parents is a predominant pattern of behavior among many children in developing a sense of autonomy. An emerging sense of self is shown in the inconsistencies of their behavior. These are evident in the swings from independent to dependent behavior and back again (see Figure 5-1). The behavior and nature of young children is unpredictable in many ways because of their attempts to develop a sense of autonomy and initiative.

The early part of this period is the time when children are first introduced

"I'm gonna run away from home?"   "Will you zip up my jacket and tie my shoes?"

Figure 5-1.

to the parents' full use of their controls over behavior. Rules begin to be defined and become modified or changed as the child grows older. The study by Clifford (1959), discussed in Chapter 2, shows how mothers of three-year-olds use a greater number of physical controls than those of older children. Children and parents both discover the power of the adult at this time in their ability to make certain demands and expect certain responses or standards of behavior from the child.

For many children, there is a change in personality at this time of the life cycle. The smiling, friendly, accepting child is replaced on many occasions by a surly, whining, little demon who gets into mischief, refuses to cooperate or obey parents' requests, and has only one very overworked word in his or her vocabulary: *"NO!"* This is the terrible two-year-old at his or her worst, according to parents. Yet parents can become so preoccupied or stimulated with using power to gain control over the child's unacceptable actions that they may be unaware that these difficult interactions are a very necessary part of the child's healthy psychosocial development.

Some biological events contribute to preparing and assisting a child to achieve the psychosocial sense of autonomy. These include learning to walk and to feed himself or herself, controlling eliminations, and so on. Other tasks that the child should learn to accomplish are introduced by parents. Generally these particular tasks are developmentally appropriate and represent society's expectations that they be accomplished in early childhood in preparation for future development. These events include, for example, the child's learning to dress himself or herself, separate easily from the mother, play alone and with others, and master certain motor skills.

The tasks, then, that a child should learn at this optimal time in life are thought to include:

1. Developing self-awareness as a distinct person from other people and things.
2. Achieving control of the body and its functions.
3. Becoming a family member and developing communication skills within the family.
4. Learning how to express and control emotions and feelings.

Developing Self-awareness

Hurlock (1975) states that the major developmental tasks of early childhood involve laying the foundations for adjustments to people and to situations away from the home. The process of developing self-awareness is based on two factors: (1) the ability to separate easily from the mother; and (2) the opportunity for exploring the environment. These factors not only lead to the toddler's discovery of herself or himself and his or her surroundings but also allow him or her to widen the world to include others in the social environment. The mastery of this process of self-differentiation affects the quality of development in the next stage of psychosocial development.

Erikson's framework of psychosocial development includes the father as a "new" significant other for the child at the autonomy stage. Although research shows that the father may begin to influence his child's development in infancy (see Chapter 2), the father is thought to serve a specific function for his child at this stage. He assists the child's development by lessening the intensity of the bonding between the mother and the child, according to Erikson. Because toddlers are showing an increasing ability to be less dependent physically on adults, the father may take an increased interest in interacting with his child, probably in terms of social interaction. Fathers are perhaps more willing to take their child with them on short errands or on special outings such as to the zoo and the library, on short walks, and so on. These experiences are stimulating psychologically and socially for both the father and the toddler. The child learns that daddies can be as trusted as mothers. The more frequently the father and the child experience enjoyable and successful interactions, the easier separations may become from the mother. The mother in these situations can influence the success of the father's initiations of the child's separations by encouraging them to occur and by reassuring the child and the father that these interactions and events are appropriate. The assumption here is that if the child learns to trust the father and has successful experiences in separating from the mother, she or he will come to generalize this trust to additional "significant others." The path is smoothed by such experiences for effective social interaction with others outside of the family.

The change in locomotor skills in infancy from the predominant use of crawling and creeping to walking affects the child's perspective on the world. The toddler moves about with increasing speed and can more freely explore the physical environment. Children of this age act on their natural curiosity to discover their surroundings. As Piaget (1967) notes, children are the world's most natural scientists, who exercise their curiosity in discovering and experimenting with things that surround them. Children who are active in their environment need these experiences to discover themselves as distinct individuals who are separate from people and things but who are also a part of their surroundings. Children act on their environment and in the process discover how their environment acts. Adults have forgotten the joy of these small but important discoveries. Young children learn that balls make intriguing movements when acted upon by kicking, bouncing, and throwing. Pots and lids make fantastic sounds when hit on the floor—the harder they are struck, the louder the sound (see Figure 5-2). Water is very attractive and makes fascinating sounds and movements, particularly when the toilet is flushed—and flushed—and flushed again!

This propensity to become involved is responsible for much of the con-

Figure 5-2.

flict between parents and children at this stage of development. Most parents can tolerate just so much noise and mess from children, and the child's safety also becomes a preoccupation of the parents. Parents learn that children's activities can lead to dangerous situations, and they react to this behavior by "child-proofing" the home (see Table 5-1) or adapting the housing arrangements to the behavior of children, as discussed by Duvall (1977). Cleaning solutions are placed out of reach, ashtrays and accessories are moved from tables, tablecloths are put away, gates are placed across doors, and electrical outlets are plugged with specially designed caps. Mothers may provide a selection of different types of toys for young children that stimulate their curiosity and exploratory behavior, but common household objects (pots, for example) may be just as fascinating as elaborate toys to the child (see Figure 5-2). Homes with toddlers or young children are easily recognized on the inside because of these protective measures taken by parents to ensure their child's safety. Such measures recognize the need for children to explore and experience objects and things within a safe environment. The life-style of the family responds and is modified by the child's behavior, demonstrating another aspect of developmental interaction between parents and children (see Figure 5-3).

Table 5-1.   Methods for Child-proofing the Home

Area	Hazard or Danger	Child-proofing Methods
Furniture	Drawers dumped on child	Place safety catches on drawers.
	Soiled upholstery	Slipcovers; or choose fabrics or materials that are easily cleaned; use patterns and darker colors that don't show dirt easily.
	Breaking valuables	Pack away in an inaccessible, safe place; use wall or hanging lamps instead of table or floor lamps.
Toys	Sharp edges and corners	Choose toys that lack these features.
	Harmful, toxic paints and surfaces	Choose toys that are nontoxic so that children can be safe from poisoning.
	Swallowing small pieces	Choose objects that are larger than a plum.
	Breaking	Give child toys that are sturdy and can stand up to heavy use.
Stairs, entrance-ways, and windows	Falling	Place gates at top and bottom of stairways; lock low windows; supervise child when she or he learns to use stairs; install safety latches on screen doors.
Kitchen	Burning	Turn pot and pan handles in toward wall; keep child away from oven.
	Poisoning	Remove cleaning solutions to inaccessible location.

Source: From *Marriage and Family Development* by Evelyn M. Duvall. Reprinted by permission of the publisher, J. B. Lippincott Company. Copyright © 1977.

Achieving Body Control

Physical development through the period of early childhood is expressed through play activities that encourage and allow refinements of gross motor skills and the emergence of fine motor skills. These skills demonstrate a

"I'm trying to remember where I hid my scissors so the children wouldn't get them."

Figure 5-3.

prominent characteristic of development in the progression from general to specific features that began in infancy. The gross motor skills progress from walking to include running, hopping, jumping, climbing, and skipping. Fine motor skills become refined during this period to include hand and finger skills that enable a child to turn pages in books, to hold crayons and pencils for scribbling and drawing, and to play with objects such as puzzles, small blocks, and construction-type toys. Beginning at three to four years of age, children enjoy an increasing number of activities that stimulate their manipulative skills, such as cutting with scissors, finger painting, stringing beads, and woodwork. All these motor skills assist children in learning autonomous as well as initiative behavior.

Toilet training usually begins when children are between eighteen and twenty-four months of age. The process of teaching a child to voluntarily control his bladder and bowels can be a difficult experience for parents. Opinions and directions for instructing children are obtained from child-care books and relatives or friends who have accomplished this task with their own children.

Toilet training a child is another example of developmental interaction in that many cues can be taken from the child's behavior that help to facilitate the learning of this task. By the time most children are of the optimal ages for learning this task, they have begun to have at least one daily bowel movement that occurs with some amount of regularity. Children provide behavioral cues when they need to move their bowels. Facial cues may be prominent, and children's behavior may be restless. The need for the bowel movement is also associated with the end of a meal because the intestines are stimulated in their actual movements at this time. The alert parent who carefully observes the child learns to place him or her on a training potty when these cues are provided by the child. Over time the experiences of internal stimulations become associated with the appropriate response.

Conflicts may occur between the parent and the child over the progress of toilet training. Some children seem to stubbornly resist training, partly because of their strong desire for freedom from direction of the parents. Difficulties in training may be associated with inconsistency of the adult's training efforts, the inability of the child to understand what is expected, or lack of sufficient positive reinforcement for the child's efforts. An analysis of the interaction pattern between the adult and the child may show that the parent expects instant results after only a few concentrated attempts in training the child. The parent may respond harshly to the child's resistance or negativism in complying with the training efforts. Feelings of shame and doubt, as discussed by Erikson, may be experienced by the child because of the vicious circle of poor training efforts and responses. Children may deeply wish to accomplish what is expected of them but are so involved with learning other things that toilet training is a bother, a nuisance, and an inconvenience to them. The parent, knowing that this is an optimal time for the child to learn this task or feeling pressures to train the child, becomes annoyed with the child's resistance and reacts by using harsh controls and exercising parental power. The result may be delayed training and the child's having negative feelings that affect his or her attitude about himself or herself. Most children at the toddler age don't like to be in dirty, wet diapers or training pants. Their feelings of doubt about their independence are reinforced by parents who make them feel guilty or unsure about their basic attitude toward accomplishing autonomous behavior. Fortunately almost every normal child comes to train herself or himself in time. Many children who may experience difficulty in being trained by parents may achieve this task through exposure to peers in preschool or day-care programs. This experience stimulates their conformity to what is expected of them.

Family Membership and Communication Skills

As children progress through the autonomy stage, parents increase their socialization efforts in teaching children appropriate behaviors, values, and attitudes. These are derived from the parents' philosophical and cultural patterns or values. The instruction of children or the shaping of their behavior is accomplished by the parents' establishing what is right or wrong for the child. No matter what the child-rearing philosophy or attitude of the parents, limits and boundaries of acceptable behavior are shown to the child and are reinforced as he or she repeatedly responds in the correct fashion.

When children are involved in the development of autonomous behavior at this age, parents eventually discover that small household tasks help the emergence of independent behavior. Taking out the trash, helping to set the table, cleaning up a room, or helping to make beds are examples of these small but necessary household tasks. What adults usually see as drudgery, children see as new adventures and responsibilities that help to increase their status and recognition as helpful, contributing members of the family. Their self-esteem is boosted by being recognized as a "good" helper to the parents, even though their help may not actually save time or work (see Figure 5-4).

The major vehicle and tool of the socialization process is language. The development of communication skills is based on the child's effective use of language. Throughout the autonomy stage, children experience numerous refinements and advancements in their ability to use language effectively in communicating with others. As infants and toddlers, children devote a great

Figure 5-4.

deal of their attention to listening to what they hear around them. They also experiment in producing various sounds with their voices. Talking and the beginnings of verbal communication occur in toddlerhood. Hurlock (1975) states that the major developmental tasks of communication skills in early childhood are building vocabulary, mastering pronunciation, and combining individual words into sentences. New words are added quickly to the child's vocabulary during these years. Short sentences are commonly used by the third year, with six- to eight-word sentences being used increasingly after this year. Nouns appear first in speech because they are probably taught first. Verbs are learned next and usually are of the present or active tense such as, "Baby want." Adjectives appear next in sentences in a simple form such as, "Doggie is nice." Prepositions and personal pronouns present the greatest difficulty for children to learn and appear last in language development. Much confusion exists about when to use words like *he, she, me,* and *her.* Words such as *over, under, around, through,* and *above* are difficult concepts for children to learn (Hurlock, 1975).

Something that may disturb some parents at this time is the degree of the child's *egocentrism,* which dominates his or her communication patterns as well as other areas of his or her life. Egocentrism is a pervading factor of cognitive development, especially in early childhood. It is readily seen in children's language and play activities. This egocentric nature may be a cause of a child's intense concentration on herself or himself in his or her growing ability to be autonomous (see Figure 5-5). Piaget (1967) believes that children of this age use themselves as the primary reference point in defining what happens in their environment and to them as participants in the environment. This is egocentrism and is seen in several ways. Young children's sentences, for example, contain an inordinate number of personal pronouns, such as *I, me, mine,* and *my.* Their conversation centers on what they've done and seen or want to do. They stimulate others to take an interest in them, particularly when they shout out, "Look at ME! Look at what *I* did!" Parents find that effective communication with their child is difficult at times because of this egocentrism. Children's intense concern with themselves prevents them from being empathetic with parents as they may be expected to be. In these instances, it is difficult for a child to understand the parents' concerns or point of view. A mother, for example, may be trying very patiently to explain to her three-year-old why he can't have some cookies when dinnertime is near. The child may resist accepting the mother's explanation by plainly but emphatically telling her, "But Mother, *I NEED* the cookies!!" This is why parents soon learn that arguing with a young child is often futile. If the child doesn't comply with the parents' requests or doesn't accept their explanations of rules or policies, then strong controls might be used to help the child to understand the parents' expectations.

The development of effective communication skills is important because a child learns appropriate behaviors by understanding what is expected. Social

"Santa WAVED at ME!"
Figure 5-5.

acceptance by others outside the family is based on effective communication skills, which are enhanced within the parent–child relationship. Parents become involved with verbal give-and-take in relating to children. This implies that parents of young children are challenged to give more in interactions with their child because of the level of the child's cognitive development. This giving may involve listening carefully to children, not becoming too impatient, and repeating requests or statements until the child accepts or understands the communication or information.

Learning to Express and Control Emotions

The sense of autonomy cannot be achieved without a child's expressing some intense emotions. Anger is the emotion most commonly associated with the earlier part of this time in children's lives. Its expression most usually is seen in negative behavior and temper tantrums of varying degrees of intensity. Both negativism (saying "no," being uncooperative, and so on) and the high frequency of temper tantrums are why two-year-olds are sometimes labeled as "terrible" by their parents.

Emotional displays in early childhood show wide and rapid swings from one state of temperament to another. Much research effort was devoted during the 1950s to studying the causes of children's expressions of anger. One of the more prominent findings was that when children are frustrated or thwarted in achieving a goal, they may express their anger by aggressive behavior. Such behavior may well describe the child's efforts toward achieving autonomy between eighteen months and three years of age. The child's goal at this time is to function as independently as possible. In attempting to teach the child appropriate behavior patterns or in protecting the child's safety, parents may frustrate or thwart goal-directed, autonomous behavior. The result, depending on the circumstances, is anger and aggression, which can range from sulking, crying, or yelling to a full-fledged, thrashing-around-on-the-floor-and-holding-the-breath type of temper tantrum.

Fears occupy a large portion of a child's emotional world in early childhood. The young child has fears of imaginary monsters, of the dark, of things and events that might inflict pain or harm, and of dreams (Jersild, Telford, and Sawrey, 1975). The increasing development of a vivid imagination, which reflects a maturing mind, is a large factor in children's fears. Hurlock (1975) states that children become afraid and show their fears in various ways. Some fears become associated with actual frightening events, such as falling down stairs. Others are learned from observing adults or older children and from anxiety-producing television programs, stories, and books.

Expressions of jealousy appear with increasing frequency during this time period and are considered normal responses to actual, imagined, or threatened loss of parental affection (Hurlock, 1972, 1975). Jealousy may stem from anger that is directed toward the parent because the child feels loss of love as a result of the parent's disapproval of much of the child's autonomous behavior. The jealousy may be expressed in various ways but commonly takes the form of aggressive acts of either a passive or an active nature. A passive–aggressive act may be when the child "accidentally on purpose" wakes up a younger child from a nap when the parent has had to spend some time in getting the child to sleep. A child may choose to have a temper tantrum that is unparalleled in intensity and duration when company arrives for dinner and he or she is sent to bed.

The intensity of a child's emotional expressions in the early part of this stage of development presents the parents with a difficult matter. The challenge is how to help children learn to control their emotional expressions within reasonable limits without repressing their expression in a harmful way. One of the initial reactions parents may have to such strong emotional outbursts of a child is not to allow or encourage them in the first place. Parents may try a variety of methods to halt temper tantrums, fears, or expressions of jealousy. Many of these include controls such as reasoning or explaining why the child must not let his or her emotions run full tilt. These controls, however, sometimes produce little effect on an angry child. Stronger controls may come into play next and include isolating the child, using physical punishments, yelling, or making threats. These also may prove to be just as ineffective, as they may frighten the child or heighten his or her anger.

Many parents learn the usefulness of distracting the young child, holding her or him close, or ignoring the aggressive behavior through trial-and-error learning. Fears may be handled in a similar manner but also may include statements that make the child feel guilty or ashamed for being afraid of something. How the parent reacts to children's emotional expressions will influence their feelings of autonomy or those of shame and doubt, according to Erikson. If children learn from parents that it is wrong to be autonomous (and this includes the freedom, within certain limits as specified by the parents, to express emotions of all types), then the attitude of shame and doubt is fostered. It can lead to unhealthy psychosocial development at this time in life. The role model that the parents present to the child invariably influences the course of the child's development as well. Some adults communicate to children through their behavior a "do-as-I-say, not-as-I-do" message. These adults may let their emotions run full tilt in social interactions while their child observes this behavior. When the child, however, incorporates these elements of the parents' behavior into his or her own and the parents observe this, the child may be punished or reprimanded for behaving just as the parent does. The result is confusion on the child's part as to what is and is not appropriate behavior.

THE PROCESS OF BECOMING: THREE TO FIVE YEARS

Children experience the challenges of developing a sense of initiative between the third and sixth birthdays. This attitude represents children's further adaptation to the world and reflects their full confidence in their abilities to achieve mastery of relationships, objects, and activities. This attitude is boosted by the accomplishments that were developed in the last stage of psychosocial development (see Figure 5-6). The sense of autonomy prepares a young child to develop the feelings of accomplishment that fully emerge during this stage of life: the pervading psychological attitude of "I CAN!"

The significant others in a child's life now come to include the family unit as a whole. These individuals, taken singly and as a group, assist and support the child in his or her efforts to establish initiative behavior and his or her adjustments to other individuals.

Children's behavior becomes directed at this time in life toward what Erikson calls "making and making like." This behavioral theme indicates children's awareness of social roles and their additional attempts to learn the order that constitutes social interactions among and between individuals.

The development of a sense of guilt, which is the alternative to a sense of initiative, is the psychosocial hazard faced by both the children and those who assist them in their development. Young children of this age show an

"We watered the living room plants for you."

Figure 5-6.

almost unlimited interest and curiosity about life and their environment. Their exuberant behavior and intense concentration on involvement in interacting with the environment leads them into conflicts with those who provide care and guidance (see Figure 5-7).

The sense of guilt may be established when children receive consistent negative reinforcement or punishment, or the parents and other family members make them feel deeply ashamed of their attempts to establish initiative behavior.

Each stage of psychosocial development presents its own unique challenges that lead toward the establishment of the particular sense at the optimal time in the life cycle. During the third to fifth years, several important tasks should be learned by children that lead toward the development of the sense of initiative. These include:

1. Discovering personal capabilities.
2. Learning to establish routines and taking responsibility for personal actions.
3. Learning to discriminate between various social roles and how to interact appropriately with others.

"We're getting our breakfast but we can't find the ice cream scoop."

Figure 5-7.

Discovering Personal Capabilities

The task of discovering limits to physical, psychological, and social capabilities is a consuming interest of a child involved in establishing initiative behavior. The behavioral vehicle for a child's discovery of personal capabilities is his or her almost limitless energy, which gives rise to what Erikson terms *intrusiveness*. Three-, four-, and five-year-olds are intrusive children. They are active children, both physically and psychologically, whose behavior is directed toward many different goals that center on discovering and exploring their world (see Figure 5-8). Their high energy level permits the development of initiative behavior that is characterized not only by intrusiveness but also by an emerging conscience about the appropriateness of their behavior.

For young children, the world is something that must be experienced, and the only way to do this is to become involved, physically and psychologically. Involvement means doing things and asking questions with the purpose of learning as much as possible about everything. Rocks cannot be experienced unless one touches and examines them, people can't be experienced unless

"YOU PEOPLE HAVE THE BEST TRASH IN THE WHOLE BLOCK!"

Figure 5-8.

one observes and talks with them, water can't be experienced without one's becoming wet, and so on.

Moral development at this age is related to intellectual development. Pre-school-aged children have a rigid conscience by which behaviors and actions are judged as being either completely "right" or completely "wrong." Piaget (1967) calls this "morality by constraint," where rules that govern many kinds of behavior are learned and reacted to automatically without the use of mature reasoning. The mental life of these young children is characterized by an active use of the imagination or fantasy. When judgments are made about why things happen as they do or about the appropriateness of some particular act, conclusions are reached by intuition rather than by deductive reasoning based on the facts at hand. Young children may react by jumping to conclusions or according to how they happen to feel at the moment. Guilt feelings may result about real or imagined actions that represent the child's struggles with handling inner conflicts coming from an emerging conscience. When children of this age experience feelings of self-recrimination, they judge themselves harshly in terms of the rightness or wrongness of their behavior. Adults serve an invaluable function when these feelings are displayed by helping children to understand that everyone makes mistakes and that their world won't collapse because of what they've done.

Discovering personal capabilities means that children have to become involved and to experience, but they also need to become aware of and accept their limitations. Limits are discovered through failures and being unable to accomplish goals, through conflicts when the established boundaries of what is appropriate and acceptable are exceeded, and when transgressions occur. Experiences in being involved in life contain elements that can lead to guilt feelings. The parents' role in interacting with children turns to verbal and behavioral instruction as to what is expected, what is appropriate, and what is right and wrong for children. When parents help children learn these limits or boundaries, routines are established and feelings of success are nurtured through accomplishments that lead the children to discover their own personal potential and capabilities.

Establishing Routines and Showing Responsible Behavior

This task of early childhood is met in two opposite ways: either children are easily persuaded to respond to certain requests (which they may consider fun to do) or they balk at the task presented to them (see Figure 5-9). Routines that are encouraged and taught in the home include dressing and undressing, mealtimes, picking up toys and other play materials, making beds, brushing teeth, and preparing for meals. Certain household tasks may be assigned to children of this age by the parents. Although perfection in performing the tasks is not expected at first, parents encourage children to perform these tasks without being asked. In other words, the parents eventually come to expect the child to show initiative in performing these routines. What is at first fun and enjoyable may eventually turn to drudgery for the child. Parents may begin to nag the child, hoping that this will make him or her do whatever tasks have been assigned. Battles may be waged daily between the parent and the child over the child's not showing responsible behavior. Child rearing by guilt, or making children feel guilty for their unacceptable behavior, may commence. Parents are challenged by the changing nature of children's interests in showing initiative behavior by helping them to establish habits and routines without the trappings of guilt at not being good enough in what is expected.

Learning Social Roles and Interactions with Others

The family is a laboratory for young children in learning how to interact with other people. Through interactions with other family members, children learn the give-and-take nature of social interactions and the roles that people assume in interactions. Parents provide children with the opportunity to learn,

"WASH, WASH, WASH! DAY 'N NIGHT! WASH, WASH, WASH!...."

Figure 5-9.

on a very elementary basis, what a marriage relationship involves and requires of both partners. By observing how parents relate as a married couple, children begin to establish an idea of what is expected of a husband and a wife, how affection is expressed, and how problems are faced and discussed.

Relationships also emerge during this time between a child and his or her siblings. Social positions are assigned to children according to their order of birth. Parents, perhaps unconsciously, react toward children and treat them differently in this manner (Bossard and Boll, 1966; Lasko, 1954). The sibling relationship may provide children with opportunities for learning and experimenting with social interactions that are not available through other means. The patterns that are learned extend throughout the growing years of childhood, and numerous changes occur in the relationship as children grow older. Researchers tend to believe that what children learn through the sibling relationship about social interaction may generalize to the way they approach their peers and other individuals outside the family (Sutton-Smith and Rosenberg, 1970).

Researchers have become more interested in the topic of sibling interaction within the past several years. An increasing number of studies have been published that investigate the value and impact of having a sibling on a child's development of many social and psychological skills. Most of these studies have used second-born children in examining the influence of an older child on the younger and the younger child's use of the older child as a role model.

One of the consistent findings of sibling interaction research is that children who have brothers and sisters learn how social power and function are used in discriminating the age and sex roles that exist in the family as representations of social roles in society (Bigner, 1974a,b; Koch, 1960; Sutton-Smith and Rosenberg, 1965, 1968). Firstborn children learn to use high-power social tactics in interacting with younger siblings to achieve their own social goals. These tactics may involve bossing, making verbal threats, using physical force, and so on. Younger children learn to react to these demonstrations of social power by sulking, tattling, teasing, harassing, and using aggression. Younger children are found to look to the older sibling as a model for how they are to interact with others (see Figure 5-10). These younger siblings learn from their interactions with the older child that older people

1974, The Register
and Tribune Syndicate

"You're lucky PJ — you don't have to be a good
example to ANYBODY!"

Figure 5-10.

have more social power than younger people (Sutton-Smith and Rosenberg, 1970).

Siblings are of value to children in their learning about sex-appropriate behaviors. Younger siblings learn that males have higher social power than females and that females facilitate social interaction whereas males are socially disruptive (Bigner, 1972, 1974a,b). Children who have an opposite-sex older sibling are presented with the opportunity to learn to discriminate the role behaviors of the other sex better than children who have a same-sex older sibling (Bigner, 1972, 1974a,b, 1977; Brim, 1957; Circirelli, 1972, 1973; Koch, 1956; Sutton-Smith and Rosenberg, 1965, 1970).

Having an older sibling may assist younger children in learning both appropriate and inappropriate role behaviors that constitute the ideas of a "good" and "bad" sibling (Bigner, 1977). Second-born children describe a good sibling in terms of positive social behavior, whereas a bad sibling is seen as being uncooperative in play activities and is described in abstract terms, such as being a "pest." A good brother is described as someone who helps with chores, plays with the younger sibling, and doesn't tattle on him or her. A bad brother is bossy and a pest, is uncooperative, and is a nuisance to have around. A good sister is seen as nice, loving, and helpful, whereas a bad sister destroys belongings, talks too much, and doesn't clean up her messes.

The older sibling acts as a teacher of younger children in other ways. Older brothers and sisters have different styles of teaching younger children how to solve problems (Circirelli, 1972). An older sister may have a special impact on younger children in that they are more likely to accept and receive help from her than from an older brother (Circirelli, 1972, 1974). Older sisters also give more explanation and feedback than older brothers when teaching younger children a problem-solving task (Circirelli, 1976).

The consensus of these research findings points to the unique properties of the sibling relationship in helping children to prepare for adjusting to social interactions with peers outside of the family group. By knowing how to relate to others in ways that are learned through interactions with brothers and sisters, children may be equipped with something like a social–psychological template of appropriate behaviors that guides the patterns of social interactions with others in the general community.

The patterns that children follow in their play activities at this time of their life show their involvement in and discovery of the social roles that are represented both in the family and in the larger society. Much of the play of three-, four-, and five-year-olds involves sex-appropriate behavior that is enriched by a vivid imagination. Play also reflects the child's increasing involvement with and preference for group activities with peers. The character of play becomes associative and cooperative, reflecting the goal-directed quality of children's behavior at these ages.

Both boys and girls may overemphasize the qualities of the sex roles they are learning at this time. Current television shows that are popular with children are reenacted through their dramatic play. Many child-care programs recognize the need for children to experiment with social roles and respond by providing play props that encourage and stimulate dramatic play. A special area may be designated as the housekeeping corner, which features dolls, play hats, adult-sized shoes and clothes, dishes, and child-sized furniture. Some centers develop prop boxes that help children to widen their awareness of social roles beyond the family. These boxes contain equipment that encourages children to play roles involved in certain social situations.

PARENTAL DEVELOPMENT DURING THE CHILDBEARING YEARS

Developmental interaction between parents and children acknowledges the impact of children on the socialization of parents into their adult roles within the family and society. When a child is experiencing the psychosocial stages of autonomy and initiative, parents are experiencing a change in the way that their sense of generativity is being developed. Children's physical and psychological needs change considerably during these stages from those that existed during infancy. As a result of the changing needs of children during the time from eighteen months to six years of age, parents change in the "need to be needed" and respond in different ways to children. The acquisition of language by children, their increased mobility, and their style of interaction force parents to reexamine interaction patterns and philosophies of socialization as children grow older. As children are developing, parents continue to develop in patterns that were begun much earlier in their own personal lives. Parents are mutually interdependent with children during this stage of the family life cycle, as each participant serves as a source of stimulation for development and socialization for the other.

Adult development during the childbearing stage of the family life cycle centers on several tasks that involve the needs of the individual adult and his or her relations to other family members. These include:

1. Meeting personal developmental needs.
2. Helping children to meet their physical and psychosocial needs.
3. Maintaining the marriage relationship.

Meeting Personal Needs

Adults face a special challenge during the childbearing stage of the family life cycle in meeting their own personal developmental needs while meeting those of their children. This is a primary adjustment that must be made if an adult is to continue his or her psychosocial development as an effective and fully functioning human being. People generally learn to juggle the alternation of meeting their own needs and those of their children, but the process of learning is more difficult for some people than for others.

Men and women share similar personal needs as developing individuals but may have specific needs independent of each other. Similar needs may include (1) occasional privacy; (2) developing and maintaining social contacts with others of their generation and stage in the family life cycle; (3) developing interests outside of the family; and (4) establishing an identity as an adult member of the community.

The recognition that both adults in the family need time for personal privacy on occasions is often overlooked. The nature of the marriage relationship and the intense interactional setting of the family may work against adults' having as much private time as they may wish during the childbearing stage. Energy is quickly depleted by the full-time mother in housekeeping duties and supervision of children. The single parent faces the additional burdens of trying to perform both parenting roles and providing the economic support of the family. What time is available in two-parent families seems to be devoted to maintaining the marriage and parenting relationship as well as social contacts with other adults. Occasionally, however, there is the need to be alone. This need should be met, as it reenergizes the self, provides the person with the opportunity to get his or her bearings on where she or he is in life, and helps the person briefly to escape the intensity of the emotional and social demands presented by family and outside interactions. Privacy is available through a variety of sources, and each adult should be encouraged to take the time and not be made to feel guilty for concentrating on his or her own need instead of those of others for brief periods of time. How the need for privacy is met by either adult is not the important issue but rather that time is taken and used to the best advantage.

Developing meaningful social contacts with other adults may seem, at first glance, to be one of the most easily met personal needs of adults at this time in the family life cycle. Families live in neighborhoods in close physical proximity to others. Neighboring, however, is becoming a phenomenon of the past. "Minding one's own business" is more common today, and the high rate of physical mobility of families makes neighborhoods change in composition very frequently. Many people feel uncomfortable in investing the time and social energy to develop friendships that quickly dissolve after a short time because a family is moving away. The economic status of a family with several young children may not allow the adults to entertain in their home as frequently as they may wish. Outside social contacts and interests change with the arrival of children. Small gatherings in someone's home or an inexpensive night out on the town constitute the usual social contacts that adults have with others their age at this time in the family life cycle. Baby-sitters are not cheap and good ones may be difficult to locate. The need is there, however, for social contact on an adult level and is met more successfully by some couples than by others.

Developing interests outside of the concerns involving the family are met in a number of ways. Some women, for example, may pursue educational goals or resume careers that were interrupted by the arrival of their children. Others may realize that they are restricted and bored by being a housebound wife and may reenter the paid labor force, become involved in volunteer work for service and charitable organizations, or become involved in religious activities. Some couples become involved with political and social causes. Involvement, in whatever regard, helps the individual to grow as a person and widens the psychological horizons beyond the demands presented by family life (see Figure 5-11). Balancing such outside interests with family concerns, however, is one of the challenges at this time of adults' lives.

An identity as an adult member of the community may come through having children. The status that comes to the person who is a parent helps to change his or her self-image from the one of a young adult without child rearing responsibilities or commitments. Having a child changes one's outlook on the nature of life and the nature of participation in this particular part of the life cycle. As experiences are gained through interacting with children, the psychological and chronological differences between an adult and a child help the adult to see how differently the world is experienced by both a child and an adult. Comparisons are made, as well, between what life

"'Dear Friends: The high points of our year were Billy's report card and PJ's new tooth. ... How's it sound so far?"

Figure 5-11.

is like for someone the same age as the parent who doesn't have children, and assessments are made that reflect on the person's satisfaction and acceptance of his or her place in life as an individual who is both a developing adult and a parent. Having children may help an individual to gauge the passage of time more accurately in reviewing his or her present status as compared with that of the past (see Figure 5-12). Certain behavior is expected of adults if they are to be accepted as members of the community. Concerns shift to the adequacy of child-care programs, whether municipal and school bonds should be approved, or if community service programs are performing as intended. These concerns reflect the involvement of adults' efforts and attention with their emerging adult role. The development of a sense of generativity is expanded to include concern for the welfare of children in general.

Women and men may have different personal needs that relate to their roles within the family. A woman confronts a psychological hazard in performing the major child-rearing function by immersing her individual identity in her role as a mother. Meeting children's needs, following and supervising

"I'd like to go through the express lane just once!"

Figure 5-12.

their activities, and assisting their growth and development may come to be the consuming interest and focal point of the full-time mother. Her personal needs and the needs of her husband are set aside in favor of meeting the needs of the children. Family life and child rearing may come to be resented or accepted as all that life can offer a woman. A woman who derives her complete fulfillment from being a wife and a mother is a person who runs the risk of stagnating her personal development as a dynamic human being. The severity of adjustment that faces many women in reorganizing their lives once the last child has grown and left the home may depend on how well interests and abilities are broadened during the childbearing stage of the family life cycle.

Men, particularly those of the middle class, who enact the traditional instrumental role of husband–father become acutely aware of their responsibility to provide economic stability for their families during the childbearing years. This aspect of their role performance is dependent on how well career and occupational goals are established and pursued. A man experiences stressful demands at this time in his life. Success in his occupation means devoting considerable time and effort to activities that may take him away from the family at a time when the mother makes increasing demands for assistance in child rearing, or when the children's developmental needs call for increasing attention from him. Maintaining an adequate balance among work, social, and family responsibilities and still finding time for privacy may make the childbearing years a stressful experience for some men.

Meeting Children's Needs

Parents continue to develop their sense of generativity in the childbearing stage of the family life cycle through their interactions with their children. The children present different challenges to parents that lead to the mastery of developmental tasks. Parents assist their children in developing a sense of autonomy and a sense of initiative. Developmental interaction between parents and children at this stage of the family life cycle implies that parents will change in the way they interact with their children in response to the changes in the children in these two psychosocial stages of early childhood.

Autonomous and initiative behavior of children is enhanced by parents who are responsive to the emerging needs of children at this time in their life. When parents recognize their children's needs, their "need to be needed" by their children is changed accordingly. Children, in effect, shape and modify the parenting behavior of adults. A parent learns that his or her growing child also recognizes the changes in his or her own maturity and will resist being "babied" or treated in a manner that was more appropriate when she or he was younger (see Figure 5-13). Older children are particularly sensitive to adults who attempt to interact with them in a patronizing manner that fails to recognize their status as "big kids." Initiative behavior, as it increas-

"That's not a choo-choo, Daddy. It's a DIESEL."
Figure 5-13.

ingly emerges in the third to fifth years, serves as a psychological flag to parents that they can no longer take their child's changing abilities for granted. Children, throughout the years of early childhood, try to prove to parents their attitude of "I can! Let me show you I can!"

As children become more capable of verbal communication, parents react by shifting to methods of child rearing that are more verbal than physical in nature. Parents who believe in permissive and authoritative methods of child rearing may begin to use an increasing amount of reasoning, verbal threats, and so on in interactions with their children. These reactions to the changing nature of children assist and guide their autonomous behavior in preparation for the next stage of psychosocial development.

Experience in child rearing produces significant changes in attitudes toward the type and choice of controls a parent uses in his or her parenting behavior. Marwell and Schmitt (1969) compared questionnaire responses of unmarried, childless female college students with those of women with children. The children of these women had a median age of four years. All of the individuals rated the likelihood of using sixteen different child-rearing methods in a hypothetical situation. Women with children differed from the college students in the probability of using seven methods of obtaining compliance with the parent's request. The proportion of mothers was greater than that of the childless college women in their estimate of (1) acting in a friendly and helpful manner; (2) using punishment until the child's compliance was obtained; (3) appealing to the good qualities of the child as a motivating factor to gain his or her compliance; and (4) telling the child that others will have a high opinion of him or her if he or she complies with the parent's request. Mothers reported that the methods they would be *least* likely to use were (1) pointing out the negative consequences of the child's behavior; (2) informing the child that he or she would feel worse if he did not comply; and (3) telling the child that only a person with "bad" qualities would not comply with the adult's request.

As children grow older, parents learn to reshape their methods of gaining a child's compliance. Marwell and Schmitt report that mothers of young children were more likely than mothers of older children to point out the consequences and the "bad" or guilt feelings the child would probably experience for not complying with the parents' requests. The greater degree of experience in discovering what worked best combined with the different ways that older children behave served in socializing the mothers of older children to be more likely to select different compliance-gaining methods. The methods that mothers of younger children said they would be least likely to use were reported by the college-aged, childless women as what they would be *most* likely to use to gain control and compliance from a child.

These differences in what methods would be used to gain compliance from a child show the influence of past experiences of the mothers in interacting with their children. They learned through these interactions what worked and what did not. This research reflects the socializing influence of parent–child interaction in teaching or conditioning the parent to those controls that are successful in gaining children's cooperation. As Marwell and Schmitt point out, the interaction between the parent and the child socializes each participant. This is what is termed *developmental interaction* in this text. The types of controls parents use may or may not affect the experiences of the child. Parents may abandon certain successful methods in favor of others that can result in achieving the desired behavior from the child. This experimentation with what controls to use leads to more efficient methods of achieving desired child behaviors. More importantly, parents learn what works successfully on the first child and may use these same methods with other children as they experience the same stages of development.

Developmental interaction during the childbearing stage of the family life cycle is shown in another manner. Experience in the parent–child interaction system may determine whether a couple decides to have other children. Paul Werner and his associates (1975) report that past experiences in child rearing may influence the decision of women, who already have two children, to have another child. A sample of these women reported what they considered to be the advantages and the disadvantages of having a third child in the near future (see Table 5-2). These responses show the women's perceptions of the impact of an additional child on their family and personal situations. Notice from the table that the reasons for having another child would be classified as altruistic motivations, whereas the reasons for not having another child might be narcissistic or instrumental motivations (see discussion in Chapter 1). Regardless of the intentions for or against having a third child, all of the reasons are based on predicting the consequences of the additional baby on the family or on personal roles. These consequences are derived in part from the mothers' past experiences in interacting with children, and these beliefs of predicted outcome were socialized partially by these past experiences.

Maintaining the Marriage Relationship

The introduction of children into the family causes a reorganization and restructuring of the relationship between a couple (see Chapter 4). The new parents adjust to the changes in their life style after the birth of the first child

Table 5-2. Advantages and Disadvantages of Having a Third Child *

Reasons Mentioned	Percentage
Advantages:	
Satisfactions with and enjoyment of children	42
Companion or playmate for existing children	37
Proper sex balance of children in family	32
Enlarging and stabilizing family as a unit	29
Small interval between children is better	20
Childbirth and development as learning experience for self and others	19
Miscellaneous	20
Disadvantages:	
Effects on economic well-being	80
Family tension or psychological well-being of the family	37
Less time for career	34
General demands on time, energy, and responsibility	32
Own psychological health	24
Concern for overpopulation and other social problems	20
Less time for leisure activities	17
Own physical health	15
Miscellaneous	36

* Total sample size was 59 women.
Source: P. Werner, S. Middlestadt-Carter, and T. Crawford. Having a third child: Predicting behavioral intentions. *Journal of Marriage and the Family*, 1975, *37*, 348–358. Copyright 1975 by the National Council on Family Relations. Reprinted by permission.

and begin to acquire the new role image and behaviors associated with being a parent. This adjustment period, however, does not ensure that everyone will live happily ever after as fairy tales would have us believe. Because of the developmental processes that work toward change among all family members, nothing remains static or unchanging in family life.

Several research studies examine what happens to what family sociologists call *marital satisfaction,* or happiness over the family life cycle. These studies are discussed here because the implications of the findings point to the influence of children, for better or worse, in shaping the degree of satisfaction in a couple's marital relationship.

Two studies delineate developmental trends in marital satisfaction over the family life cycle (and were briefly mentioned in Chapter 4). The degree of satisfaction that is reported by middle-class couples follows a U-shaped pattern that corresponds to the stage of the family life cycle being experienced by the couples (see Figure 5-14). The degree of marital satisfaction reported

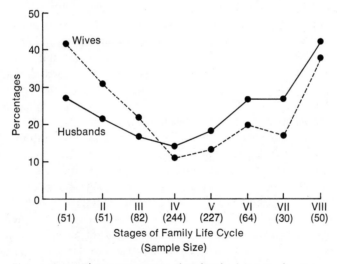

Figure 5-14. The percentage of individuals at each stage of the family life cycle that reported their marriage to be going well "all the time." A reanalysis of scores on a 6-point scale with 1 equaling "never" and 6 equaling "all the time" indicated that only 4 per cent of the variance of marital satisfaction scores was associated with the family life cycle stages. This is because a large percentage of those in the middle stages are satisfied "most of the time." (Source: Rollins, B., & Feldman, H. Marital satisfaction over the family life cycle. *Journal of Marriage and the Family,* 1970, *32,* 20–28. Copyright 1970 by the National Council on Family Relations. Reprinted by permission.)

by couples studied by Rollins and Feldman (1970) shows a general decline as the first child grows older. This decline changes to an improvement in marital satisfaction as children are raised and launched into lives of their own, with the happiness of the couples showing a recovery to a degree that is greater for men and about the same for women prior to the introduction of children into the family. This trend in marital satisfaction over the family life cycle has been confirmed by another study by Rollins and Cannon (1974). Other studies (Gurin, Verhoff, and Feld, 1960; Bradburn and Coplovitz, 1965; Burr, 1970) have shown only a decline in marital satisfaction without a recovery in degree when the children are no longer present in the family. Data from a study by Ryder (1973) suggest that the general decline in marital satisfaction may begin shortly after the birth of the first child. The mothers who participated in this study when compared with childless women reported that husbands paid less attention to them after the baby's birth than before it was born. This report reconfirms the data discussed earlier in the last chapter on studies of the transition to parenthood.

One explanation provided by Rollins and Cannon (1974) as to why the U-shaped curve of marital satisfaction exists is that *role strain* takes an increasing toll on the satisfaction gained from the marriage relationship of parents as children grow older. Role strain, in a general and broad interpretation as discussed by Burr (1973), occurs when three factors coincide: (1) *role conflict* creates incompatible expectations for a person holding several roles at the same time; (2) *role incompatibility* produces demands on one social role that are incompatible simultaneously with those of another social role; and (3) *maximum role activity* places demands for optimal role proficiency in all social roles. These three factors are thought to combine to produce role strain during the middle stages of the family life cycle (when children are present) and affect the degree of satisfaction within the parents' marriage. What is plain here is that it becomes increasingly difficult for both the husband and the wife to pay close attention to the needs and demands of their marriage relationship while attending to the needs and demands of their growing children. The obligations and responsibilities of parenting often take precedence over those relating to the marriage.

This research suggests few positive values to having children in order to improve a marriage. The results serve as a warning to adults that children can be disruptive to their relationship and that the problems associated with children and marriage relationships won't improve perhaps until the children are raised and gone from the home. What is positive from the research is that adults can be informed of the overcommitments in adult social roles that lead to conflict and stress. Preventative measures can be taken when warnings or signals of this stress are noticed by the couple. The research also speaks of the importance of developing a strong emotional commitment between marriage partners before children are produced to sustain them through the role-straining years of having and raising children to maturity.

Notice from Figure 5-14 that men and women differ in their reactions through the life cycle. Men begin to experience disenchantment with the marriage earlier than women, but recovery takes place sooner and is stronger, whereas women are happier with their marriages in the early stages of the cycle but recover more slowly from the disenchantment. Men have been reported by Harry (1976) to define and perceive happiness in terms of their involvement in family life during the childbearing and school-aged–child stages of the family life cycle. As children grow older, however, men find happiness in other aspects away from and not involving the family, such as in their occupational roles. This research supports the trend reported by the marital satisfaction studies just discussed. Although there are no empirical data on women that are similar to Harry's data on men regarding how happiness in life is defined, we might speculate that the trend for women reflects their socialization to become mothers, the degree of their involvement with children as a fulfillment of a social goal in life, and the devastating reaction that requires adjustment to life as well as an identity crisis when the children leave the home.

From a practical point of view, some preventative measures can be taken by adults to mend their marital fences and to maintain the emotional bonds of the marriage while meeting their parental responsibilities. One of the most useful methods, which many middle-class couples find to be successful, is the occasional weekend or overnight escape from their parenting duties. A competent, trusted sitter or relative stays with the children while the parents take off for a romantic rendezvous at a local motel or resort. These brief but helpful vacations from parenting assist couples in becoming reacquainted with each other and renew their relationship. Some couples are disturbed to discover that sexual relations become stale and uninteresting as the marriage continues. Volumes of material are available that discuss new and different ways to spice up and restimulate sexual interest and enjoyment. These are usually discovered by couples sometime during the childbearing stage or shortly into the next stage of the family life cycle. When a couple has produced as many children as they wish or believe that they can afford to support, an increasing number of couples initiate some type of permanent birth control, such as a vasectomy, which is performed on the man, or a tubal ligation on the woman. The general consensus of research shows that sexual interests and frequency of coitus improve considerably for the majority of couples when these measures are taken because the fear of pregnancy is completely removed from sexual relations.

Children may be a factor in marital satisfaction in a different manner. Luckey and Bain (1970) report that children were mentioned as the only mutual factor of satisfaction between couples who were identified as having an unsatisfactory marriage. Couples with children who were identified as having a satisfactory marriage found companionship and fulfillment in each other, whereas those who were unhappy in their marriages turned to their children to fulfill their emotional needs. Such couples are in danger of jeopardizing their marriage. Although couples who have children are married longer than those who do not, the absence of children may cause marriages such as these reported by Luckey and Bain to lose their reason for existing once the children are gone from the home. Marriages work best when based on mutual companionship between adults. Although companionship with children may temporarily fulfill emotional gratification needs of adults, problems may eventually result in a pathological relationship between parents and children.

The research on marital satisfaction serves as an indication that adults need to be aware of the stress that begins during the childbearing years. The general decline in satisfaction may continue throughout the periods of the life cycle while children are present, but preventative measures can be initiated to safeguard the integrity of the marriage.

SUPPORTS FOR CAREGIVING IN EARLY CHILDHOOD

Community supports for alternative forms of caregiving are more numerous and available to families with young children than to those with infants. A variety of child-care programs often are present in larger communities and cities that offer numerous types of experiences for young children. Depending on the needs and the financial status of a family, young children may be enrolled in full- or halfday programs in child-care centers that operate during the week, during daytime hours only, seven days a week or only during business days. Other families may desire their child to have the more intensive but short-term experience offered by a preschool program. Others may wish their child to take advantage of opportunities offered through compensatory programs such as Head Start. Child-care programs, through the nature of their goals and objectives in working with young children, offer a number of alternatives to families as community supports for caregiving during the childbearing stage of the family life cycle.

Child-Care Centers

Americans have been rather reluctant to become involved in establishing and operating child-care centers until recently. The increasing numbers of facilities and their use by families is a reversal of negative public attitudes in the past toward day care, according to Angrist and Lave (1973). Day care was viewed as a custodial service that met the needs of poor and more unstable families for child care. This view, according to these authors, is perpetuated today through the visibility of child-care delivery services to welfare mothers and others supported by public assistance. Europeans, on the other hand, have long supported and approved of day-care services for children (Bronfenbrenner, 1970). Although attitudes toward substitute child care (whether home- or agency-based) are improving, there continue to be many questions and controversies surrounding the issue of day care. One of the primary questions relates to the immediate and long-range effects of substitute care on children and on family functioning.

WHO USES CHILD-CARE CENTER SERVICES, REASONS, AND COSTS.   As with infant-care services, the majority of individuals who purchase day-care services are families in which both parents work or in which the single parent is employed or in training for employment. The increasing number of women in the paid labor force accounts for the increasing use of day-care services today. When women enter the labor force, research shows that satisfaction with work outside the home and substitute child care go hand-in-hand (Harrell and Ridley, 1975). In other words, when mothers feel comfortable about using substitute child care and feel that the quality of care is adequate, they become more satisfied in their occupations. Heckman (1974) also reports that women's work efforts are considerably improved by the degree of their satisfaction with substitute child-care programs.

Child-care services are increasingly available on university campuses throughout the country (Cargill, 1977). These facilities are often a component of laboratory programs of academic departments that teach and perform research in child development and family relationships or in early childhood education. Many of these programs have been established by university administrations in response to pressure from students for assistance with child care. These facilities aid students by providing adequate care for their children when they attend class and/or work.

Family or home-based care is another option for parents, rather than agency-based substitute child care. Although services offered by this type of arrangement vary, family day care is characterized by featuring (1) the smaller numbers of children who receive care (usually six at a maximum); (2) a "warmer," more homelike atmosphere; and (3) more individualized attention from adults in providing caregiving (Sale, 1973; Wallach and Piers, 1973). For these reasons, this type of substitute child care is used by more individuals than any other type of group care for children. Parents may feel that the more intimate, homelike environment improves a child's adjustment and reduces his or her fears of prolonged separation from the family.

The costs of substitute child-care services are difficult to determine or estimate accurately because of rapid fluctuations in cost within communities, the wide range of services available, and poorly developed means for gathering such information on a national scale. One study (Bedger, 1973) reports that costs per child/hour in day-care centers ranged from 32 cents to $2.69. Annual costs for services at these figures based on an eight-hour day, five-day week purchase of services for fifty weeks per year range from $640 to $2,320. The National Council of Organizations for Children and Youth (1976) states that an annual family expenditure of $2,400 for child-care services is not unreasonable. What is unreasonable is the lack of federal and state assistance to all individuals using child-care services. Although assistance is available for those families who qualify under poverty guidelines or where the single parent is gaining job training, the federal government has only recently granted a limited tax exemption for payment of child-care services on annual income tax returns. Quality programming of child-care services does not come cheaply, and the lack of federal and state support raises questions about the priorities of government regarding human services.

WHAT PARENTS WANT FROM DAY-CARE SERVICES.   A number of issues reflect the concerns of parents about the safety and well-being of children when care is provided in group settings. Agencies that provide such services are responding in an appropriate manner to these expectations of parents. Day care in the past primarily was a custodial service that consisted of rather limited experiences that lacked enrichment for children. As the public became more aware of the importance of early education, ideas of quality child-care services changed. Today many day-care centers offer a developmental rather than a custodial program. The increased availability of trained child-care professionals in such centers has also improved the quality of services offered to families.

Two surveys (Auerbach-Fink, 1977; Handler, 1973) report that parents expect quality child-care services to consist of (1) custodial care; (2) socialization experiences (how to relate to others); (3) activities that help children acquire new skills; (4) provision of a safe environment; (5) provision of adequate nutrition through meals and snacks; (6) the presence of qualified, trained staff members; and (7) parental involvement of some nature. Handler's survey indicated that expectations of parents differ according to the type of center used by a family. Parents who used the services of nonprofit centers favored custodial care over socialization experiences. These feelings reflect the older attitude toward day care, particularly among working-class families or those receiving public child-care assistance.

WHAT PARENTS CAN EXPECT FROM CENTERS.   Parents can anticipate a number of services from child-care centers that provide a quality developmental program for children. These include (1) a full range of experiences (small- and large-group as well as individual activities, field trips, art and science activities, and so on); (2) the acquisition of new skills in all areas of development; (3) the maintenance of children's health through screening procedures, immunization programs, proper nutrition, and adequate rest; (4) the maintenance of emotional attachments to family members; (5) the development of a sense of community gained through socialization experiences and social interactions with peers and adults; and (6) the socialization of children into a democratic style of life (Caldwell, 1973).

Professionals are increasingly aware of the potential of substitute child care in influencing the mental health of children and families (Heinicke, Friedman, Prescott, Puncel, and Sale, 1973). Quality child-care centers recognize their role in promoting the emotional development of children and strive through activities and style of interaction with children to meet the personal needs of children and to help them cope with their crucial needs. For many children, the child-care setting becomes a surrogate family that works in conjunction with the parents to provide nurturance, socialization experiences, and enhancement of development. Child-care workers can play an important role in helping parents to understand the reasons for problems in the development or behavior of young children and in helping both children and parents to adjust to a variety of family crises. Staff members can also act to recognize developmental delays in children so that referrals can be made to appropriate professionals. When physical or psychological abuse of children is observed by staff members, referrals can be made as well to help these parents and children.

The success of quality day-care programs is interdependent with community involvement in providing services for children. Parents must be involved in planning and implementing services to ensure that expectations are met. Large day-care centers, and most often those that are publicly funded, respond by forming parent advisory committees that provide input and evaluation of services to staff members. Although problems exist in soliciting the voluntary participation and time of parents, these groups accomplish a great deal in assisting centers to be responsive to parental needs for and concerns about substitute child care (Auerbach, 1975).

Preschool Programs

The specialization of preschool programs is a recent development. Most programs have a common objective of educating children, whereas less attention is given to physical development and parent involvement (Smart and Smart, 1977). The programs are seen by parents as an extension of and supplement to experiences available in the home and as excellent sources for introducing children to their peers. Several descriptions of types of preschool programs are available (Leeper, Dales, Skipper, and Witherspoon, 1974; Reed, 1971; Smart and Smart, 1977; Todd and Heffernan, 1977) and are summarized here. Most preschool programs are short-term, meaning that sessions are held for a two- to three-hour period.

1. *Nursery schools* represent a traditional approach to early education that emphasizes social development, acquiring cognitive skills, encouraging a child's sense of autonomy and initiative through activities and interactions with others, and creativity. Most schools of this type typically enroll children who are three to four years old. A purpose of these programs is seen by both parents and staff as preparing children for entrance into public school. Parent involvement is encouraged primarily through parent-education programs.

2. *Cooperative preschools* feature parent involvement in the actual operation of the program. This involvement by parents acts to reduce operating costs and fees as well as to educate parents (usually mothers) about child growth and development during early childhood. Cooperative programs are commonly sponsored by churches and religious organizations as well as by neighborhood or community parent groups. The curriculum varies among these programs as a variation of the traditional nursery school curriculum. Resources are more limited in these operations because of the concern of cooperative programs to provide services to families at a reasonable cost.

3. *Specialized curriculum programs* focus on a particular educational philosophy for young children. Programs can include an emphasis on Piagetian theory, the Montessori method, or the open-classroom approach, for example. These programs attempt to educate children using theoretical frameworks.

4. *Programs for children with special needs* feature educational activities that are adapted to the needs of atypical children. Children who have physical or mental handicaps, for example, attend these programs, which are privately or publicly funded through local, state, and federal resources. There is a growing trend to incorporate these young children with handicaps into other preschool programs. There are two central purposes for including these children in programs that also enroll children without handicaps: (1) handicapped children can profit from interacting with normal children and are assisted in developing healthy self-concepts; (2) normal children are aided by having experiences with those who have handicaps to develop greater empathy with and acceptance of these special children. Rehabilitative services are an integral part of programs that serve children with special needs.

5. *Compensatory programs* act to provide disadvantaged children with experiences that may be lacking from their home or neighborhood environment. Head Start programs are typical of such programs. Activities provided for children emphasize language, social, and cognitive skill acquisition; enhancement of children's self-concepts; and a variety of "hands-on" experiences with the physical environment. Additional services provided by these programs are directed to meeting the health and nutritional needs of the children. Parent involvement occurs through advisory committees to ensure that programs meet parental expectations.

What Parents Can Expect from Preschools

In discussing the elements of a better preschool, Day and Sheehan (1974), state that three primary differences emerge from observation of the variety of programs available to parents. These include (1) the organization and utilization of space; (2) children's access to materials and the ways they are used; and (3) the degree and type of adult–child interaction (see Table 5-3).

Most programs feature learning centers within the physical environment to promote interest in a number of areas. These centers usually consist of areas

Table 5-3. Factors of Preschool Programs Relating to Child Behavior

Space, Materials, Adult Roles Integrated	*Space, Materials, Adult Roles Not Integrated*
1. Many instances of adults and children working cooperatively.	1. Little long-lasting adult–child contact.
2. Children have considerable autonomy within expanding limits.	2. Unnecessary constraints for each learning–play area established by adults well in advance of children's use. The children's behavior in each learning area prescribed by staff.
3. Most materials available to children, with their use of them in constructive, developmental ways.	3. Only a few, routine materials available. Most materials are not accessible to children; they are brought out and put away by staff.
4. Much child–adult and child–child communication and activity.	4. Much child–child talk is often transitory and uncommunicative.
5. Children's efforts seemed to be focused on completing play or work.	5. Children inattentive, listless, and easily distracted. Great amounts of random undirected movement.
6. Little acting out and aggression being directed at other children.	6. Children using toys in a very aggressive manner. Aggression often directed at other children.
7. Program directed by the staff but evolved with the participation of the children.	7. Not much of a program. Much teacher-directed activity. Long periods of adult inattention to children.

Source: D. Day, and R. Sheehan. Reprinted by permission from *Young Children*, Vol. 30, No. 1 (Nov. 1974), p. 23. Copyright © 1974, National Association for the Education of Young Children, 1834 Connecticut Avenue, N.W., Washington, D.C. 20009

for blocks, reading, art and science activities, and social play, for example. Space within a classroom may be open or closed. Open-space environments feature small room dividers with a minimum degree of privacy for adults and children. Closed-space environments may have quiet areas that are well defined and can be composed of several separate rooms.

Better preschool programs provide easy access to a wide variety of materials for children. Restricted use of materials such as clay, paper, small manipulative materials, and blocks is minimized. Materials are rotated or replaced frequently by the staff, who assist the children in using these resources for learning.

Adult–child interactions in quality preschool programs are frequent but also selective. Adults in such programs interact verbally with children on an individual basis as well as in small groups. The adults listen to what the children say and respond in a manner that expands their vocabularies and concepts about their world of people and things. The adults know when to interact with the children and when not to interfere with the children's interactions with each other. The children's interactions with the adults lead to cooperative behavior. Programs where the adults spend much of their time in performing housekeeping duties instead of in active involvement with the children encourage considerable aggressive acting-out and attention-getting behaviors from children, according to Day and Sheehan. Active involvement of the adults with the children promotes increased involvement with materials and prosocial behavior among children.

Child-care programs in general can function to promote the mental health of children by expanding the functions of the teacher. Stein, Beyer, and Ronald (1975) describe a four-year project that involved psychiatric assistance to teachers in their responses to a variety of family and individual problems that affect young children. The project demonstrates how the preschool teacher can assist the parents of young children in their child rearing and its associated problems. For many parents the preschool is the first experience with extrafamilial agents of socialization for their children. The teacher can provide assistance for the parents in their learning to cope with separation from their child and his or her incorporation into the larger community. Preschool teachers can assist families and young children to adjust to numerous crises by performing the therapeutic functions of advising, listening, eliciting feelings and attitudes, and counseling. Such crises include helping children and adults adjust to situations involving death, illness of the child or family members, surgical procedures and hospitalization, and separation or divorce of the parents. By playing a supportive role, the preschool teacher can play a vital adjunctive role in socializing young children.

POINTS TO CONSIDER

- Two psychosocial stages of development occur during the early childhood period of the life cycle: (1) the *sense of autonomy* versus *shame and doubt;* and (2) the *sense of initiative* versus *guilt.*
- The major developmental tasks that children should accomplish during these psychosocial stages center on laying the foundation for adjustments to people and to situations away from the home environment.
- Adults who provide care for children also continue to develop in their personal achievement of a sense of generativity during their child's early childhood years.

- The developmental changes that children experience during early childhood prompt corresponding changes in their parents' styles of interaction, their child-rearing methods, and their use of controls.
- Adults face certain tasks during their child's years of early childhood that involve their changing personal needs, their roles as parents and spouses, and their relationships with other family members.
- Community supports for alternative forms of caregiving are more numerous and available to families with young children. Child-care programs vary according to philosophy and objectives in assisting families in the socialization of young children.

REFERENCES

ANGRIST, S., and LAVE, J. Issues surrounding day care. *Family Coordinator*, 1973, *22*, 457–464.

AUERBACH, A. Parents' role in day care. *Child Care Quarterly*, 1975, *4*, 180–187.

AUERBACH-FINK, S. Mothers' expectations of child care. *Young Children*, 1977, *32*, 12–21.

BEDGER, J. Cost analysis in day care and Head Start. *Child Welfare*, 1974, *53*, 514–523.

BIGNER, J. Sibling influence on sex-role preference of young children. *Journal of Genetic Psychology*, 1972, *121*, 271–282.

BIGNER, J. A Wernerian developmental analysis of children's descriptions of siblings. *Child Development*, 1974, *45*, 317–323. (a)

BIGNER, J. Second-borns' discrimination of sibling role concepts. *Developmental Psychology*, 1974, *10*, 564–573. (b)

BIGNER, J. Children's perceptions of "goodness" and "badness" in sibling roles. Unpublished manuscript, 1977.

BOSSARD, J., and BOLL, E. *The sociology of child development* (3rd ed.). New York: Harper & Row, 1966.

BRADBURN, N., and CAPLOVITZ, D. *Reports on happiness*. Chicago: Aldine, 1965.

BRIM, O., JR. Family structure and sex-role learning by children. *Sociometry*, 1957, *21*, 1–16.

BRONFENBRENNER, U. *Two worlds of childhood: U.S. and U.S.S.R.* New York: Russell Sage, 1970.

BURR, W. Satisfaction with various aspects of marriage over the life cycle: A random middle class sample. *Journal of Marriage and the Family*, 1970, *22*, 29–37.

BURR, W. Theory construction and the sociology of the family. New York: Wiley, 1973.

CALDWELL, B. Can young children have a quality life in day care? *Young Children*, 1973, *28*, 197–208.

CARGILL, G. Child care on campus. *Young Children*, 1977, *32*, 20–23.

CICIRELLI, V. The effect of sibling relationship on concept learning of young children taught by child-teachers. *Child Development*, 1972, *43*, 282–287.

CICIRELLI, V. Effects of sibling structure and interaction on children's categorization style. *Developmental Psychology*, 1973, *9*, 132–139.

CICIRELLI, V. Relationship of sibling structure and interaction to younger sibling's conceptual style. *Journal of Genetic Psychology,* 1974, *125,* 37–49.

CICIRELLI, V. Mother–child and sibling–sibling interactions on a problem-solving task. *Child Development,* 1976, *47,* 588–596.

CLIFFORD, E. Discipline in the home: A controlled observational study of parental practices. *Journal of Genetic Psychology,* 1959, *95,* 45–82.

DAY, D., and SHEEHAN, R. Elements of a better preschool. *Young Children,* 1974, *30,* 15–23.

DUVALL, E. *Marriage and family development* (5th ed.). Philadelphia: Lippincott, 1977.

GURIN, G., VERHOFF, J., and FELD, S. *Americans view their mental health.* New York: Basic Books, 1960.

HANDLER, E. Expectations of day care parents. *Social Service Review,* 1973, *47,* 266–277.

HARRELL, J., and RIDLEY, C. Substitute child care, maternal employment, and the quality of mother–child interaction. *Journal of Marriage and the Family,* 1975, *37,* 556–564.

HARRY, J. Evolving sources of happiness for men over the life cycle: A structural analysis. *Journal of Marriage and the Family,* 1976, *38,* 289–296.

HECKMAN, J. Effects of child care programs on women's work effort. *Journal of Political Economy,* 1974, *82,* S136–S163.

HEINICKE, C., FRIEDMAN, D., PRESCOTT, E., PUNCEL, C., and SALE, J. The organization of day care: Considerations relating to the mental health of child and family. *American Journal of Orthopsychiatry,* 1973, *43,* 8–22.

HURLOCK, E. *Child development* (5th ed). New York: McGraw-Hill, 1972.

HURLOCK, E. *Developmental psychology* (4th ed.). New York: McGraw-Hill, 1975.

JERSILD, A., TELFORD, C., and SAWREY, J. *Child psychology* (7th ed.). Englewood Cliffs, N.J.: Prentice-Hall, 1975.

KOCH, H. Sissiness and tomboyishness in relation to sibling characteristics. *Journal of Genetic Psychology,* 1956, *88,* 231–244.

KOCH, H. The relation of certain formal abilities of siblings to attitudes held toward each other and toward their parents. *Monographs of the Society for Research in Child Development,* 1960, *25,* Whole No. 78.

LASKO, J. Parent behavior toward first and second children. *Genetic Psychology Monographs,* 1954, *49,* 99–137.

LEEPER, S., DALES, R., SKIPPER, D., and WITHERSPOON, R. *Good schools for young children* (3rd ed.). New York: Macmillan, 1974.

LUCKEY, E., and BAIN, J. Children: A factor in marital satisfaction. *Journal of Marriage and the Family,* 1970, *32,* 43–44.

MARWELL, G., and SCHMITT, D. Childbearing experience and attitudes toward the use of influence techniques. *Journal of Marriage and the Family,* 1969, *31,* 779–782.

National Council of Organizations for Children and Youth. *America's children.* Washington, D.C.: The Council, 1976.

PIAGET, J. *Six psychological studies.* New York: Random House, 1967.

REED, K. *The nursery school* (5th ed.). Philadelphia: W. B. Saunders, 1971.

ROLLINS, B., and CANNON, K. Marital satisfaction over the family life cycle: A reevaluation. *Journal of Marriage and the Family,* 1974, *36,* 271–282.

ROLLINS, B., and FELDMAN, H. Marital satisfaction over the family life cycle. *Journal of Marriage and the Family,* 1970, *32,* 20–28.

RYDER, R. Longitudinal data relating marriage satisfaction and having a child. *Journal of Marriage and the Family,* 1973, *35,* 604–607.

SALE, J. Family day care: One alternative in the delivery of developmental services in early childhood. *American Journal of Orthopsychiatry,* 1973, *43,* 37–45.

SMART, R., and SMART, M. *Children: Development and relationships* (3rd ed.). New York: Macmillan, 1977.

STEIN, M., BEYER, E., and RONALD, D. Beyond benevolence: The mental health role of the preschool teacher. *Young Children,* 1975, *30,* 358–372.

SUTTON-SMITH, B., and ROSENBERG, B. Age changes in the effects of ordinal position on sex-role identification. *Journal of Genetic Psychology,* 1965, *107,* 61–73.

SUTTON-SMITH, B., and ROSENBERG, B. Sibling consensus on power tactics. *Journal of Genetic Psychology,* 1968, *112,* 63–72.

SUTTON-SMITH, B., and ROSENBERG, B. *The sibling.* New York: Holt, 1970.

TODD, V., and HEFFERNAN, H. *The years before school.* New York: Macmillan, 1977.

WALLACH, L., and PIERS, M. Family day care: the humanistic side. *Child Welfare,* 1973, *52,* 431–435.

WERNER, P., MIDDLESTADT-CARTER, S., and CRAWFORD, T. Having a third child: Predicting behavioral intentions. *Journal of Marriage and the Family,* 1975, *37,* 348–358.

6

Developmental Interaction During Middle Childhood

The period of life labeled as middle childhood occurs from the time of a child's entrance into school (at about six years of age) and extends to the time he or she becomes a teenager at thirteen years of age. During this period of time a number of developmental events and changes occur that lead toward increased maturity and responsibilities for individual behavior.

School-aged children are faced with a central psychosocial task of developing a *sense of industry* as opposed to a *sense of inferiority*. Although this crisis constitutes the major concern of children at this time in life, many supplementary developmental tasks arise during this period as well. These tasks complement a child's emerging sense of self. Achievement of these skills assists in developing a healthy self-concept.

Parents continue to experience the challenges of interaction with a child whose emerging self-concept is sensitive to psychological bruises inflicted by increasing interactions with others outside the home. The adults' sense of generativity or caring for growing children becomes modified during this time. The changing nature of the school-aged child requires major modifications in the style and nature of parental interactions. Methods and techniques of parenting or guiding children that were successful during the child's earlier years are no longer as efficient or effective during this period. Essentially parents must become more psychological than physical helpers of a child at this time. The change in the nature of caregiving often comes about rather subtly as the child progresses through the years of elementary school.

THE DYNAMICS OF BECOMING: CONTINUED

The events of early childhood laid the foundation for the developmental events that occur during the middle childhood years. Erikson (see Chapter 3) believes that the development of a sense of industry becomes the primary psychosocial task for children during these years. A sense of industry can be described in several ways. Taken literally, it is the development of a positive attitude toward work and mastery of the "tools" or academic and social skills that are appropriately learned at this time in life. The development of a healthy attitude toward work means learning to apply oneself to a task and completing it satisfactorily. The task itself may vary considerably from moment to moment and from child to child. Regardless of the nature of the task, the feeling that should emerge during this stage is one of enjoyment in performing tasks and a sense of pride in accomplishment. This stage of psychosocial development differs from the previous one (the *sense of initiative*) in that new expectations are determined for the child and his or her efforts are evaluated more objectively. In the initiative stage, curiosity about the world and what children can discover about themselves were the primary objectives of psychosocial development. In the middle childhood years, this curiosity is transformed into exploring the nature of the environment and achieving goals and skills that "everybody" knows how to do.

The entrance into an all-day school environment is a new experience for many children. Teachers and other adults become additional caregivers and authority figures for children. This new order of life signifies a change in the child's status both in his or her own eyes and in those of his or her parents and teachers. The entrance into school brings another social group into focus in influencing a child's development. This group is composed of other children of similar ages and abilities who become a child's peers or contemporaries. As children progress through school, this group becomes an increasingly important socializing influence in their lives.

The process of becoming a self-actualizing individual continues through middle childhood as children attempt to achieve the goals society expects of them. These goals are communicated through their parents, the school environment, and their peer group to include:

1. Developing a new individuality.
2. Establishing relations with peers.
3. Refining existing skills and acquiring new ones that are physical, social, and mental in nature.

Developing a New Individuality

The years of middle childhood constitute a period in which a child's interactions with the environment and those who populate it assist him or her in developing a new sense of individuality. The seriousness with which life is approached through work and a preoccupation with what can be accomplished or produced aid children in developing a sense of industry. In Erikson's framework of psychosocial development, the theme of this period in a child's life is one of "making things together," referring to the involvement children have with their peer group in developing their skills. "Making things" relates to how children become very involved in acquiring the skills and abilities that are expected to be accomplished during this period of their life.

Success in mastering a wide variety of physical, social, and mental skills helps children to realize their own uniqueness and potential in the world of adults. The experiences that a child encounters in mastering this range of skills prepares her or him for eventual acceptance into the adult world. School-aged children, however, have ambivalent feelings about attaining the ultimate status of adulthood, according to Elkind (1974). From their particular point of view, school-aged children strongly desire to enter the fascinating world of adults, whose skills and abilities are admired. Adults are not-so-secret heroes of children early in this stage of development. They are aware of the power and respect commanded by adults and strongly wish for their approval. The ambivalence in their feelings about growing up and achieving these skills, however, comes with the realization that adults may not have as much fun in life as children do (see Figure 6-1). This realization, erroneous as it may actually be, shows the increasing ability of children to see situations in life from a variety of views.

This example of contradictions in the nature of school-aged children is also evident in what Elkind (1974) describes as the pragmatic–optimistic nature of school-aged children. The pragmatic aspect of these children appears in their efforts to achieve a sense of industry. Their concern is with how things work and how to produce things of meaning and value that will receive the approval of others. The culture of childhood at this time in life is geared to this preoccupation with "making things," especially with other children. Toys, which are still acceptable and desired, are of the type that help children to achieve a sense of success and accomplishment in making things. Kits are especially popular, and they allow a child to produce a mind-boggling array of products. Such products range from pot holders to models of various objects to paint kits. Although these assist and promote the development of large and small muscle skills, it is the end product as well as the process of creation that provides a sense of well-being and accomplishment. These products are treasured by children and may be placed on display for all to admire and praise.

The optimistic nature that accompanies the new sense of individuality asserts itself as children grow older during these years. Success in small endeavors feeds this sense of optimism about mastering new skills and acquiring new abilities. As Elkind states, a source of this optimism for children is their belief that there are an unlimited number of years in which to attain their goals and master the skills necessary to become an adult. The pragmatism that accompanies this optimism about themselves and the world they live in results in an attitude that persistent effort at a task eventually ends in its accomplishment.

The emergent individuality of children is also evident in their increasing

"The thing that bothers me most about growing old is the probability of becoming an unemployed teenager!"

© 1977 by NEA, Inc.

Figure 6-1.

involvement with others outside of the family. The striving for a sense of industry dictates involvement not only with material, concrete things but also with interpersonal relations with others. By interacting with a number of children, a child is afforded feedback and an evaluation of his or her abilities, strengths, and weaknesses. As she or he determines areas of strength as compared with others of the same age, individualism emerges in attempts to attain superiority and accomplishment that will result in the anticipated admiration of others.

Fears that are generated by a child's encounters with the competitive world of peers are another example of the contradictory nature of development in middle childhood. Fears of not being good enough at tasks and skills that "everybody" is learning or already has learned generate concerns from a child about his acceptance by others the same age. Children make numerous derogatory remarks about their abilities and general self-worth with increasing frequency during middle childhood. Remarks such as "Nobody likes me" or "I can't do *anything* right" are common and reflect a child's increasing ability to understand how he or she compares with peers. These remarks indicate his understanding of how he evaluates himself with others, a skill that is necessary to healthy personality development. The ability to see ourselves through the opinions and reactions of others whom we value helps us to form ideas of our worth as individuals during this stage of development.

Contradictions are evident as well in school-aged children's relations with adults and with the family as a group. The achievements in attaining a sense of trust, autonomy, and initiative in the earlier stages of psychosocial development enable children to create a culture to which adults are not admitted although there is an admiration of the qualities and strengths that adults possess. Toward the end of this period, the culture of childhood represents a rejection of adults and the standards of behavior that they ask of children on the one hand, while the desire and need for adult approval and security is evidenced on the other. The rejection of adult authority increases dramatically toward the end of this stage as identification with the peer group is established. Children of this age poke fun at anything and everything that adults represent, for example, by creating ditties and chants such as "Trick or treat!/Smell my feet/Give me something good to eat!" Adult activities and institutions also fail to escape the mockery of school-aged children when they sing, "Here comes the bride/Big, fat, and wide!/Here comes the groom/ Sweeping up the room!"

Problem behavior among peer groups increases considerably, particularly among sixth-grade children, whose apparent goal is to exasperate adults to the *n*th degree. Yet adults are admired in spite of the problems that children sometimes feel they create. Older children, especially, focus this admiration specifically on adults who have glamorous or attractive occupations and professions, such as sports figures and television personalities.

The family still remains a center for security throughout the years of testing and experimenting with an emerging individuality. The authority of the family is recognized by school-aged children but is questioned by negative assessments such as "You always pick on me," or "You don't make anybody else around here do as much as I have to." The family provides security for experimenting with a variety of social interactions with others both inside and outside the group. It also acts as a source of love and acceptance when children experience social battles and failures.

Establishing Relations with Peers

Our culture is a composite of different subcultures. Many subcultures are familiar to us and include racial, ethnic, or age groupings of individuals. A number of subcultures are experienced by individuals throughout the life span, and it is during the middle years of childhood that one of the first and most important subcultures is experienced. This is the subculture of the peer group of childhood (see Figure 6-2).

The peer group does not begin to establish its cohesiveness or strength during the early part of middle childhood. It increases in prominence in children's lives as they progress through the later years of this period. Peer groups in middle childhood are highly subject to change in composition within a short period of time. The subculture of the peer group is similar to other subcultures in having its own traditions, activities, values, acceptable behavior patterns, and rules of conduct. Participation in peer groups is an indication of healthy social development, and the peer group acts as an important source of socialization for children.

Williams and Stith (1974) list the following five functions of the peer group in middle childhood in preparing children for adult life.

"A BIG GUY IN THIRD GRADE CALLED ME 'PAL' TODAY. HOW *BOUT* THAT?"

Figure 6-2.

1. *Companionship.* Young children's play activities evolve from being solitrary to cooperative as children grow older. During middle childhood, the cooperative nature of play includes close friends. Play during middle childhood occurs within the context of small groups that may not be larger than three to four children at the most. The neighborhood gang may constitute the most active grouping of children during these years, although companionship during and after school is established with classmates. The companionship of the peer group teaches children numerous social skills, such as learning to compromise and to give and take in social interaction. Tree houses can't be built or fully enjoyed alone, exploring the neighborhood is best accomplished with several good buddies, and secrets are of no use if there is no one to share them with. Collections of whatever composition (stamps, coins, dolls, rocks, and so on) increase in quantity and quality through bargaining and exchange with friends.

2. *Testing Ground for Behavior.* The peer group provides children with opportunities to perform acts that may be forbidden by adults in authority. Such behavior can range from swearing to protesting against what is considered to be unfair treatment to vandalism against others' property. Name calling may act to motivate others into performing acts that otherwise would never be considered or to test other children for their reactions to the labels. This can include taunting others by labeling them as a "scaredy cat, crybaby, tattletale, show-off, turkey, or dummy." The peer group provides the opportunity for children to explore their independence from adult standards, which results in their learning two unique patterns of behavior: the one acceptable to adults and the one acceptable to peers. Adults may accept crying, for example, in reaction to frustration, whereas peers may reject such behavior. As children experience what is acceptable to their peers, a new standard of behavior emerges that requires strict loyalty and careful adherence in order to maintain acceptance by the group. Some adjustments are necessary as well between what kinds of behavior are approved by adults and what is acceptable to peers. Making a neat appearance or keeping one's room straight may be pleasing to adults, but keeping a neat desk or being a fastidious dresser may be strictly unacceptable at school among friends if a child really wants to be thought of as being a "neat" kid (see Figure 6-3).

3. *Transmitting Knowledge.* The peer group functions to transmit knowledge on numerous subjects. Children of this age will more readily believe the pronouncements and facts offered by their peers than their parents at times. Much accurate information is exchanged on innumerable topics, as each child brings a different background and source of knowledge to the group. Misinformation can be transmitted as well, particularly on mysterious or complicated subjects. Many school systems and individual teachers recognize the impact of the peer group on learning in middle childhood and capitalize on children's acceptance of other children as teachers. Peer education

Figure 6-3.

has assisted many children who have otherwise had difficulty in some particular academic matter.

4. *Teaching Rules and Logical Consequences.* Rules are a way of life among school-aged children, and adherence to rules helps them to learn acceptable behavior patterns. Rules that are learned through games and play activities spill over into the ways that social interactions are conducted and controlled within the peer group. The peer group uses an increasingly strict code of acceptable behavior as children grow through the years of middle childhood. Elements of these codes usually accentuate the negative side of behavior, and children develop a set of rules composed of a list of don'ts rather than do's. These may include don'ts such as tattling, crying, cheating, or seeking too much adult attention. When a child accidentally or intentionally violates this code of conduct, he or she experiences the logical consequences of the error by being ostracized by the group. This takes the form of ignoring the offender and punishing his or her actions by refusing his or her participation or interaction with the group. This action by itself serves several purposes: (1) it teaches conformity to group values to all members; (2) it demonstrates the results of inappropriate behavior to all; (3) it encourages cooperation among those who perform the ostracism; and (4) it encourages the development of a strong general code of conduct.

5. *Sex-Role Identification.* Even in these times of increasing sex-role equality, children continue to gravitate into groups that are organized according to biological sex. This has several possible explanations. Adults may continue to expect differences, however slight, in the behavior of boys and girls. The pressure to conform to patterns of behavior considered appropriate by the peer group may also contribute to the segregation of the sexes. Freudian psychology points to this period as the time when a clear, unquestioned identity emerges because of a child's experiences with the peer group. In this

Figure 6-4.

regard, the peer group may serve to reinforce traditional ideas and standards of sex-role behavior. Boys, for example, may value physical activity and aggressive behavior toward each other and support an intolerance for interactions with girls. Whatever the reasons, children organize their groups according to biological sex membership, and the peer group is used to seek a definition of who a child is and how he or she is to behave. This tendency toward sex cleavage in peer groups emerges in the second or third grade and persists through middle childhood until adolescence, when groups become integrated once again (see Figure 6-4).

Refining Skills and Acquiring New Ones

The nature of psychosocial development during middle childhood reflects the strivings of children to master a variety of physical, mental, and social skills. Children become increasingly involved in refining existing skills and in acquiring new ones (see Figure 6-5). Growth rates are slower during middle childhood, and maturation increases in both fine and large muscle skills. The greater strength and endurance of school-aged children allows for more strenuous play activities over a longer period of time. Experiences with the environment coupled with different expectations for development lead to changes in mental skills during this time of life.

Williams and Stith (1974) state that attainment of the skills necessary for playing sports and games is an index of the level of a child's physical development in middle childhood. Our culture emphasizes the development of general or gross motor skills as opposed to acquiring superior fine motor skills. Physical education programs in elementary grades focus on improving the performance of these general motor skills by both boys and girls. Because many peer group activities emphasize such skills, it is important that children have opportunities to develop the abilities involved in these activities. Ac-

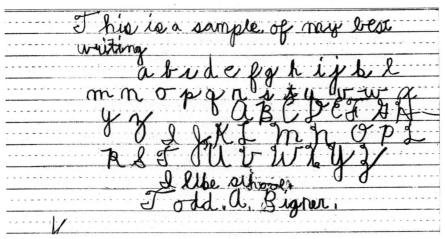

Figure 6-5. Characteristic writing skills demonstrated by a nine-year-old boy in the third grade. These skills are typically acquired by children in American public schools at this time in their education.

tivities involving gross motor skills include hiking, skating, ball games, jumping rope, biking, and so on. Acceptance by peers often is dependent on the ability of a child to perform these gross motor skills adequately. Acceptance by others leads to a sense of well-being and pride as well as independence. Success also encourages a willingness to try new and different skills. Failure or difficulty in acquiring these skills may result in rejection by the peer group, limited involvement with normal peer group activity, and the development of a sense of inferiority.

The nature of development in infancy and the preschool years is characterized by curiosity about the environment, which guides a child's learning. These experiences lay the foundation for the mental development that occurs in the middle years of childhood. The school-aged child approaches the world in a manner that is characteristically different from that of a preschooler. The preschooler is inevitably bound by his or her rigid egocentricity in perceiving, assimilating, and accommodating to information gathering. Egocentricity continues to be present through middle childhood but diminishes in strength as developmental progress is made during these years. In contrast to a preschooler, who would angrily grab a ball from a playmate when she or he feels it is his or her turn to play, the school-aged child realizes that he or she could lose a friend by this action. A solution instead might be attempted through persuasion.

Piaget (1967) refers to cognitive development during middle childhood as the period of *concrete operations*. By the time children reach school age, they can understand and use certain principles or relationships between events and things. In using and comprehending these relationships, children operate with objects, symbols, and concepts. They are now able to internalize. They learn to add and subtract, classify and order, apply rules of logic to reach conclusions, and apply rules to their conduct. They become system-oriented in learning that certain operations result in addition, for example, whereas others result in subtraction. They are now able to use imagery to perform mentally certain actions that were performed physically in the past.

The application of operations is seen first in the child's preoccupations with learning to group and to classify objects and events. The school-aged child develops the ability to think about parts and the whole simultaneously. For example, if a four-year-old is shown a box of wooden beads that contains more brown beads than white beads and is asked, "Are there more brown beads or more wooden beads?" he or she responds that there are more brown beads, being unable at this time to deal simultaneously with two separate concepts, such as color and type of material. The child who is in the concrete operations period is able to comprehend that an object can be classified in two or more ways, and the same question would appear to be senseless.

The preoccupation with classification is evident in the collections that are loved and cherished by children during this time in their lives. The collections that are started by school-aged children are numerous and varied, ranging from the more common stamp, comic, coin, and doll collections to pine cones, bubble gum wrappers, and bottle caps. At first, there is the collection and classification of anything and everything, but as a child grows older and has broader experiences with the environment, the collections become more specialized. Specialization of interest reflects the child's ability to recognize more complex systems of classification.

Two other major cognitive events occur during middle childhood: the attainment of an understanding of *conservation* (of mass, volume, and so on) and an awareness of *reversibility*. *Conservation* means that something retains the same properties even though it can be rearranged differently or reshaped. A classic Piagetian example of the understanding of mass involves the rearrangement of the shape of two clay balls. The child is shown two clay balls of equal size and amount of clay. One clay ball is flattened, and the child is asked to judge which ball now has more clay. The child who has acquired the skills of conservation of mass understands that only the shape of the clay ball has been altered and that each ball has the same amount of clay.

Reversibility means that certain operations can be completed in reverse order and end up the same. Science experiments, which appeal to children of this age, can be used to demonstrate the concept of reversibility. For example, water has properties that allow it to exist in several physical states. The process of freezing water and then allowing it to melt back to its liquid state helps children to acquire the understanding of reversibility. One can also use prisms to teach the concept of reversibility by showing children how sunlight can be divided into its component colors and returned back to white light, a composite of all the spectra.

Like preschoolers, school-aged children suffer from limitations in their cognitive approach to understanding the world. The preschooler is bound by his or her egocentric perceptions and point of view, whereas the school-aged child is confined by his or her own hypotheses and assumptions about the world. After forming such hypotheses and assumptions, school-aged children search for evidence to support their thoughts while disregarding evidence to the contrary. Such an approach results in what Elkind (1970) terms *cognitive conceit*. At some time during middle childhood, children discover that parents are not entirely right all the time. This discovery leads them to the conclusion that the parent is wrong a good deal of the time and his or her credibility is diminished. Likewise, if a child learns that he or she is right on one matter, then it logically follows that he or she is right on all matters.

Appropriate physical, mental, and social skills are acquired unevenly in middle childhood. Equal attention is not given to success in each of these areas. Discontinuity in developmental rates and a wide range of individual differences result in normal or advanced development in one or more of these areas for some children while others lag considerably behind. Children who develop outstanding reading skills, for example, may lag behind other children in their level of general motor skill development, and a child who has advanced motor skills may struggle to keep up with classmates in the development of reading and mathematical skills.

The optimistic nature of the middle childhood years occasionally is dampened by failures or slow progress toward levels of skill performance in things that "everybody knows how to do except me." School-aged children can be their own harshest judges of their successfulness in these areas of development. Unrealistic standards of performance and high expectations of accomplishment work to make many children feel that their skills or "tools" are inferior and unacceptable.

These years of development during middle childhood culminate in much developmental progress. Children, with their limited perspective of their past, underestimate where and how far they have come toward the goal of maturity and mastery of their environment. A "new" child emerges in the process of growing up who is more skilled in social interaction with adults and others of the same age. Children at this age have acquired new skills to help them cope with the environment and the challenges of formal education. They have developed an attitude of "anything worth trying can be performed well." In the end, they are prepared for the next stage of psychosocial development in determining who they are and where they will fit in society during their years of adolescence.

PARENTAL DEVELOPMENT IN THE SCHOOL-AGE YEARS

Parents remain a source of security and stability for the school-aged child during this relatively busy time in life. Children value their parents and other family members, although there is a gradual tendency not to admit this openly during the later years of this period.

School-aged children generally view their parents in an idealistic way. Their dad is seen as the greatest in every matter he undertakes, and their mom is the very best in the whole world! Parents begin to lose their infallible status in their child's eyes during the ninth year. Children react to the realization that parents are capable of making errors and mistakes with feelings of resentment, and their disappointment is shown through hostile, sarcastic remarks. Relations with parents can become strained at the end of the middle childhood period because of the harsh unacceptance of parental imperfections. Despite these negative assessments of parents' abilities and nature, school-aged children express a general satisfaction and approval of their relations with parents. Research also shows that children have attitudes that are generally more favorable or neutral than unfavorable toward mothers and fathers (Harris and Tseng, 1957).

Parents continue their psychosocial development as adults during the school-age period of their first child's life. Because of the interaction processes during these years, the child affects changes in styles of caregiving and interaction with parents. Personal developmental tasks of the adults center on a number of issues that relate to their parenting and family activities as well as individual needs at this time of the family life cycle. These tasks include:

1. Responding to the changing demands of child rearing.
2. Redefining personal identities and goals.

Responding to Children's Developmental Demands

Developmental interaction between parents and a school-aged child affects the manner in which caregiving will change during these years. The developmental tasks and challenges that face the school-aged child differ considerably from those encountered in infancy and early childhood. A child's developmental progress during these years occurs in a manner that is more psychological and social than physical. These physical skills, however, play an important role in the development of children's self-concepts. A child's world during middle childhood is one of confrontation with peers in a competitive social environment. Peers act as a source of a child's measurement of his or her developmental progress, for assessing his or her weaknesses and strengths, and for his or her identification as a person of worth. The changes that are experienced in cognitive skills lead toward greater use of language for communication, information gathering, and problem solving. The use of elementary logic emerges during this period and assists children in reaching conclusions, establishing beliefs and opinions, and defining values despite errors that may occur in the logical process.

Parenting in middle childhood focuses on children's attainment of developmental tasks but becomes increasingly focused on psychological assistance and guidance. The study of Clifford (1959) shows that psychological controls are used more frequently and effectively by mothers of nine-year-olds. These controls include reasoning and taking privileges away as compared with physical controls such as spanking.

Psychological guidance consists primarily of reassuring children, helping them to bounce back from social blunders with friends, and providing positive reinforcement for their efforts in acquiring new skills. The competitive culture of school-aged children and the high degree to which they expect immediate success in any endeavor sets them up for needing secure and stable adults who seem, from the child's perspective, to weather any imaginable difficulty.

Duvall (1977) states that responding to a child's changing developmental demands means learning to let her or him go during the middle childhood years. The increased involvement of children with peers and activities outside of the home and in school means increased periods of absence from the home. Mothers, especially, may find it exhausting to try to keep a stable and predictable schedule of routines in the home. Meeting a hectic schedule of activities such as music and dance lessons, ball games, scout meetings, and other extracurricular activities tempts many adults to obtain a chauffeur's driving license, particularly when there are several school-aged children in the family.

Most parents are genuinely interested in having their child become involved in peer group activities because these associations indicate a new degree of social sophistication, independence, and healthy emotional development. Parents signify their trust and acceptance of the changing status of their child as a maturing person by encouraging her or him to become involved with others. A price may be paid, however, in attempting to help children meet these social needs. Williams (1968), for example, found that full-time mothers of school-aged children have fewer close friends and more restricted outside interests because of commitments to helping their children become involved in peer group activities. Full-time mothers, who continue to hold the major responsibilities of caregiving during this time, are challenged to discover and provide activities that will meet these needs of children.

Letting go of school-aged children also means dealing with their increasing valuing of peers and best friends over family members, according to Duvall (1977). Letting children go involves allowing them to take overnight trips to a friend's home and in later years going on weekend slumber parties and camping trips with Scouts and other groups.

Erikson believes that when children of school age encounter a number of experiences that reinforce doubts about their abilities, a sense of inferiority becomes the predominant attitude rather than a sense of industry. They feel that they are not as good or as capable as their peers, that they cannot succeed at the same tasks and skills, and that no amount of effort or trying will solve their dilemma. Derogatory remarks about self-worth are commonly expressed at this age. Children who consistently demonstrate an attitude of helplessness over a long period of time are essentially children who are discouraged about their abilities and themselves.

Interactions with peers provide children with a source of self-evaluation that is graphically presented and understood. Peer groups have never had the reputation of being especially kind, accepting, or understanding of a child's weaknesses or failures. Every child is at one time or another made to feel inadequate, and feelings are easily hurt by negative interactions and assessments. One child in particular may be chosen to be a scapegoat by the entire peer group and is tormented unmercilessly for behavior patterns, style of speech, or physical appearance. For children who are seen as "different" by the peer group, the school-age period, with its heavy emphasis on interactions with other children, becomes an especially critical challenge. The situation that these children encounter causes them either to learn to defend themselves or to become discouraged by their attempts to gain acceptance.

At this stage of a child's psychosocial development, the caregiver should give close attention to what children can do or accomplish while avoiding excessive attention to their faults, shortcomings, or weaknesses. Encouragement or positive reinforcement of what a child can accomplish or what he or she attempts leads to feelings of self-worth over time. Adults can create situations where children can experience success. The adult can assign simple but positive attention-getting jobs for children that others will notice. Adults can verbalize the positive aspects of a child to others while in the child's presence. This helps the peer group to focus on these characteristics. All children need assistance from adults in learning and developing the social skills of empathy, or understanding the emotions and feelings of others. Although it is unreasonable to expect children of this age to practice the Golden Rule consistently ("Do unto others as you would have others do unto you."), they can learn to develop the maturity and social sophistication involved in empathetic understanding with the guidance provided by adults.

Parents begin to shoulder new concerns for their child's ability to cope, adjust, and succeed in the demands and expectations of society at this time. These expectations center largely on the child's progress in acquiring mental and social skills. Middle-class families are well known for placing achievement pressures on children, and educational achievement is high on the list of priorities (see Figure 6-6). Normal progress in mastering academic skills means expecting children to learn to read at their appropriate grade level or better, to comprehend and calculate mathematical operations, and to develop an interest in and a bank of knowledge about their environment and the world at large.

Much research has been performed on children's educational achievement and the factors that distinguish the attainments of children of the middle and lower classes. Consistent differences in child-rearing patterns and the values that are transmitted by parents to children are the most prominent general

"Poor kid! He has a 'stage mother' and a 'little league father'!"

Figure 6-6.

factors. Chilman's (1966) review of research identifies a number of factors within the family environment that promote or limits the level of children's educational achievement (see Table 6-1).

Redefining Personal Identities and Life Goals

Most individuals are in their late twenties or early thirties when their first child enters school. Children master their own unique set of problems and tasks over a six- to seven-year period. Adults continue to develop and change in achieving a sense of generativity through this period as well.

Gail Sheehy (1976) describes this particular time (between the ages of twenty-eight and thirty-two) as a transition period in adults' lives. The years

Table 6-1. Child-rearing Patterns of Families of Children Who Are Educationally Achieving Compared with Those of Low-Income Families

Conducive	*Low-Income*
1. Infant and child given freedom within consistent limits to explore and experiment.	1. Limited freedom for exploration (partly imposed by crowded and dangerous aspects of environment).
2. Wide range of parent-guided experiences, offering visual, auditory, kinesthetic, and tactile stimulation from early infancy.	2. Constricted lives led by parents: fear and distrust of the unknown.
3. Goal commitment and belief in long-range success potential.	3. Fatalistic, apathetic attitudes.
4. Gradual training for and value placed on independence.	4. Tendency for abrupt transition to independence: parents tend to "lose control" of children at early age.
5. Educational–occupational success of parents; model as continuing "learners" themselves; high achievement needs of parents.	5. Tendency to educational–occupational failure; reliance on personal versus skill attributes of vocational success.
6. Reliance on objective evidence.	6. Magical, rigid thinking.
7. Much verbal communication, with a flexible, conceptual style and emphasis on both speaking and listening.	7. Little verbal communication, especially of an interactive, conceptual, flexible kind.
8. High value placed on academic achievement.	8. Academic achievement not highly valued.
9. Democratic, rather than authoritarian child-rearing attitudes.	9. Authoritarian child-rearing attitudes.
10. Collaborative attitudes toward the school system.	10. Fear and distrust of the school system.
11. Values placed on abstractions.	11. Pragmatic, concrete values.

Source: C. Chilman. *Growing up poor.* Washington, D.C.: Welfare Administration Publication No. 13, 1966.

of the "trying twenties" (when the family was being established) have been devoted to laying the foundations for life's work, establishing goals, and making concrete choices in seeking these goals. During the "Catch 30" transition period, adults confront a crisis in evaluating their progress according to the choices and goals that were established earlier. Both men and women may feel the restrictions of the choices made earlier, yet they should experience a sense of action rather than resignation or complacency in reaching a solution to their dilemma. Dissatisfaction with the way life is proceeding is the general reaction at this time, and depression and inner turmoil are also experienced while adults seek to reach positive, workable solutions to their own unique life situation (see Figure 6-7).

© 1977 by NEA. Inc.

"I think I've finally pinpointed your problem — too much awareness!"

Figure 6-7.

The passage of time, the launching of all the things that should be done, and a preoccupation with these endeavors consume much of adults' energy and attention during their twenties. The thirtieth birthday, however, has become a traumatic event in our culture. From the youthful perspective of those who haven't yet reached this pinnacle in the life span, the event of becoming thirty years old is seen as no longer being "with it." The saying "Never trust anyone over thirty," communicates this underlying message of being out of touch with the mainstream of youthful culture. The thirtieth anniversary of one's birth is but another punctuation mark that divides the transition from one period to another in the life cycle. It marks the fact that one's life is nearing its halfway point, and this realization is cause enough to motivate a reassessment of the direction that life is taking. Perhaps it is not just an accident that the oldest child's entrance into school coincides with the "Catch 30" transition period in many adults' lives. While this child is struggling to master the requirements of development that society calls for at this time in his or her own life, his or her parents are also grappling with mastering the direction that their lives will take in their future. A child who is of school age also acts as concrete evidence of the passage of time. Almost suddenly there is the realization by parents of something like "She can't be ready for school now! It seems like only yesterday that she was just learning to walk." The pressures that are felt by this passing of time may result in feelings that life will pass by if action is not taken to remedy feelings of discomfort or discontent.

The feelings that appear at this time in adults' lives are the result of taking stock of the outcome or progress toward reaching goals that were set earlier in life (see Figure 6-8). According to Sheehy, the middle-class man now feels a drive either to make a deeper commitment to his occupational goals or to make a clean break into a new vocational world to do what he's "always wanted to do with his life." Middle-class women, who may have chosen from one of the three interrelated choices available to them during their twenties (marriage, career, or parenthood), begin to experience the inner rumblings of discontent with the choice or choices made earlier. This dissatisfaction with the direction they have chosen for their lives stems partially from a desire to break loose and explore new personal horizons. Their husbands, who are also experiencing a reassessment of their own situation in life, may apply pressure to them to take advantage of the opportunity to develop new interests or acquire new skills that are marketable for employment. Most women, however, are threatened enough by the psychological events that characterize the "Catch 30" transition period to interpret this well-intentioned pressure from their husbands as an indication of rejection or dissatisfaction with them as wife or mother.

Something obviously has to happen to resolve this crisis for both adults in the family. One possible solution is for the marriage to dissolve through di-

"Huh, that's funny. I've been looking at myself in the
mirror for years and I still don't recognize myself."
Figure 6-8.

vorce. The studies by Rollins and Feldman (1970) and Rollins and Cannon (1976) show that the degree of satisfaction with the marriage relationship is at its lowest during the school-aged-child stage of the family life cycle because of the role strain experienced by both adults (see Chapters 4 and 5). Statistical evidence gained from analysis of the frequency of national divorce rates supports this possible outcome as a very real solution to the "Catch 30" problems of many couples. Glick and Norton (1973) report that for the past fifty years, the median length of marriages before divorce has been 7.2 years. This makes the years of the school-aged-child stage of the family life cycle the divorce-prone years for couples. (The ramifications of divorce on parenting are discussed in Chapter 8.) In other instances, however, divorce may serve to complicate the confusion and disruption of this time of life for adults.

Sheehy (1976) believes that another possible solution to the dissatisfaction with one's progress at this time is entrenchment or deeper involvement in reaching goals. Adults experience a "rooting and extending" adjustment period that follows some type of decision to get a firmer grip on life's goals. With the assessment of progress up to this point, positive and vital efforts may be made to ensure that goals are reached. Men, for example, may determine new approaches and begin to become deeply involved in efforts to establish a new business, develop a solid and respected reputation in the academic or professional world, or make their first million dollars by age forty. Deadlines and timetables are set to guide them in the attainment of their goals. Women, according to Sheehy, also determine the future direction of their lives by taking strong and definite actions to establish their individual independence. A woman's course of action is seen by Sheehy as a strong indication to the husband of the reality of her individuality. Any number of alternatives can be available, such as completing a college degree, establishing a business of her own, entering into postgraduate or professional training, or returning to a career or occupation interrupted by marriage and child rearing.

According to Sheehy, the mandate is for change of some type for both adults at this time. Regardless of the nature of this change in personal direction or status in life, decisions must be reached that lead to deeper commitment to goals that have been reassessed and rearranged in priority. Strains are experienced in the personal development of adults at this time. Challenges are presented by a school-aged child who is trying to cope with encounters with age-mates and acquiring skills that prepare him or her for adulthood. The school-aged-child stage of the family life cycle is perhaps the most hazardous to the integrity of the family.

SUPPORTS FOR CAREGIVING IN MIDDLE CHILDHOOD

Community supports for families of school-aged children vary in the type and nature of caregiving assistance. Children of this age respond to more structured group activities. Communities respond to this need of school-aged children by providing programs that are peer group oriented.

Larger communities and cities usually have extensive recreational programs for school-aged children. Arts and crafts programs are especially popular with children of this age as well as organized sports and game activities. Enrollment is usually limited to a small group of children to facilitate supervision and interaction. The costs of participation in these activities are usually minimal. These programs are often held during after-school hours or on weekends.

School-aged children have a particularly strong desire to belong to groups. As they progress through the years of middle childhood, children become eligible for membership in more formal groups that promote social development, moral responsibility, vocational interests, and recreation (Williams and Stith, 1974). Membership in these groups is sometimes segregated by sex, but this aspect of group composition is disappearing in light of recent federal government policies. Examples of these more formalized groups are the Cub Scouts, Brownies, Camp Fire Girls, 4-H, and so on. Most of these groups serve as a cooperative socialization agent with the family in promoting children's sense of industry and their involvement with age-mates. Many of the activities provided by these groups, such as camping trips and project development, serve to enhance school-aged children's self-confidence and social skills with others both their own age and older.

These organizations are more commonly composed of children of middle-class families. These families promote children's participation in a number of extrafamilial socialization activities as a reflection of their status in the community. Because many of these groups also promote values such as achievement, honesty, and neatness, they provide a continued socialization process into a middle-class life-style for children. Children from the lower social classes may or may not participate in these groups. Families that are attempting to rise in social status probably use these organizations and activities to gain acceptance by other families. Some philanthropic organizations recognize the particular needs of school-aged children in inner-city environments from poverty-level families and provide opportunities for group activities. Such organizations as Boys' and Girls' Clubs hope to promote "juvenile decency" rather than juvenile delinquency by providing facilities where children can experience a wholesome, accepting atmosphere through group activities.

A continual concern for working parents of school-aged children is adequate care during after-school hours for children. Most child-care centers are neither equipped nor willing to accept these children. A number of communities are recognizing this problem of inadequate after-school care. An increasing number of programs are offered by recreation departments or school systems to provide supervised activities at elementary schools for these children.

School-aged children are involved in a wide range of lessons, if parents can afford such instruction, in such areas as speech, music, dance, gymnastics, and swimming. Such lessons may be exploratory at first to determine if children have abilities that can be developed over time. These experiences can lead to self-confidence in developing children's concepts of their ability to achieve in these endeavors and skills.

Day camps during summer months are used by some parents to extend socialization experiences for school-aged children. These camps are more concentrated group experiences that are based on the organized group activities during the school year. When children are older, parents sometimes place children in camps for varied periods of time away from home. Although this is an exciting experience for many children, others have difficulty in adjusting and become homesick. If these summer camp experiences are positive, children grow in their self-confidence to function in a new environment away from the security provided by family members.

POINTS TO CONSIDER

- Development in middle childhood focuses on a child's attempts to master a number of developmental tasks that lead to the achievement of a sense of industry.
- The peer group becomes a significant influence during this period of a child's life and has several socialization functions.
- Success in mastering a wide number of physical and social skills in middle childhood prepares a child for the next stage in psychosocial development.
- Caregiving by adults increasingly shifts to psychological assistance and guidance when children are of school age.
- Developmental interaction between parents and children results in parents' learning to begin "letting go" of children so that they can increase peer involvement and activities outside the home.
- Parents experience a transition period in their personal development during the school-aged–child stage of the family life cycle.
- Evaluations that parents make of their personal progress toward choices and goals made in their twenties may result in some type of change in direction or status in life.
- Alternative supports for caregiving in middle childhood are based on the peer group orientation of children.

REFERENCES

CHILMAN, C. *Growing up poor*. Washington, D.C.: Welfare Administration, 1966.

CLIFFORD, E. Discipline within the home: A controlled observational study of parental practices. *Journal of Genetic Psychology*, 1959, *95*, 45–82.

DUVALL, E. *Marriage and family development* (5th ed.). Philadelphia: J. B. Lippincott, 1977.

ELKIND, D. *Children and adolescents: Interpretative essays on Jean Piaget*. New York: Oxford University Press, 1970.

ELKIND, D. *A sympathetic understanding of the child: Birth to sixteen*. Boston: Allyn & Bacon, 1974.

GLICK, P., and NORTON, A. Perspectives on the recent upturn in divorce and remarriage. *Demography*, 1973, *10*, 301–314.

HARRIS, D., and TSENG, S. Children's attitudes toward peers and parents as revealed by sentence completions. *Child Development*, 1957, *28*, 401–411.

PIAGET, J. *Six psychological studies*. New York: Random House, 1967.

ROLLINS, B., and CANNON, K. Marital satisfaction over the family life cycle: A reevaluation. *Journal of Marriage and the Family*, 1976, *36*, 271–282.

ROLLINS, B., and FELDMAN, H. Marital satisfaction over the family life cycle: A reevaluation. *Journal of Marriage and the Family*, 1970, *32*, 20–28.

SHEEHY, G. *Passages: Predictable crises of adult life.* New York: Dutton, 1976.

WILLIAMS, J. Close friendship relations of housewives residing in an urban community. *Social Forces*, 1968, *36*, 358–362.

WILLIAMS, J., and STITH, M. *Middle childhood: Behavior and development.* New York: Macmillan, 1974.

7

Developmental Interaction During Adolescence and Early Adulthood

THE INDIVIDUAL IN ADOLESCENCE

The *families-with-teenagers* stage of the family life cycle begins with the oldest child's thirteenth birthday and extends to the time when she or he leaves the home to begin life as an adult (Duvall, 1977). The adolescent stage of development is technically divided into two periods: early and late adolescence (Hurlock, 1975). Early adolescence is recognized by the initiation and completion of puberty and ends with the child's entrance into the senior year of high school at about seventeen years of age. Late adolescence begins at this point and extends through this year to the eighteenth birthday, the age of legal maturity. Parents typically are in their mid-thirties or early forties when their first child grows through the adolescent years. Other children in the family are usually of school age at this time in the family life cycle.

This six- to seven-year period of the family life cycle is characterized by the oldest child's involvement in establishing a *sense of identity* versus *role confusion*. Parents of teenagers draw nearer to the completion of the sense of generativity stage in their personal psychosocial development. The mesh or correspondence between the psychosocial stages of parents and child results in changes in the style of interaction. The child's attempts to fit together the puzzle of his or her own personal ego integrity coincides with the parents' realization that they, too, must begin to recognize the fulfillment of their identities as caregivers and mature individuals. The challenges that confront both parents and child may result in conflicts of varying intensities as each individual experiences his or her own inner conflicts.

The completion of this stage of the family life cycle should culminate in a resolution of basic personal identities and crises for both parents and child.

THE EMANCIPATED CHILD

The concept of adolescence as a stage in the life span is unique to Western culture in its definition and length. The idea that the years between puberty and legal maturity involve special developmental tasks and challenges is a relatively recent concept. G. Stanley Hall and Sigmund Freud are credited with publicizing this period as a time of "storm and stress" in an individual's life. These theoretical explanations about adolescence appeared in the late nineteenth century. Previously there had been no transition period between childhood and adulthood. As soon as children became physically capable of performing as workers, they entered into adulthood, gaining many of the privileges and responsibilities associated with this status. Western cultures have rarely recognized the physical and psychological event of puberty with the rituals and rites that exist in more primitive cultures. These rites often serve as an indicator of a child's transition to adulthood.

Hurlock (1975) states that the adolescent stage of development has the following characteristics.

1. *It is a transition period.* Industrialization and increased technology have changed the cultural definitions of when childhood ends and adulthood begins. Adolescence has evolved into a transition period between those two broad stages in human development. Our highly industrialized society demands a lengthy period of training for vocations that have become increasingly specialized each year. Such specialized occupations call for advanced training and education for adult jobs and can extend far beyond the years after legal maturity has been reached. The nature of adolescence as a transition period from dependence to independence is emphasized by Erikson's belief that a sense of identity is established at this time (see Chapter 3). The establishment of this attitude prepares the teenager to assume the major roles of adulthood.

2. *It is a period of change.* Adolescence is a period of metamorphosis in an individual's life (see Figure 7-1). Dramatic changes in body proportions coincide with changes in attitudes and behavior, including a heightened emotionality, feelings of inadequacy, heightened egocentricity, and shifts in values.

3. *It is a dreaded age.* A teenager's caregivers perceive this stage as troublesome and full of potential conflicts, and the teenager may come to view adults as potential adversaries or as the "enemy." The clash that often results between these individuals makes the adolescent period one that is dreaded for its consequences in the interpersonal relations between parents and teenagers.

4. *It is a time of unrealism.* Adolescents are characterized by unrealistic expectations and aspirations. These attitudes are expressed in relations with both peers and family members. The high hopes for their participation in the future lead teenagers to create dreams and idealistic notions about their own abilities and skills to cope with the world. This tendency can create, in turn, disappointment and disillusionment with themselves. This stage of discon-

Berry's World

© 1977 by NEA, Inc.

"When did the Disneyland poster get replaced
by the Farrah Fawcett-Majors one?"

Figure 7-1.

tentment may be remedied through increased social experiences that lead to more rational ways of viewing society and relations with others.

Developmental tasks that individuals encounter during adolescence center on developing more advanced skills, abilities, and attitudes that lead to preparation for adulthood. These tasks include:

1. Establishing a sense of identity versus role confusion.
2. Adjusting to physical changes in body proportions and body image.
3. Establishing independence as a mature person.
4. Adopting new codes of conduct and clarifying values.
5. Exploring vocational objectives and adult roles.

Establishing a Sense of Identity

Erikson (1950, 1964) speaks of identity formation as being the primary psychosocial crisis of adolescence. Identity formation in adolescence is the understanding that many different roles are assumed in life and that numerous alternatives are available for the direction that life can take in the future. Teenagers attain an awareness that they have many different but related selves. They come to recognize that they have a true identity that is integrated from these various selves into a wholeness of individuality. A variety of selves are fused into a composite picture of who the teenager is. These selves that make a wholeness come from the teenager's recognition that she or he is a student, a worker, a lover, a family member, and so on.

The identity crisis of adolescence is a crossroads in the teenager's psychosocial development. Erikson describes this crisis in identity formation as a time when teenagers need to experience continuity between what they have learned about themselves from their experiences in childhood and what their development holds for their future. The adolescent's attempts to develop a wholeness of self is the product of his or her past experiences in growing up. This process of determining who one is, what values are important, what attitudes should be held, and what direction should be taken in life began long ago in the development of the previous psychosocial senses. Society helps to focus the sum of these experiences on a clearer idea of personal identity during the years of adolescence. Children are given some indication by society that they will eventually need to establish some idea of who they are and where they will go in life when they are asked, "What do you want to be when you grow up?" During adolescence, this question is rephrased by the teenager into "Who am I and what can I be?" Hopefully his or her experiences at this time in life will result in the answer, "I am all of these selves and I can do many things."

Teenagers are assisted in their identity formation by their peer group and by adults whom they respect and idealize. Adolescence is a tribal experience with others of a similar age. The interactional experiences shared with the peer group at adolescence are similar in purpose to those that occurred in the school-age years, but the peer group takes on additional functions in adolescence. Teenagers, like school-aged children, use the peer group as a device for making self-evaluations. The peer group in adolescence, however, becomes a new source of redefinition of the teenager's identity. The school-aged child began to admire the glamorous or popular individuals in sports, the professions, and other fields. In adolescence, the nature of this admiration is magnified into the tribal gatherings seen at rock concerts and is reflected in the enormous popularity of a host of rock musical groups and other folk heroes of adolescence.

Both of these "significant others" (the peer group and the idealized figures) are found outside the family group and assist the teenager in his or her development. Experiences with these individuals lead to another developmental task that is related to identity formation: the establishment of independence from the controls of the family. Independence leads to identity formation in helping the adolescent to develop feelings that she or he has some control over destiny. By establishing their own pursuits and interests away from the family, cultivating their own group of friends, taking a job, and so on, teenagers communicate an increasing desire to break loose from the identity they have gained from the family and into the discovery of their own personal identity.

Role confusion is the alternative to a sense of identity. When the efforts of the teenager to establish self-identity become too difficult to allow the creation of a clear picture of his or her composite self, Erikson believes that a central idea of identity fails to develop. A disjointed, fragmented concept of self is the result of lack of integration of the various selves and roles that have been encountered. There is a tendency to focus on the totality of the self rather than on the wholeness of the self. *Totality* refers to the inability to see beyond the various roles we play and what we are to what we can be. There is only partial identification in role confusion, and the boundaries that separate the various roles and selves are distinctly recognized. True and whole identification, according to Erikson, is the result of connecting links between the selves we discover we have. Role confusion is the result of inabilities to establish these links, and the self is seen as compartmentalized.

The sense of identity that is forged in adolescence is not an achievement of a final destiny or a static goal in the search for who we are and where we can go with our lives. This sense is a foundation of personal identity that retains certain constants throughout the rest of life about who we basically believe ourselves to be. Other roles and selves are acquired, developed, and recognized and become integrated into the basic sense of identity.

Adjusting to Physical Changes

The initiation of puberty around age eleven among girls and age twelve among boys signals the beginning of numerous physical and psychological changes. Puberty is the developmental event by which a child becomes a sexually mature individual. The changes that are stimulated during puberty occur rapidly and affect increases in body size and proportions as well as maturation of the sexual organs. Increases in height and weight are associated with what is called the *adolescent growth spurt*. These rapid increases occur over a period of about three years. Approximately 13 centimeters (about 5 inches) in additional height gains are experienced by girls and about 18 centimeters (approximately 7 inches) by boys by age fourteen. Weight gains average almost 13 kilograms (30 pounds) for girls and about 20 kilograms (45 pounds) for boys over this same period of time (Krogman, 1970). Although these dramatic gains in height and weight occur over a three-year period, the most rapid increments occur in the early part of the period for both boys and girls. Growth rates in both height and weight decelerate slowly after the fifteenth birthday for boys and after the fourteenth birthday for girls (see Figure 7-2).

Changes that occur in the proportions of body parts follow a dramatic course similar to the increases that occur in body size (Tanner, 1970). The

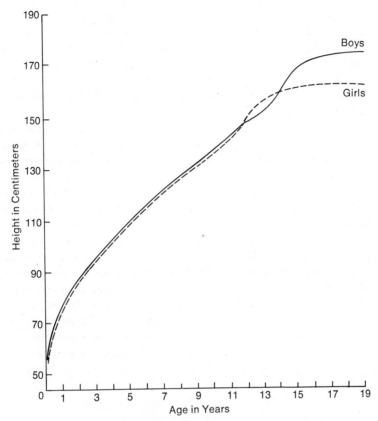

Figure 7-2. Height curves for boys and girls. (Source: Tanner, J., Whitehouse, R., & Takaishi, M. Standards from birth to maturity for height, weight, height velocity, and weight velocity: British children 1965. *Archives of Disease in Childhood*, 1966, *41*, 454–471; 613–635.)

extremities of the body grow earlier and more rapidly than other areas of the body at the beginning of puberty. These increases in proportion give the preadolescent or young adolescent the appearance of being "all hands and feet." Those who begin the growth spurt early have body proportions that differ at maturity from others who begin the process at a later age. Early-maturing boys, for example, have broader hips and shoulders, more stocky legs, and shorter arms and legs than later maturers. The legs and arms of most teenagers are disproportionate to their trunk. The synchronization of the growth of all body parts occurs over the period of early adolescence, when the body eventually comes to take on more adultlike proportions.

Just as the body proportions and size generally show a rapid increase in growth, the event of puberty produces rapid changes in the growth of the reproductive organs. Growth of the testicles in boys precedes that of increases in length and circumference of the penis, beginning at about age twelve. Growth of the pubic hair commences at about the same age. Growth of hair on the face, chest, and armpits appears after the pubic hair has almost completed its growth. The change to a deeper voice begins shortly after the appearance of pubic hair, with breaks in tone and pitch occurring when the larynx is growing rapidly (see Figure 7-3).

Growth of the reproductive organs in girls is not as noticeable as in boys, but the initial functioning of these organs is marked by the *menarche* or first menstrual period at about age thirteen. The occurrence of menstruation is variable in intervals and duration for approximately the first year, which is known as the period of adolescent sterility. Although a girl may be menstruating, irregularly, during this time, ovulation or the production of mature eggs from the ovaries usually does not occur.

With the appearance and regulation of the menstrual cycle, other sexual developments occur in girls. The hips become enlarged and widened as a result of the growth of the pelvis. The breasts begin to develop shortly after the widening of the hips, with the nipples showing increases in size before the mammary tissue enlarges. Pubic hair appears next after the enlargement of the hips and breast commences. Growth of hair at other locations on the body is associated with the menarche but is light in pigmentation and soft in texture except at the armpits and on the legs (because of the practice of shaving these areas). Voice changes are noticeable in girls at this time, but breaks in tone

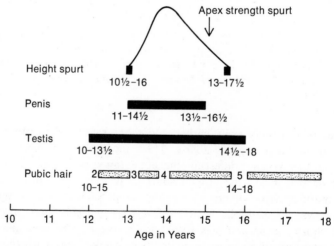

Figure 7-3. The sequence of events in physical maturation in adolescence among boys. Figures below the events shown represent the range in time of occurrence. (Source: Tanner, J. *Growth at adolescence* (2nd ed.). Oxford: Blackwell Scientific Publishers, 1962.)

and pitch are uncommon (see Figure 7-4). In both boys and girls, the glands that are located in the armpits also become active during this time, resulting in the production of perspiration and changes in body odor. Similar glands located on the face also begin to function at this time, and infection or lack of proper hygiene can result in acne.

Hurlock (1975) lists several psychological changes in early adolescence that are associated with or are a result of the physical changes produced by puberty: (1) *a desire for isolation,* which teenagers demonstrate at times by withdrawing from interaction with peers and family and devoting much time to daydreaming, being alone, and craving privacy; (2) *heightened emotionality,* which is demonstrated by emotional outbursts of anger, pouty behavior, and crying easily; (3) *excessive modesty,* which is shown through a heightened sensitivity and embarrassment about changes that are occurring in the body; (4) *lack of coordination* due to an inability to adjust quickly to rapidly changing body size and proportions; and (5) *heightened insecurity,* which appears in the form of decreased self-confidence. This may also be due to changes in the behavioral standards set up by parents as well as a decreased level of strength and energy.

These psychological changes associated with puberty and early adolescence may be due to an interaction between rapid physical changes and heightened social pressures from peers, parents, and other adults. This time in an individual's life has been characteristically labeled as a "storm and stress" period.

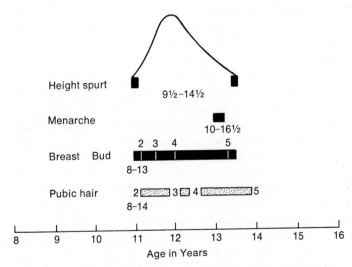

Figure 7-4. The sequence of events in physical maturation in adolescence among girls. Figures below the events shown represent the range in time of occurrence. (Source: Tanner, J. *Growth at adolescence* (2nd ed.). Oxford: Blackwell Scientific Publishers, 1962.)

Girls may react more strongly to the rapid body changes than boys because they experience the changes of puberty earlier than boys but recover quicker and establish a stable pattern of behavior sooner.

By experiencing rapid growth and development over a relatively short period of time, adolescents are forced to seek a redefinition of their body image. Body image is the perception of our physical attributes and our assessment of satisfaction with how we are endowed physically. The image we have of our bodies comes from a variety of sources based on social interactions with others. Mass media advertisment, for example, heavily emphasizes stereotypical body images of beauty, grace, and good proportions and features. Shoenfeld (1963) believes that the body image of adolescents is derived from both real and fantasized social experiences that come from peers' emphasis on good physiques, the individual's own attributes and development, and cultural stereotypes of the "body beautiful." Much research shows that the type of body image held by adolescents influences their self-concept. For example, Gunderson (1965) reports that males of late adolescent age expressed a desire to be six feet tall and weigh between 170 and 180 pounds. As their own weight and height deviated either below or above these ideal figures, there was an accompanying decrease in the degree of their satisfaction with their bodies.

The individual difference in the time of puberty influences the psychological reaction of the teenager. Researchers have known for some time that children who mature earlier than their peers encounter a different set of social circumstances and expectations than children who mature later than the majority of their peers. For example, the boy who is an early maturer may be more admired by peers and assume leadership roles in sports and social activities (Jones and Mussen, 1958; Tanner, 1963). Boys who are late maturers may suffer socially from their individual difference in that they cannot or are not allowed to participate in athletic activities. Their appearance and behavior may bring rejection or isolation from the peer group, who consider these children to be immature. Reaction to this assessment of the late maturer is often one of heightened sensitivity and anxiety or a variety of negative attention-getting behaviors (Eichorn, 1963; Jones and Bayley, 1958).

The timing of puberty has a different effect on girls. Early maturation for girls creates social problems, especially in their relations with boys of the same age. These girls orient more toward older boys, which very likely creates friction and heightened animosity between themselves and boys of their own age (Jones and Mussen, 1958). Parents and teachers may show disapproval of the behavior of girls who show an early interest in boys. These girls' preoccupation with appearance is also a concern of adults. Early-maturing girls also may develop a strong sensitivity toward their bodies and an exaggerated image of their appearance because of these reactions from others. The late-maturing girl may experience a negative body image and self-image in early adolescence. The differences between early- and late-maturing girls, however, have less of an effect on personality development than what occurs for boys (Weatherly, 1964). Late-maturing girls may have a more negative body image in early adolescence when compared with early-maturing girls (Mussen and Jones, 1958).

Early physical maturation of both boys and girls may affect their relations with adults. The larger size and more mature appearance of these teenagers may cause adults to expect higher standards of behavior, which are more appropriate for older adolescents. There is a tendency to react to the visible physical attributes of these teenagers in assuming that increased height and weight and more advanced development are accompanied by similar increments in social and emotional development. Unrealistic expectations of the early maturer may cause behavior problems to increase above those that may normally be expected at this time in an early-maturing adolescent's life.

The degree of adjustment to physical changes in adolescence increases with age during this period. As teenagers experience a decline in the rate of their physical changes, there is an increase in the degree of control over body parts and their use that gives rise to better coordination and less awkward activity. As adolescents gain confidence in their body coordination and physical appearance, they become more accepting of their body image and psychologically adjusted to the limits and strengths of their physical attributes.

Establishing Independence

The experiences of adolescence are a struggle toward an emancipation of the individual from the behavior patterns and restraints that characterized his or her development as a child. An adolescent is an emancipating child who seeks a new definition of self through interactions with others. The self that is constructed during adolescence is dependent on the ability of the individual to explore a variety of personal dimensions. What emerges from the process is a reintegration of the central tasks of infancy (trust) and childhood (autonomy, initiative, industry) at a more advanced level. This is the recognition that identity is formed through independence of choice and that one can act on the environment and react to it in turn.

Throughout the adolescent period there is an increasing tendency to drift further away from the dependencies of childhood. The push away from the family and more toward the peer group is especially characteristic of social and personality development in adolescence. The family has acted to protect and nurture a growing child during the previous years of development, exerting controls and providing encouragement when needed to help her or him cope with and achieve the developmental tasks. During adolescence, this dependency is no longer as appropriate as in childhood. Dependency and controls come to be resented, and a teenager increasingly resists being unjustly treated as a child.

Adolescents demonstrate their independence in a number of ways. Their increasing involvement with peer group activities away from the home provides prominent avenues for escape from adult supervision. Overnight and weekend trips with friends, getting a driver's license, taking a part-time job, after-school activities, and involvement in sports all lead to the teenager's taking increased responsibility for his or her own behavior.

Independence is shown as well in the teenager's choice of friends. Approval of friends was sought from parents in childhood. One of the most likely ways for parents to invite conflict between themselves and teenagers is to be critical and unapproving of their choice in friends. Teenagers may show a seeming lack of discrimination in their choice of friends in early adolescence. This situation often changes as the teenager clearly delineates what is desired in friendships with others.

At times, the desire for independence is so strong that irrational and radical attempts are made by adolescents to prove to the world at large, but especially to parents, that they are autonomous individuals. Such behavior often results when parents attempt to exert control over the teenager's behavior too severely. These less positive independence-achieving types of behavior are expressed in a variety of ways, such as driving recklessly, using theatrical-like makeup, dressing in a sloppy or revealing manner, or having unusual eating habits and tastes. Many of these behaviors give rise to the negative image that many adults have of adolescents in general and also of the individual teenager.

The following are five prominent categories of behavior that characterize what is termed *acting-out* behavior among adolescents.

1. *Use of drugs* includes alcohol, cigarettes, marijuana, hallucinogens, barbiturates, amphetamines, and other related substances. The strict laws that govern the availability and use of many of these drugs demonstrate the "forbidden fruit" attitude that is connected with these substances. This in itself may make using drugs an appealing experience for teenagers as a demonstration of their independence from adult controls. Drugs may be used by adolescents for other reasons as well. Most of these substances produce euphoric effects. A sense of well-being is experienced, tensions and anxieties are relaxed, and inhibitions are freed. The attention-getting effects of drug use on peers cannot be minimized. Most drugs, and alcohol in particular, may be seen as devices that do things *for* adolescents rather than as substances that do things *to* them (Maddox, 1964). Alcohol and tobacco are the drugs that are more widely used by adolescents than other substances (see Figure 7-5).

Adolescents who use drugs on a regular basis often begin at an early age, and their use of drugs follows a pattern of development through this age period. The findings of a survey of adolescent drug use (Smart, 1970) show that the peak use of drugs is between the ninth and eleventh grades. The economics of drug use may account for the wider use of alcohol and tobacco. Most illicit drugs, such as marijuana and stimulants, are relatively expensive and somewhat more difficult to obtain than alcohol and tobacco products.

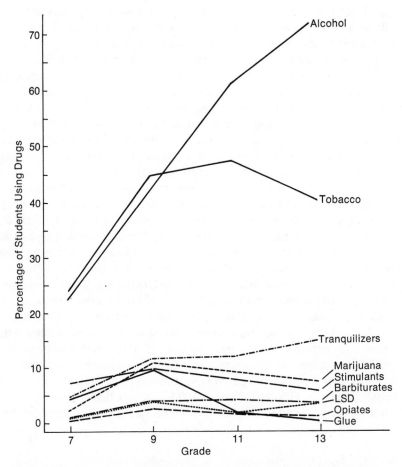

Figure 7-5. Drug use among teenage students (expressed in percentages). (Source: Smart, R. Some current studies of psychoactive and hallucinogenic drug use. *Canadian Journal of Behavioural Science,* 1970, *2,* 232–245. Copyright 1970, Canadian Psychological Association. Reprinted by permission.)

The use of drugs by adolescents is commonly assumed to be more widespread in the lower socioeconomic groups (Hager, Vener, and Stewart, 1971). A survey conducted by Guinn and Hurley (1976) compared drug use among high school students who attended an urban heterogeneous grouping school and those who attended a school largely composed of Mexican-American students. The results show that self-reported drug use was higher among the students who attended the urban school. The results of this study also support the finding that more alcohol and tobacco are used than other drugs.

2. *Premarital sexual behavior* may represent another outlet for expressing

independence from adult standards. Both males and females may use sexual activity as a device to gain popularity and status with peers or as a means to express hostility and revenge toward parents. Contrary to what the popular press may imply, premarital intercourse is not a normative behavior of adolescence. Accurate information on the incidence of sexual intercourse is difficult to obtain, but several investigations show that more adolescent females become active sexually at younger ages than in the past (Bell and Chaskes, 1970; Sorensen, 1973; Vener, Stewart, and Hager, 1974). Sorensen, for example, found that 13 per cent of the sexually experienced adolescents he studied had their first encounter at age twelve or younger and that forty-seven per cent had experienced intercourse for the first time by age fifteen (see Table 7-1). Other studies show different results in age at first intercourse, however (Bauman and Wilson, 1974; Zelnick and Kantner, 1974).

3. *Running away* from home has been considered a form of juvenile delinquency that occurs more frequently among lower socioeconomic groups. Shellow and his associates (1967), however, report that runaway youths represent all socioeconomic levels and that repeated runaways often come from families with incomes that exceed $12,000 annually. These investigators found that serious conflicts with parents represented the most common reason for teenagers' running away. The conflicts that culminated in the teenagers' leaving home were over personal issues relating to style of dress, hair length, and choice of friends (Justice and Duncan, 1976). There has been an increase in the number of teenagers who attempt to communicate their frustration and independence to parents by running away (Bayh, 1973). The National Center for Health Statistics (1975) reports that approximately one of ten adolescents between the ages of twelve and seventeen have left home

Table 7-1.   Age of First Intercourse of Nonvirgin Adolescents

	All Nonvirgins	Nonvirgin Boys	Nonvirgin Girls
12 or under	13%	17%	7%
13	15	18	12
14	15	18	11
15	22	18	26
16	15	12	21
17	9	12	6
18 or 19	11	5	17
Total	100%	100%	100%

Source: R. Sorensen. *Adolescent sexuality in contemporary America.* New York: World Publishing Co., 1973. By permission of Harry N. Abrams, Inc.

at least once. Girls run away from home almost as frequently as boys (8.7 per cent as compared to 10.1 per cent of the total teenage population).

It is easier for today's teenagers to divorce themselves from an intolerable home or school environment by leaving with the intention of never returning. Most runaways gravitate to large urban settings, where their anonymity can be fairly assured. Runaways chance the risk of being questioned and detained by police and have a greater probability of becoming involved in criminal activities to support themselves (Ambrosino, 1971). Howell, Emmons, and Frank (1973) state that almost two thirds of the runaways in their study said that running away from home had been a positive experience; 74 per cent of the boys and 86 per cent of the girls felt that their return to the home made their lives much better, however.

A federal law (The Runaway Youth Act) was passed by Congress in 1974. It recognizes the high nationwide incidence of running away from home during adolescence. This act provides funds for shelters and for counseling runaway teenagers in addition to providing a toll-free telephone number that offers help to teenagers who have or are contemplating running away from home.

4. *Early marriage* may represent another means of demonstrating independence or may serve as an escape from an intolerable home or school environment. Although the percentage of teenagers who become married has declined from the 1950s (see Figure 7-6), this option remains a definite possibility for many teenagers today.

Teenage marriages do not fare well in terms of long-range stability. An analysis of divorce rates for 1969, for example, shows that approximately half of the women granted divorces through that year had married before age twenty (Plateris, 1973). Glick (1975) reports that women whose first marriage ended in divorce were married at an age that was almost two years younger than women whose marriages had not ended in divorce.

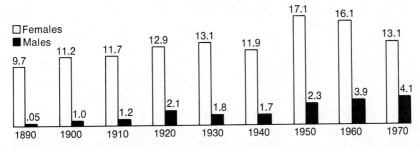

Figure 7-6. Per cent of teenagers married by age and sex in the United States between 1890 and 1970. [Source: Hetzel, A., & Capetta, M. Teenagers: Marriages, divorces, parenthood, and mortality. *Vital and Health Statistics*, 1973, *21*(23). DHEW Publication No. (HRA) 74-1901.]

Teenagers who marry to escape or to prove independence encounter many difficulties that reflect on their failure to complete the developmental tasks of adolescence before undertaking those of young adulthood. Marriage may be entered by teenagers with many assumptions that focus on the romantic aspects of this intimate relationship. The possibility of an extended relationship may elude teenagers because their struggles to establish a sense of identity and their strong drive for independence interfere with the give-and-take nature of a marriage between mature individuals.

5. *Suicide* attempts are the most drastic actions that can be taken by adolescents to prove a point to the world. Miller (1975), in reviewing studies of adolescent suicide, identifies the individual and environmental factors that relate to suicide attempts and the actual act as (a) feelings of social isolation due to loss of a love object; (b) stress due to strained relations with parents or in reaction to parental abuse; (c) depression; (d) high suggestibility to suicidal ideas; (e) internalized aggression, that is, anger that is directed by the individual toward himself or herself; and (f) a need to communicate a cry for help. Miller estimates that suicide may be the third leading cause of death among fifteen to nineteen-year-olds. Although suicide may not represent an act of independence in every case, its occurrence is perhaps the ultimate answer to the question of whether life is worth living for those adolescents who attempt the act.

Adolescence is an emancipation process in many areas of development. Changes in mental, social, emotional, and physical development lead to horizons that were less clear in childhood as the teenager approaches adulthood. One of the most dramatic demonstrations of this emancipation is the shift from needing the external controls provided through family members to the adolescent's acquiring fully functioning inner controls. This internalization helps to guide the adolescent in making the numerous choices that face her or him as a young adult.

Adopting New Conduct and Values

An adolescent's first steps toward independence are explored through the peer group. This group comes to have greater influence on his or her behavior, values, and attitudes than does his or her family at this time in life. The influence of the peer group shows in styles of dress, musical tastes, the reliance on slang vocabulary for communication, and acceptable behavior patterns. The peer group in adolescence also serves as a laboratory for developing a variety of skills and social roles. As groups shift and change in composition, adolescents explore their abilities to assume the roles of leader, follower, activist, or rebel. The fear that underlies much of the teenager's concern about acceptance by peers is that of being a nonconformist or being different from others in some way. Identification comes through the group in early adolescence and later is derived from inner resources as a result of these activities with peers.

A more definite pattern in the development of peer groups occurs in adolescence than during middle childhood. Dunphy (1963) describes this development in five stages from early through late adolescence. The first is the *precrowd* stage. This stage is characterized by small cliques that are usually composed of less than nine boys or girls. The clique acts as a conduit for membership in a crowd. Acceptance into a clique is based on achievement, recognition, and demonstration of conformity to rules of conduct. The second is the *beginning crowd* stage, when initial, timid attempts are made at heterosexual contacts between members of same-sex cliques. These contacts take place as a group activity instead of on an individual basis. The third stage is a *transition period* to the heterosexual activities of the crowd. Members of both same-sex cliques who have high status in their groups initiate dating activities on a one-to-one basis. Individuals who hold acceptance in one or more cliques act to assist the formation of the isolated cliques into the crowd through these heterosexual contacts. Stage four is the *crowd* stage, when heterosexual cliques are formed to constitute the crowd. The last stage occurs in late adolescence and is labeled the *disintegration* period, when the organization of the crowd is replaced by an informal grouping of couples who go steady or are engaged. The purpose of these developments, according to Dunphy, is to encourage and sanction the emergence of the heterosexual involvement of adolescents with each other. Taken in a step-by-step manner, teenagers learn new codes of conduct that lead toward the next stage of psychosocial development: establishing a sense of intimacy.

The transition to adulthood involves the adoption of new attitudes and values that are considered characteristic of mature individuals. The issue that confronts adolescents in this developmental task is one of conflict in resolving ways of thinking and logic that were developed in middle childhood. Piaget (1967) labels adolescence as a time when individuals enter the stage of *formal operations* in their cognitive development. Development of the cognitive skills required at this stage involves an increased ability to use logic and reasoning based on hypotheses and deduction to reach conclusions and solve problems. There is a decrease in egocentricity in the later adolescent years that allows the individual to reach solutions to problems from a number of approaches. Greater flexibility of thought characterizes the cognitive skills that are developed in adolescence.

An individual emerges from the middle childhood period by viewing the world in absolute terms. Issues and behavior are seen in terms of polar extremes. Something is definitely either right or wrong to do, people are treated fairly or unfairly, and someone is either good or bad, for example. A major task of the adolescent is to reconcile this approach to categorizing values and behavior by developing an ability to perceive gray areas and to develop a rationale for understanding rules of conduct. During this stage the teenager must move from knowing and acting upon specifics in values, attitude, and behavior to understanding the broader, more general philosophies that govern an adult approach to life (Hurlock, 1975).

The peer group experiences of adolescents play a significant role in determining what values, attitudes, and behaviors are important to the individual. The rigidity with which most peer groups enforce conformity to their specific moral and behavioral codes indicates to the individual that acceptance and continued membership are conditional upon the adoption of these codes. No longer do parents find their child accepting without question what they consider important values or behaviors. The striving for establishing a personal identity and independence from adult control encourages the teenager to evaluate what she or he has learned from parents and teachers within the context of peer group interactions. Peer group experiences of this nature assist the adolescents in modifying and reshaping their basic moral values into what is acceptable not only to themselves but also to their peers. The ultimate goal or objective of this challenge to reconcile differing values and behaviors is the internalization of a general and more abstract scheme of controls to guide the choices and decisions that govern adult behavior.

Exploring Vocational Objectives

The experiences of the school-age period that help to develop a sense of industry laid the foundation for exploring future vocational choices in adolescence. The adolescent observes the occupational roles that adults hold and is confronted with choosing a vocational direction from an overwhelming number of alternatives. The ideas developed in middle childhood toward work and work interests are explored in depth during adolescence.

Our culture places the teenager in a contradictory position regarding his or her future in an occupational role. Initial decisions about occupational choice and preparation for a vocation are ordinarily made in the ninth grade. This initial decision is crucial because other courses of action and decisions regarding preparation for the future are contingent on what direction seems to best fit the teenager's interests and abilities. Teenagers have not developed sufficient values or knowledge about occupational skills and roles when they are fourteen or fifteen years old to enable them to make sound decisions about where their future lies occupationally. A decision must be made, however, at this time if the teenager is to begin the various educational programs that lead to the intended fields of interest.

In reviewing the research on vocational choice development, Robert Grinder (1973), identifies five factors that influence career choice in adolescence: (1) *place of residence* can determine the level of adolescents' vocational aspirations in that those from rural areas and small towns tend to choose occupations that are lower in pay and prestige than those who grow up in metropolitan settings; (2) *socioeconomic status* has a similar influence in affecting occupational choice because of life-styles and values regarding educational achievement; (3) the *sex of an individual* may play an important role in vocational choice despite the effects of the women's movement on making vocational choices equally available to both sexes; (4) the *occupation of the father* may act significantly to influence a boy's choice in his future occupation because boys tend to identify strongly with the father as a role model; and (5) *occupational attractiveness* may influence vocational choices, which are evaluated in terms of their level of prestige, power, income, and psychological rewards.

Parents' encouragement is an important determinant of career choice for adolescents. Jacobsen (1971) states that parents of ninth-grade boys make serious attempts to socialize their sons toward occupational roles. He found that two types of encouragement are used frequently by parents: (1) job possibilities may be explored abstractly by discussion or by a verbal encouragement of interests along certain lines; or (2) job choices are more concretely explored by encouragement of the adolescent to take specific vocational courses or to take a job, for example. Jacobsen also found that it is not one parent (usually the father) who takes the more active part in encouraging vocational interests but rather that both parents are involved in this process.

As teenagers evaluate and explore the wide variety of vocational choices available, initial attempts are made at discovering the degree of congruence between interest and choice. Part-time and summer jobs may be used as an effective means to discover the possibilities of a vocation. Such jobs, however, may be difficult to obtain, resulting in a large number of unemployed individuals at this crucial time in the decision-making process.

The inability to begin thinking about a career or vocational objective during adolescence may contribute to feelings of role confusion. The ability to pursue an exploration of job choices leads to a sense of identity and develops the feelings of independence that are essential to adolescent psychosocial development.

THE INDIVIDUAL IN EARLY ADULTHOOD

The period of early adulthood begins with the teenager's eighteenth birthday and extends through age forty (Hurlock, 1975). The family, however, is concerned with limited child-rearing responsibilities for only a six- to seven-year period at the beginning of this stage. This constitutes the "launching" stage of the family life cycle. The stage is characterized by the events of the first child's leaving the family home to begin his or her own life and ends with the "empty nest," when the last child has been launched from the home base.

Erikson (1950) describes this period as most appropriate for the young adult to develop a *sense of intimacy*. This stage of psychosocial development precedes the stage of generativity, which the parents are completing when the first child is being launched. It is the initial preparation stage for the next stage in selecting a mate and establishing a close, nurturant relationship with this person before beginning a family.

The primary developmental tasks for the individual are unique at this stage of the family life cycle and include:

1. Achieving a sense of intimacy versus isolation.
2. Achieving full autonomy as an individual.

Achieving a Sense of Intimacy

Graduation from high school serves as one of the delimiters that signals the end of adolescence. New cultural expectations now center on the behavior, attitudes, and values of young adults. These expectations focus on the idea that the swings of indecisive adolescent behavior are left behind to be replaced by the increasing maturity of the individual.

Young adulthood is, on the one hand, a settling-down period (Hurlock, 1975) as patterns of behavior emerge to provide a more stable life-style. Sheehy (1976), however, calls this period in early adulthood the "trying twenties" in characterizing the difficulty of the decisions and choices that are made at this time in life. Both viewpoints are acceptable. The experiences of childhood and adolescence are concerned with the discovery of the self and the environment as well as with exploring one's place in life. Young adulthood witnesses the application of choices tentatively explored in these earlier years.

One of the most pressing choices is deciding whom one wishes to spend his or her life with or who is the most appropriate person with whom to develop a close, intimate relationship, leading to the establishment of a family. The lessons experienced in learning a sense of trust that were developed long ago in infancy are evoked once again at this stage in development. Consistencies in learning to trust and anticipate the behavior and attitudes of another individual act to enhance the development of a sense of intimacy. One of the most essential consistencies that influences the choice of an intimate partner is learning to distinguish between sexual attraction and feelings of love. Social scientists continue their attempts to identify and describe the elements and stages involved in mate selection. The roots of these explanations may lie in a number of factors and variables that are derived from our experiences in childhood and adolescence and acquaint us with a variety of different kinds of love. The effects of these experiences should crystallize into some idea of whom we wish to become intimate with, what kinds of similarities between ourself and the other person are important, and what personal attributes will serve as the basis of a nurturant relationship conducted in a mature manner.

Sheehy (1976) believes that during the "trying twenties" the individual exercises and enacts a number of "shoulds." This involves a variety of expectations of appropriate behavior that are largely cultural in nature and are enforced by the peer group. One of the most pressing "shoulds" is getting engaged to, marrying, or living with another person of the opposite sex (see Figure 7-7). Duvall (1977) points to two factors from research on mate selection that serve to guide our decision in making this particular choice. *Homogamy,* or the tendency of individuals to be similar in traits, life-style, and value systems, is one of these factors. Such similarities may be socio-economic status, religious beliefs, or ethnic group membership. *Propinquity,* or physical closeness, is another factor that strongly influences a choice of partners. We tend to gravitate toward individuals who come from peer groups established in high school or college or from our own neighborhoods. Geographic region may qualify as a factor in propinquity, as the life-styles of others from the same area are more familiar and predictable to us.

Social isolation is the hazard of inadequate psychosocial development in early adulthood from Erikson's point of view. This *sense of isolation* comes from the inability to develop a close relationship with another or from withdrawing from the peer group before having the opportunities to develop such close associations. The peer group provides the principle contacts for locating a promising mate. With the close of adolescence or the completion of educational training and the shift to an adult occupational role, the peer group is frequently replaced by a more heterogeneous grouping of people involved in related work roles. Unless the individual is able to seek out age-mates with similar interests and life-styles, a sense of social isolation may be experienced in early adulthood. This situation may not be as extreme as what existed when Erikson formulated his theory. For example, since the 1950s a number of apartment developments have been built that cater to single individuals. Singles' bars are commonplace locations in large urban areas and attract a large number of available young adults.

Figure 7-7.

Self-centeredness or a sense of isolation is the predicted result of not establishing a sense of intimacy in early adulthood. The fear of isolation may motivate individuals into pseudointimacy or to become married or to live with someone, even an individual who may not even remotely fulfill their romantic ideals, in order to avoid loneliness.

Achieving Full Autonomy

Early adulthood brings the launching of the individual into full responsibility for his or her actions. The weight of this responsibility is felt in Sheehy's (1976) description of the period as the "trying twenties." The pressure increases to make choices after exploring the alternatives in life that are available during the adolescent years. These choices revolve around mate selection, vocational objectives, and eventual life-styles.

The first years of early adulthood may be devoted to detaching oneself further from the trappings and obligations of parents and family members. Although the process of removing oneself physically and psychologically from parental control and influence has begun in adolescence, early adulthood sees the individual truly embarking on his or her own style of life. Financial responsibility for oneself is only one of the many ways that this is assumed. During this time of life we also rely on what we learned as very young children in establishing a sense of autonomy: that freedom is essential for personal growth but may be bought at the expense of inner turmoil and anxiety over the "rightness" of these personal choices. Sheehy believes that young adults are compelled to view the choices made at this time in life as irrevocable and unchangeable. The great desire and pressure now centers on an individual's capitalizing on all the years of socialization and training that should bear fruit in early adulthood in wise personal choices that are made. The feeling that is experienced is that the course of life and its work can now be fixed on a definite pattern with no questions as to the certainty of fulfillment. In reality, questions will rise to tempt the young adult about the correctness or wiseness of his or her choices but become buried by denial that one's past could have shaped a wrong or improper choice. Only later, when the individual has had time to evaluate the nature of these choices, will the confrontations be made with how satisfied one is with a marriage, life's work, or the goals of life that were chosen in early adulthood.

PARENTAL DEVELOPMENT IN ADOLESCENCE AND EARLY ADULTHOOD

The families-with-teenagers stage of the family life cycle signals the approaching end of child-rearing responsibilities for adults. As the first child grows through adolescence, parents must once again adapt to the changing developmental demands of their child in providing their caregiving. This is a period of conflict and strained communications between parents and teenagers. Differences in value orientation and life-styles between the generations may become apparent as the teenager approaches early adulthood. With the completion of the adolescent stage and the exit of the last child from the home, the parents face the challenge of adjusting to new roles as adults as they enter the last stage of psychosocial development.

Developmental interaction during the families-with-teenagers and launching-of-young-adults stages centers on developmental tasks that include:

1. Maintaining effective communications with children.
2. Meeting individual and shared needs.

Maintaining Communications with Children

One of the most significant criteria of the successfulness of parents and teenagers in meeting the challenges of the adolescent period is the effectiveness of communications among all individuals. The question that rises at this point is whether conflict between parents and teenagers is a natural phenomenon that can't be avoided. This issue of conflict between the generations is more commonly known as the *generation gap* and focuses on differences in values, attitudes, and life-styles between adults and teenage children.

Support can be found for both the explanation that conflict is expected and unavoidable or that conflict is unnecessary and nonnormative behavior. Freudian psychology has promoted the first notion, that conflict between generations is essential to the development of the adolescent's sense of identity as a mature, autonomous individual. This viewpoint removes all responsibility for conflict from the parents and focuses on the teenager. Because she or he is experiencing a difficult adjustment period, she or he is seen as deliberately starting arguments as well as being generally disagreeable or uncooperative. The other viewpoint is expressed by contemporary writers (Meissner, 1965; Offer, 1969; Weiner, 1970, 1977), who feel that the generation gap is a creation of the mass media in responding to the actions of a small group of disturbed adolescents.

The central issue surrounding the issue of conflict between parents and teenagers revolves around the exercise of adult controls on adolescents' behavior. One of the primary goals of socialization throughout the years of childhood has been to prepare children to assume responsibility for their own behavior. Yet parents may experience contradictory feelings about the means by which teenagers express their independence as well as having doubts about their ability to make reasonable or wise decisions.

Conflict between parents and children comes from a variety of sources at this time of the family life cycle. The majority center on disagreements between parents and teenagers about the child's personal conduct and activities, according to Chand, Crider, and Willits (1975). Conflict between parents and teenagers, however, is most pronounced when the adolescent reacts with negative attempts at autonomous behavior, such as running away from home. Blood and D'Angelo (1974) have found that adolescent runaways identify more items on a scale as major issues of conflict and report more conflicts with parents than nonrunaway adolescents. Running away stemmed from these adolescents' perceptions of inadequate demonstrations of affection and love from parents. Another area pinpointed as a topic of conflict by the runaways was the issue of feeling unaccepted by parents and their failure to listen to the teenagers.

Elkind (1974) describes conflicts between parents and children as a process in the growth toward maturity of both individuals. Elkind outlines three types of arrangements between parents and children that are used to govern and regulate child behavior: the *bargain,* the *agreement,* and the *contract.* Conflicts result at all stages of development when these arrangements are violated by the actions of the child or the parents.

A bargain is established between a parent and a child when the parent offers some type of reward or withholds a punishment in return for the child's cooperation. In early childhood, for example, such a bargain might be "You can have some ice cream if you finish your dinner." In adolescence, the bargaining may be initiated by the teenager: "I'll do all the laundry if you'll let me stay out late tonight."

In arranging an agreement, both parents and child agree to comply with specified rules over an indefinite period of time. Rules can be negative in childhood in the attempt to teach children appropriate conduct and carry a condition, expressed by "If you don't brush your teeth after eating, you can't have dessert for a week." In adolescence, agreements become more positive and change in their content, such as "If you want to keep the privilege of driving the car, you'll have to agree to be home on time."

According to Elkind, contracts between parents and children are less explicitly defined and are usually acknowledged only when they are violated by parents or child: "The mother, for example, who says, 'Look how they treat me after I worked and slaved for them,' reveals her belief in an implicit contract as does the remark of an adolescent, 'No matter how much I do around the house, it is never enough' " (Elkind, 1974, pp. 86–87). Contracts between parents and children involve the three following clauses, which vary in content, according to Elkind.

1. The *responsibility–freedom* clause to a contract features the parents' expectations that certain personal responsibilities will be taken by children in return for degrees of freedom and autonomy. In early childhood, the parents demand that the child take responsibility for dressing, feeding, and control of bodily functions, for example, in return for freedom of movement and exploration of the environment. In middle childhood, parents demand that the child take care of property and pursue educational achievements in return for the freedom to stay away from the home longer and become more in-

volved with peers. Adolescence sees the clause rewritten in terms of parents' demands that responsibility be taken for sexual behavior and finances, for example, in return for new privileges in style of dress and choice of friends.

2. The *achievement–support* clause relates to the development of personal competencies. In early childhood, parents expect children to achieve certain skills in all areas of development, such as learning appropriate speech patterns and learning to relate to others. In middle childhood, parents expect children to develop academic competencies and more advanced social skills. In adolescence, parents accelerate expectations to a more advanced level. Throughout childhood and adolescence, children expect emotional support for their efforts in developing these competencies.

3. The *loyalty–commitment* clause deals with maintaining bonds and emotional ties between parents and children. Infants are expected only to respond positively to parents' affectional advances. Children are expected to maintain their emotional loyalty to parents despite relationships with the peer group and new adults, such as teachers. At adolescence, loyalty is expected to the beliefs and values that the parents hold.

Relations between parents and teenagers may become tense as teenagers come to expect and demand freedoms that violate these contractual agreements with parents. Parents may fail to respond to the adolescent in ways that demonstrate their support and trust in the teenager's emerging individuality. Both parents and adolescents come to perceive each other as being insensitive to the other's needs. Grinder (1973) identifies two reasons that parents may have difficulty in recognizing an adolescent's need to achieve recognition as a maturing, responsible individual: (1) cultural impoverishment of the parents and (2) personality constrictions of the parents. Cultural impoverishment of the parents, according to Grinder, refers to the problems of anticipating events that the teenager will confront in his or her future. Because there have been numerous changes and questioning of traditional social structures in recent years, parents come to fear that recognized institutions and values may not persist into the future. This fear results in more authoritarian controls to enforce conformity. Personality constrictions relate to parents' conflicts over recognition that their increasingly autonomous child is removing their "need to be needed" in depending on them for guidance and care. This recognition is threatening to the deeply ingrained sense of generativity. The maturing adolescent pushes his or her parents toward a transition to new adult roles that affect the parents' self-concepts. Any transition is uncomfortable and tense and may result in conflicts between teenagers or young adults and their parents.

Meeting Individual and Shared Needs

Parents are usually in their mid-thirties or early forties when the first child becomes a teenager. They are usually of this age when the last child begins school. Many parents will be in their late forties to early fifties when these stages are completed. Throughout the six- to seven-year period of the first child's adolescence and the first years of his or her early adulthood, the adults should be expected to experience a recovery or increase in the degree of satisfaction with their marriage relationship (see Figure 7-8). The research of Rollins and Feldman (1970) and Rollins and Cannon (1974) shows that the recovery is experienced differently by men and women. Women show a slower rate of recovery or increase in marital satisfaction through these two stages of the family life cycle. Men and women are similar in the degree of reported general satisfaction with family life at these two stages (see Figure 7-9). Both report a sharp decline in happiness followed by a rapid increase in satisfaction as adjustment occurs during the families-in-middle-years stage. These reactions can be traced to the stressfulness of family life and interpersonal interactions with children during these stages as well as to the transi-

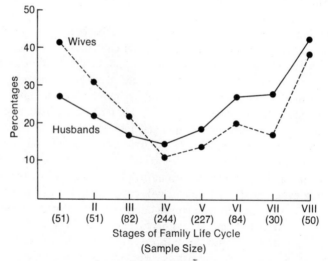

Figure 7-8. The percentage of individuals at each stage of the family life cycle who reported their marriage was going well "all the time." A reanalysis of scores on a 6-point scale with 1 equaling "never" and 6 equaling "all the time" indicated that only 4 per cent of the variance of marital satisfaction scores was associated with family life cycle stages. This is because a large percentage of those in the middle stages are satisfied "most of the time." (Source: Rollins, B., & Feldman, H. Marital satisfaction over the family life cycle. *Journal of Marriage and the Family*, 1970, *32*, 20–28. Copyright 1970 by the National Council on Family Relations. Reprinted by permission.)

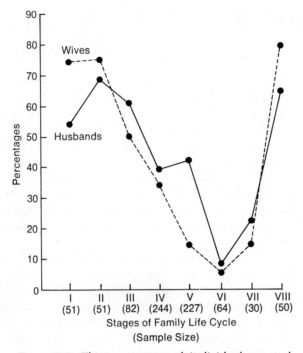

Figure 7-9. The percentage of individuals at each stage of the family life cycle reporting that their experiences at their present stage of the cycle was very satisfying. (Source: Rollins, B., & Feldman, H. Marital satisfaction over the family life cycle. *Journal of Marriage and the Family*, 1970, *32*, 20–28. Copyright 1970 by the National Council on Family Relations. Reprinted by permission.)

tions to new roles being precipitated by the launching of the oldest child into his or her own life.

Sheehy (1976) describes the years from thirty-five to forty-five as the "deadline decade." This is the period when adults reach yet another identity crisis in their lives, but this is a different type of crisis than those confronted in earlier years. These years of the deadline decade are perceived as the opportunity for a last-ditch effort to determine and live true identities. The growing, developing adult experiences a parallel period with the teenager in questioning the purposes of life, the functioning of society's institutions, and the values that are important to guide life's work and future behavior. The teenager's struggles in the search for personal identity may stimulate a similar experience for adults.

Both men and women who confront this crisis in midlife pause psychologically to take stock of the progress made thus far in life and to determine the options that are still left. This survey, according to Sheehy, is initiated by women at about age thirty-five and by men at about age forty. The reactions and courses of action taken by women differ from men as well (see Box 7-1).

Sheehy lists several reasons why women experience the midlife survey earlier than men. This is the age when the average woman or mother: (1) sends her last child off to school; (2) is most likely to be unfaithful to her husband; (3) reenters the work force and becomes employed outside the home; (4) is apt to remarry if she is a divorcee; (5) is most likely to run away from home or desert her family; and (6) sees the end of her years of childbearing coming into sight. All of these factors taken together or singly act to stimulate the woman to take bearings on where her life has been headed, to evaluate and assess her available options to remedy any feelings of discontent, and to take positive actions toward recovery. Women, then, try to rebalance their lives.

The reaction of men to the midlife identity crisis is delayed, according to Sheehy, until about age forty, when they, too, feel that time is slipping by rapidly. Men react by accelerating their efforts at achievement of personal goals, especially their vocational objectives. Men may react differently than women at this time in the way in which the sense of generativity is developed. Women, by virtue of their socialization and assumption of the role of primary caregiver to children and the family group, have had more direct, hands-on experiences to develop the strength of their generativity through child rearing than men. Men usually are not permitted these experiences to the same degree as women, so that the achievement of a sense of generativity may be delayed until the midlife crisis forces them to "discover" their children. This discovery that they can be nurturant or the desire to become involved in teaching skills to and sharing knowledge with children comes at a time when the children are demanding release from parental involvement in their lives. Women, who have been carrying the major responsibility of involvement with the children, may find it easier to accept adolescents' strivings toward independence. The growth and development of the children symbolizes a release from these responsibilities to many mothers. Having an "empty nest" causes realignments in their attitudes and perceptions. The future is anticipated rather than dreaded. Men may react to the "empty nest" or the approaching end of child rearing with depression or guilt over the lost opportunities for involvement with their children.

When men confront the nurturant aspect of their personalities that emerges from their survey at midlife, they may feel threatened by what seems to be a feminine quality. Coupled with this may be the realization that their sexual abilities are declining. Erections are not as easily produced, and impotence may be experienced for the first time at midlife. Reactions may vary from depression to becoming a Don Juan-type character who attempts to seduce younger women to prove masculinity. The more hopeful course is a man's

BOX 7-1. SHE LIKED HERSELF BETTER
BEFORE THIS SELF-ANALYSIS

Ten years ago I didn't know anything about myself. I didn't know who I was, where I was or where I was going.

I didn't know how I felt about my plants, my tennis game, breast-feeding, nicknames, waxed dental floss or premarital sex. I had never analyzed my marriage, my dreams, my hostilities, or my reasons for taking a tape recorder with me to the labor room.

I crossed my legs at the ankle and slept with my fists closed, but never knew why. I fantasized about Paul Newman calling me out of a high-level Girl Scout cookie meeting because he was unable to sleep. My marriage was working, but the reason was something I couldn't put my finger on.

Then came the tide of self-analysis books—one, two, sometimes three and four a month inviting me to dissect my motivations for living and understand myself.

So, I became my own best friend, went around saying, "I'm okay, you're okay" and opened our marriage at both ends. It has taken 10 years of self-analysis, but I've discovered something I never knew about me before. I'm boring.

I liked me better when I was mysterious and shallow. Even my anxiety attacks aren't any fun anymore. What good does it do me to get uptight when deep down inside I know it's merely a psychological signal to myself to alert me to future dangers and threats?

My friend, Mayva, is really into self-analysis and continues to drive me crazy. The other day I tried to down a vitamin pill when Mayva said, "Are you having trouble swallowing that pill?"

"Yes."

"What year did your dog die?"

"Two years ago. What's that got to do with swallowing a pill?"

"Why are you so hostile about the dog's death?"

"I am not hostile!"

"Have you ever felt you were too assertive and tended to dominate your marriage?"

"Mayva, I am sick to death of analyzing my every move."

"You're uptight. Maybe you should meditate for 30 minutes."

"I can't. I forgot my mantra."

Her eyebrow rose. "That's rather Freudian, isn't it?"

"I call it old age."

"I think you're going through a predictable life crisis."

"Which one?"

"I don't know. Gail Sheehy only went through age 40 in 'Passages.' You're probably right. We think too much about ourselves."

"Tell me about it," I said, putting my arm over her shoulder.

Source: From *At Wit's End* by Erma Bombeck. Copyright 1977 Field Enterprises, Inc. Courtesy of Field Newspaper Syndicate.

acceptance of his caring nature and the development of a closer intimacy with his wife. In essence, these developments at midlife may promote rather than hinder marital satisfaction.

The close of adolescence and the departure of the last child from the home brings the parents to the full development of their sense of generativity. By caring for others, they have prepared the way for growth in their next stage of psychosocial development: the *sense of integrity* versus *despair*. This stage challenges the individual to reconcile himself or herself with the realities of his or her life. The essentials of the self are examined and brought out on display in everyday behavior. There is no longer a preoccupation with how one should act or false beliefs held about what should be right. The period is one of integration of all the senses that have been developed through life. The future is less demanding in its urgency for promised fulfillment. The boundary of temporal existence comes closer into view, and for many individuals, life is lived for the self rather than for others, as in the past. Sheehy describes this time as one of renewal, basing her view on Erikson's label of integration of the self. Growth of the self continues until death and is motivated by the courage of an individual to face himself or herself with all his or her virtues, strengths, and weaknesses. There is acceptance of the self and others. Renewal is gained also by involvement with the continuation of life through children and grandchildren. The cycle of developmental interaction is observed as it is repeated once again from generation to generation.

POINTS TO CONSIDER

- Adolescents encounter developmental tasks that center on developing the more advanced skills, abilities, and attitudes that lead to preparation for adulthood.
- The developmental tasks of early adulthood focus on developing a close, intimate relationship with another and achieving full autonomy as an individual.
- Developmental interaction during the years of adolescence and early adulthood forces parents to adjust to new roles as adults.
- The central challenges of interaction with children during these stages involve resolving conflicts and maintaining lines of communication while meeting individual needs.
- Adults may experience a period of self-examination during this stage of the family life cycle that parallels the experiences of teenagers and young adults in establishing self-identities.

REFERENCES

Ambrosino, L. *Runaways*. Boston: Beacon Press, 1971.

Bauman, K., and Wilson, R. Sexual behavior of unmarried university students in 1968 and 1972. *Journal of Sex Research*, 1974, *10*, 327–333.

BAYH, B. Runaway youth hearings before the Subcommittee to Investigate Juvenile Delinquency, Committee on the Judiciary, United States Senate. Washington, D.C.: Government Printing Office, 1973.

BELL, R., and CHASKES, J. Premarital sexual experience among coeds, 1958 and 1968. *Journal of Marriage and the Family*, 1970, *32*, 81–84.

BLOOD, L., and D'ANGELO, R. A progress research report on value issues in conflict between runaways and their parents. *Journal of Marriage and the Family*, 1974, *36*, 486–491.

CHAND, I., CRIDER, D., and WILLITS, F. Parent–youth disagreement as perceived by youth: A longitudinal study. *Youth and Society*, 1975, *6*, 365–375.

DUNPHY, D. The social structure of urban adolescent peer groups. *Sociometry*, 1963, *26*, 230–246.

DUVALL, E. *Marriage and family development* (5th ed.). Philadelphia: J. B. Lippincott, 1977.

EICHORN, D. Biological correlates of behavior. In H. Stevenson (Ed.), *Child psychology*. Chicago: University of Chicago Press, 1963. Pp. 4–61.

ELKIND, D. *A sympathetic understanding of the child: Birth to sixteen*. Boston: Allyn and Bacon, 1974.

ERIKSON, E. *Childhood and society*. New York: Norton, 1950.

ERIKSON, E. *Insight and responsibility*. New York: Norton, 1964.

GLICK, P. A demographer looks at American families. *Journal of Marriage and the Family*, 1975, *37*, 15–38.

GRINDER, R. *Adolescence*. New York: Wiley, 1973.

GUINN, R., and HURLEY, R. A comparison of drug use among Houston and Lower Rio Grande Valley secondary students. *Adolescence*, 1976, *11*, 455–459.

GUNDERSON, E. Body size, self-evaluation, and military effectiveness. *Journal of Personality and Social Psychology*, 1965, *2*, 902–906.

HAGER, D., VENER, A., and STEWART, C. Patterns of adolescent drug use in middle America. *Journal of Counseling Psychology*, 1971, *18*, 292–297.

HOWELL, E., EMMONS, E., and FRANK, D. Reminiscences of runaway adolescents. *American Journal of Orthopsychiatry*, 1973, *43*, 840–853.

HURLOCK, E. *Developmental psychology* (4th ed.). New York: McGraw-Hill, 1975.

JACOBSEN, B. An exploration of parental encouragement as an intervening variable in occupational–educational learning of children. *Journal of Marriage and the Family*, 1971, *33*, 174–182.

JONES, M., and BAYLEY, N. Physical maturing among boys as related to behavior. *Journal of Educational Psychology*, 1958, *41*, 129–148.

JONES, M., and MUSSEN, P. Self-conceptions, motivations, and interpersonal attitudes of early- and late-maturing girls. *Child Development*, 1958, *29*, 492–501.

JUSTICE, B., and DUNCAN, D. Running away: An epidemic problem of adolescence. *Adolescence*, 1976, *43*, 365–371.

KROGMAN, W. Growth of the head, face, trunk, and limbs in Philadelphia white and negro children of elementary and high school age. *Monographs of the Society for Research in Child Development*, 1970, *35*, Whole No. 136.

MADDOX, G. Teenage drinking in the United States. In R. McCarthy (Ed.), *Alcohol education for classroom and community*. New York: McGraw-Hill, 1964.

MEISSNER, W. Parental interaction of the adolescent boy. *Journal of Genetic Psychology*, 1965, *107*, 225–233.

MILLER, J. Suicide and adolescence. *Adolescence*, 1975, *10*, 11–24.

MUSSEN, P., and JONES, M. The behavior inferred motivations of late- and early-maturing boys. *Child Development*, 1958, *29*, 61–67.

National Center for Health Statistics. Self-reported health behavior and attitudes of youth 12 to 17 years, United States. *Vital and Health Statistics*, 1975, *11*, Whole No. 147.

OFFER, D. *The psychological world of the teenager: A study of normal adolescent boys*. New York: Basic Books, 1969.

PIAGET, J. *Six psychological studies*. New York: Random House, 1967.

PLATERIS, A. Divorces: Analysis of changes, 1969. *Vital and Health Statistics*, 1973, *21*, 1–58.

ROLLINS, B., and CANNON, K. Marital satisfaction over the family life cycle: A reevaluation. *Journal of Marriage and the Family*, 1974, *36*, 271–282.

ROLLINS, B., and FELDMAN, H. Marital satisfaction over the family life cycle. *Journal of Marriage and the Family*, 1970, *32*, 20–28.

SHEEHY, G. *Passages: Predictable crises of adulthood*. New York: Dutton, 1976.

SHELLOW, R., SCHAMP, J., LEIBOW, E., and UNGER, E. Suburban runaways of the 1960s. *Monographs of the Society for Research in Child Development*, 1967, *32*, Whole No. 111.

SHEONFELD, W. Body-image in adolescents: A psychiatric concept for the pediatrician. *Pediatrics*, 1963, *31*, 845–855.

SMART, R. Some current studies of psychoactive and hallucinogenic drug use. *Canadian Journal of Behavioural Science*, 1970, *2*, 232–245.

SORENSEN, R. *Adolescent sexuality in contemporary America*. New York: World Publishing, 1973.

TANNER, J. The regulation of human growth. *Child Development*, 1963, *34*, 817–847.

TANNER, J. Physical growth. In P. Mussen (Ed.), *Carmichael's manual of child psychology* (3rd ed.). New York: Wiley, 1970. Pp. 77–155.

VENER, A., STEWART, C., and HAGER, D. Adolescent sexual behavior in middle America revisited: Generational and American–British comparisons. *Journal of Marriage and the Family*, 1974, *36*, 728–735.

WEATHERLY, D. Self-perceived rate of physical maturation and personality in late adolescence. *Child Development*, 1964, *35*, 1197–1210.

WEINER, I. *Psychological disturbance in adolescence*. New York: Wiley, 1970.

WEINER, I. The generation gap: Fact and fancy. *Adolescence*, 1977, *12*, 155–166.

ZELNICK, M., and KANTNER, J. The resolution of first pregnancies. *Family Planning Perspectives*, 1974, *6*, 74–80.

THREE

Developmental Interaction: Implications for Parenting

All families are not alike in their structure and manner of functioning. Differences in family composition most likely result in differences in the way that the adult conducts his or her parenting functions. The impression has been created over the years that families differing from the norm are pathological or abnormal. The experiences of individuals growing up in such families have also led to the impression that these individuals have pathological personality traits because of their family background and experiences.

The last part of the text explores the implications of developmental interaction on parenting behavior in three different family forms. The issue of how developmental interaction between parents and children is affected by differences in family structure is also explored. The last chapter examines the problems of parents, who as developing individuals themselves must socialize and be socialized by a child who is acquiring values, beliefs, and skills for coping with the ever-changing world of the future.

8

Family Variations and Parent–Child Relations

We have a number of impressions regarding the composition, style of life, and patterns of child rearing among families that lead us to believe that most of us fit a particular pattern. The "typical" family is assumed to be composed of two opposite-sex adults and their children who live in a home that is comfortably furnished. The father is seen as being the provider and the decision maker, and the mother is occupied with performing the major responsibilities of full-time caregiving to children. The children are thought to be healthy and busily involved in growing up, giving both parents plenty of headaches and concerns in the process. The mother is thought to approach her child-rearing activities in either an authoritative or a permissive manner, whereas the father is seen as being more authoritarian in his interactions with children. Although problems are encountered in interpersonal interactions and in other areas (finances, for example), nothing is seen as insurmountable, and the family lives happily ever after.

This description of the "typical" family is a stereotype, or an impression that is formed from limited information, exposure, or experience. Stereotypes are often erroneous and misleading. For example, athletes are stereotyped as having limited intelligence, women are stereotyped as being physically weak and highly emotional, and men are thought to be generally stubborn.

The stereotype of a "typical" family is also erroneous. Every family does not include a man in the husband–father role or a woman in the wife–mother role; all parents do not necessarily fit the descriptions discussed in previous chapters of this text; and some families do not include children. Families that do not represent the norm are considered to have more problems than those that approximate the idea of the "typical." These divergent families are thought to be more vulnerable to stress and receive less support from society.

© 1977 by NEA, Inc.

"What kind of family are we, anyway? Nuclear, extended or what?"

Figure 8-1.

Researchers have known for some time that stress coming from outside the family tends to solidify rather than disorganize the group (Hill, 1958). Outside sources of stress that affect family functioning include wars and economic problems in the larger society, such as inflation and recession. Sources of trouble that come from within the family are more likely to produce stress leading to disorganization. These include loss of a member through illness, death, separation, or divorce as well as situational events such as alcoholism, delinquency, and infidelity.

When a family experiences stress from within itself, the result often is disorganization that affects the family's ability to function in a healthy, efficient manner. Solutions are sought and compromises are made to compensate for these changes.

A family that is atypical from the norm is not necessarily a family that is in stress. Such families, however, may not operate as efficiently as possible. Problems in functioning are unique to the particular family. This chapter discusses the particular problems and concerns of three different family forms and the manner in which caregiving is affected and responded to by children. These family forms include one-parent families, reconstituted families, and the adolescent or unwed parent.

ONE-PARENT FAMILIES

The Single Mother

The problems of a single-parent family are generally those that involve the woman in her role as a parent. The number of families in which there was only one parent was 3.5 million in 1970, and over 85 per cent of these single parents were women (U.S.. Bureau of the Census, 1970).

There are several ways that a family loses the functions and presence of one of the adults, usually the husband–father: (1) divorce, desertion, or separation; (2) death; or (3) having a child illegitimately. Of the total number of white females who headed a family in 1975 (almost 5.2 million), over 32 per cent were divorced, 14.6 per cent were separated, 18.3 per cent were not divorced but the spouse was absent, 39.4 per cent were widowed, and 9.4 per cent were unwed mothers (U.S. Bureau of the Census, 1976). Comparable figures relate to black women who were family heads, although there were fewer total female-headed black families during this year. About 25 per cent of the white female family heads had one child, and almost 17 per cent had two children.

Researchers have been aware of the differences in child-rearing patterns and personalities of children in homes where the father is absent. A considerable amount of study has been devoted to determining the effects of father absence on children's development, particularly that of boys (see Chapter 3). Researchers, however, are increasingly turning their attention to the problems faced by the single-parent family as a group. The problems and situations encountered by women as single parents depend on the nature of their circumstances. Women who are divorced have problems that differ from widowed or never-married women in their parenting roles and life-styles.

A number of different descriptions emerge from research conducted on the family life, styles of parenting, children, and status of the family headed by a single mother.

1. *She heads a low-income family.* The median income in 1975 of families headed by a woman was $6,884. This figure compares with a median income of $14,867 for two-parent families headed by a male during the same year (U.S. Bureau of the Census, 1976). There may be two reasons that the single-parent female-headed family faces a future of relative poverty. First, there is a strong association between family income and family stability. The probability of divorce, separation, or desertion is less likely as family income increases (Carter and Glick, 1970). As applied to the single-parent family,

if the mother was poor before the loss of the father, she is likely to be just as poor or more so after his departure. The economic status of the family prior to the loss of the husband–father partially accounts for the low-income status of these families. Second, economic discrimination against women may also account for the reduction in income after the departure of the husband (Brandwein, Brown, and Fox, 1974). These researchers note that women are given less job training, receive lower incomes, have less-secure positions, and are less likely than men to have a job in the first place.

A study by House (1976) on the economic impact of divorce found that women receive a more equitable settlement if they are white, are thirty years of age or older, have at least a high school education, were married more than five years, had been employed outside the home prior to or during the marriage, and had an annual family income of approximately $15,000. Obviously, all women do not fit this description.

2. *She experiences additional role strain as a parent.* With the loss of the husband–father from the family, a woman must now perform his functions as well as her own as a parent. In addition to becoming the primary wage earner, the woman is forced to shoulder the other responsibilities of the ex-husband and attempt to compensate for his absence in performing child-rearing and other functions. One of the major findings along these lines is the shift to more authoritarian patterns of child rearing by the woman when she becomes a single parent (Kriesberg, 1970). Other investigators find that the fathering function is assigned to an older child or to a relative (Glasser and Navarre, 1964; Marsden, 1973). Kogelschatz, Adams, and Tucker (1972) report a variety of reactions by women to single parenthood. All were hostile and depressed about the departure of the husband. Among those whose husbands had been absent for more than two years, none expressed satisfaction with their daily circumstances of life. These women were found to be highly dependent emotionally, focusing their needs on their child and on the child's grandmother in providing emotional reassurance and caregiving support.

3. *She experiences negative community attitudes and support.* The single mother is much maligned and generally lacks the sympathy and understanding of others in her community. Many women are forced to apply for public assistance through the Aid to Families of Dependent Children Program for child care and economic support. This drain on taxpayers' dollars does not enjoy wide popular support in the United States. Marsden (1973) reports that single mothers feel that they have little respect from neighbors. Many of these women feel that they are being left out of the mainstream of society (Burgess, 1970). There is a definite decline in social activities, particularly with friends who remain married, when a woman becomes a single parent. Unless the woman joins a support group, such as Parents Without Partners, she may live in a social vacuum in a world populated by couples and their children.

The Single Father

Relatively little is known about the functioning of a single-parent family that is headed by a man. The 1970 Census of the United States indicated that over 600,000 single fathers with children were present in the population (U.S. Bureau of the Census, 1970). By 1974, this figure had increased to slightly over 1 million single fathers with dependent children (U.S. Bureau of the Census, 1976). Approximately 15 per cent of all single-parent families in 1974 were headed by men.

A man becomes a single father through the same causes that affect a woman. Divorce is the leading factor, followed by death of the spouse through natural causes, accidents, or suicide. Changes in the structure of laws regulating custody of children after divorce have brought an increasing number of men into single-father status. Prior to 1960, a father had to prove that a mother was "unfit" or that the environment provided through the mother was detrimental to the children's welfare in order to gain custody of his children. Courts have tended to presume that the mother was more capable than the father of being the primary caregiver. No-fault divorce laws and changes in attitudes toward full-time mothering among women are resulting in more cases of fathers being awarded custody of their children (Schlesinger 1966).

Several studies (Gasser and Taylor, 1976; Mendes, 1976; Orthner, Brown, and Ferguson, 1976) confirm similar reactions and adjustments among single fathers as a group. Some parallel problems are experienced to those encountered by single mothers, although reactions differ for single fathers.

1. *He experiences role strain.* Like the single-parent mother, the single father must adjust to the added responsibilities of child rearing in addition to providing the family income. The adjustment of single fathers differs from that of mothers, however, in a variety of ways. It would be expected that men would have a more difficult time adjusting to performing routine household management tasks because these were usually performed by the wife during the marriage, and men are not usually taught these skills as children. Researchers report that this may be the case for certain home management skills for some but not all men. Meal preparation was reported most often as a problem area (Gasser and Taylor, 1976; Mendes, 1976). The majority of these management tasks were shared by the children rather than by outside help. The majority of fathers studied by these investigators complained of conflicts in synchronizing child care, household duties, and wage-earning responsibilities in a workable routine.

2. *He experiences changes in relating to the children.* Becoming a single parent brings new insights to men about their responsibilities in child rearing. Mendes (1976) reports that the fathers of her study seemed to be more aware of their preadolescent children's need for affection and nurturance and made efforts to show their affection by hugging, touching, and kissing the

children. She states that the fathers of adolescents reported fewer physical demonstrations of affection and instead expressed their love more indirectly by how well they performed their parenting role and by being a stable presence in their children's lives. The men thought that teenaged children showed their love by being cooperative and by showing respect to the fathers. The fathers in the study by Orthner, Brown, and Ferguson (1976) reported that they demanded more independence from their children than other parents. These fathers, however, were found to change their attitudes and practices in child rearing upon assuming the primary caregiving role. They became less traditional in approach, less discipline-oriented, more concerned with the quality of child-care agencies, more interested in their children's educational experiences, and more protective toward their children. A common concern expressed by the fathers of daughters in these studies related to the problems of raising a daughter in a motherless home, such as anxieties over the "proper" socialization of girls and their emerging sexuality. There was a reported reluctance to discuss sexual matters and concern about the lack of an adequate social role-model for the girl.

3. *He experiences a less disrupted life-style than a single mother.* The fathers in these studies reported changes in their life-styles as adults. By being more intimately involved with their children, single-parent fathers experienced a decline in social activities, including activities with former friends of the couple, especially if the fathers were divorced rather than widowed. Social activities revolved around participation in single-parent groups and activities, the children, or a female friend. Most of the men in the study of Orthner, Brown, and Ferguson (1976) reported involvement in dating activity but had no concrete plans to remarry at any time in their near future. Sexual activity was present, but the majority of men in this study felt that discreetness in such behavior was necessary and that living with a woman was inadvisable as a model for the children.

A striking difference among the single-parent fathers compared with single mothers was the fathers' assessment of their life-styles. The majority of the fathers reported feeling satisfied and happy in their new status as a single father. Most reported having a good relationship with their children and feeling well-adjusted, especially the divorced fathers. Widowed fathers were having a more difficult adjustment to their status because of the suddenness and lack of psychological preparation for the separation (Gasser and Taylor, 1976). This more positive reaction to single parenthood in comparison to the more negative reaction among women relates to the lack of social stigma that is attached to the single male versus the single female. Orthner, Brown, and Ferguson (1976) state that single-parent men may be seen as less threatening to intact marriages than single-parent women. Economic factors may also play an important role here, in that men do not face the immediate loss of financial support that women experience when the spouse departs from the family. Men are generally able to maintain their level of income more easily under these circumstances.

Children in One-Parent Families

One of the leading causes of single-parent families is divorce of the parents. Divorces have been increasing in recent years (see Figure 8-2), showing a 22 per cent increase during 1968–1969 (Plateris, 1973). More recent data show that 4.8 marriages per 1,000 population ended in divorce in 1975 (U.S. Bureau of the Census, 1976) and that slightly less than two children were

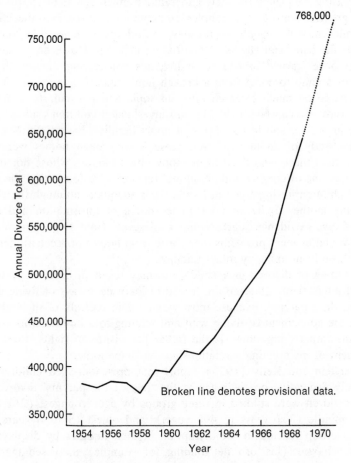

Figure 8-2. Frequency of divorce from 1954 to 1971. (Source: Plateris, A. Divorces: Analysis of changes, 1969. *Vital and Health Statistics*, 1973, *21*, 1–58.)

involved in each divorce. In 1969, for example, there were an estimated 840,000 children under eighteen years of age involved in divorces in the United States (Plateris, 1973). Although other research has shown that the presence of children may not contribute to marital satisfaction, census data from 1969 show that the length of marriage before divorce increases not only with the presence of children but also with increases in the number of children. The median duration of marriages before divorce in 1969 for couples with no children was 3.8 years as compared with 13.8 years for couples with three or more children (Plateris, 1973). This pattern is consistent with patterns of the past.

Divorce has carried a considerable degree of social stigma in the past, but its increasing frequency has acted to remove much social disapproval. One of the greatest concerns of couples contemplating divorce is the effect on their children. It is difficult, even today, to find any evidence that completely supports the beneficial effects of divorce on children. However, family practitioners have learned to counsel individuals considering divorce that it is better for a child to come from a broken home than to live in one. This advice is based on much research into this topic and particularly relates to a classic study of Ivan Nye (1957), who investigated children's adjustment to divorce in broken and in unhappy but intact families. Essentially Nye found from his study of adolescents that those from broken homes were better adjusted than those who lived in unhappy intact families whose home atmosphere was one of conflict and emotional turmoil. Nye found that the adjustment of children in single-parent families was adequate, although the children found the mother to be an inadequate source of information and advice. None of Nye's evidence suggests that adolescents from single-parent homes have more adjustment problems than those from homes of reconstituted families or those from unhappy intact families.

The timing of divorce in a child's life may result in different levels and types of adjustment. Children are forced to learn new ways of living and relating to their parents. Because most women gain custody of their children, there is the adjustment of living with and relating to a mother who also performs the father's functions. If the father has visitation rights, there is the adjustment of maintaining a relationship that is periodic.

Wallerstein and Kelly (1975) report that preschool-aged children react differently depending on their age at the time of the parents' divorce. Preschool children were studied in three groups by age: youngest (2½ to 3¼ years), middle (3¾ years to 4¾ years), and oldest (5 to 6 years). The youngest group reacted to the disruption in their families by displaying regressive behaviors (loss of toilet training, for example), increased aggression, fretfulness, confusion, and attention-getting behaviors. Regressive behaviors occurred more frequently among the children who had not been informed of the reason for the father's withdrawal from the family. When this group was seen a year later by the investigators, these behaviors had largely disappeared.

The variable that seemed to determine the children's recovery was the quality of caregiving performed by the mother, the father, or the substitute caregiver. If the caregiver was a consistent figure and was nurturant, the source or location of the caregiving was irrelevant (in the home, in a child-care center, or elsewhere). Only half of the children who were between 3¾ and 4¾ years old (the middle preschool-aged group) showed regressive behaviors, but many of these children were reported to be whiny, irritable, and fretful as well as aggressive. The more advanced level of cognitive development among these children led them to be mistrustful of the stability of relations with adults. Some children felt responsible for the parents' divorce. The oldest group (those between 5 and 6 years old) showed general restlessness, heightened anxiety, irritability, and moodiness. This group, however, showed a better degree of adjustment to the parents' divorce than the youngest or middle groups of children. These older children were the least affected in their developmental progress. The role of the school environment and involvement with peers may have assisted these children in compensating for a difficult home environment.

Wallerstein and Kelly (1975) report sex differences in the adjustment of children to the parents' divorce a year later. A significantly larger number of preschool-aged girls were more troubled than boys at the end of this period. Changes in relations with both parents were described also. In contrast to 30 per cent of the mothers who felt that their relationship with their child had not changed after their divorce, 44 per cent of the mothers stated that the relationship with their child was less gratifying, had more conflict, and was more limited in scope than before the divorce. The reverse was true for the child's relationship with the father. Of the fathers, 44 per cent reported an improved relationship with their child that was more consistent and satisfying in quality as compared with 26 per cent of the fathers who reported a decline in interest as shown in decreased visits and attitudes toward being involved with their child. These differences in relations between mothers and children and fathers and children can be traced to the increased role strain of the mothers who took on the additional role functions of the father as well as their own in child rearing. Fathers, being freed considerably from the daily interactions that inevitably produce conflicts of varying degrees, could more freely explore the dynamics of interaction with their child after the divorce. The prolonged absence of the child from the fathers' lives before the divorce perhaps led many of these to value their child even more after the divorce had occurred.

Wallerstein and Kelly (1976) studied the reactions of nine- and ten-year-old children to divorce. These reactions included feelings of hurt, rejection by the absent parent, helplessness over the situation, and loneliness. The investigators found that the school-aged children of their study were angry at either one parent or both, a reaction similar to that found in preschool-aged children. The school-aged children were found to have pervasive fears, and one fourth of the group were worried about being forgotten or abandoned by their parents. Few children were found to feel that they were the cause of their parents' divorce. Although identity with the family group generally shifts to that of the peer group in middle childhood, the authors noted that the family identity of these school-aged children was threatened by the divorce. Another outcome of divorce was an alignment with one parent following the divorce that actively worked to exclude or reject the other parent. This reaction occurred in slightly over one fourth of the sample studied and was found to be initiated by the parent rather than by the child. A reassuring reaction also reported was the school-aged children's empathetic response to a distressed parent or siblings by being especially sensitive to the emotional needs of the others.

Adolescents' reactions to divorce can be expected to differ from those of younger children. Sorosky (1977) describes the varying reactions among adolescents according to factors that include (1) the emotional environment of the home prior to the divorce; (2) the nature of the divorce; (3) the relationship of the parents following the divorce; (4) the age of the adolescent at the time of the divorce; and (5) the strength and coping mechanisms available to the adolescent in adjusting to the divorce.

Sorosky (1977) states that the turmoil and bitterness of a bad marriage ("emotional divorce") can cause more inner turmoil to an adolescent than the actual divorce of the parents. This report reconfirms Nye's (1957) earlier findings on the emotional climates of broken versus unhappy intact families. Reactions of teenagers to the divorce of parents can occur and include (1) a fear of abandonment, rejection, or loss of love; (2) interference with psychological and developmental progress toward personal identity; and (3), most important, a fear of failure in their own future marriage, according to Sorosky (1977). Most adolescents were not surprised by their parents' divorce. Many reported a sense of relief that an end was in sight to the emotional upheaval in the family. An abrupt dissolution of the parents' marriage gave teenagers a more difficult adjustment problem than an anticipated divorce. In reviewing research on the effects of divorce on children, Sorosky notes that continued conflicts between parents after the divorce can produce pathological reactions in adolescents. He notes as well that the younger a teenager at the time of the parents' divorce, the more likely he will be to experience the departure of a parent as a personal abandonment and loss of the parent's love. Regressive behaviors have been noted in young adolescents whose parents divorce as well as hostile and sexual acting-out behaviors. The older adolescent shows a better degree of adjustment and approaches the situation with a more mature perspective. Sorosky finds that the adolescent who has the greater skills in adapting to change fares better than the one who experiences separation anxiety.

The findings of these studies on children's reactions to divorce are highly negative and represent a dour, depressing picture. It is important to note, however, that the findings of these studies were largely based on small samples of children who were being seen by medical personnel because of their problems in adjusting to their parents' divorce. Not all children who experience the divorce of parents react as described by these studies, although most researchers agree that no children escape completely the impact of family disruption.

Support Systems for One-Parent Families

The single-parent family has some assistance in making adjustments to the variety of changes resulting from this new status. Although the one-parent family's greatest strength may come from its own members, support systems in the community are helpful in assisting the adults to make the transition to new roles and responsibilities.

Single-parent organizations may offer the best opportunities for therapeutic support, services, and information for many single mothers and fathers. These organizations, such as Parents Without Partners (PWP) and programs offered by the Family Life Council or by religious groups, are found more commonly in large urban settings. Patricia Clayton (1971) and Robert Weiss (1973) describe the functions of Parents Without Partners in meeting the needs of the single parent. Weiss identifies four types of support that PWP provides its members.

1. *The organization acts as a sustaining community* because it is composed of people who accept the single parent and can share the problems that are experienced, particularly those that relate to child rearing. Because many single parents experience social isolation in their new status, PWP promotes social activities for both single families and single adults. In providing this highly visible service, PWP chapters sponsor activities that provide an opportunity for members to meet prospective spouses or to find companionship. Although this can be advantageous, it may tend on the other hand to drive some men away because they fear "being trapped" by aggressive women who seek a new father for their children (Hunt, 1966; Orthner, Brown, and Ferguson, 1976).

2. *The organization brings people together who share common concerns.* Weiss reports that women find PWP activities particularly valuable in providing opportunities to form friendships with other women who are experiencing problems of adjustment similar to their own. This function fulfills an emotional as well as a situational need.

3. Parents Without Partners acts *to promote a sense of personal growth* by recognizing members' service to the organization.

4. The group also provides a means for *establishing a new emotional attachment to others*. This service acts to combat the feelings of loneliness and isolation that the single parent experiences in role adjustment. Most of these functions are served through social activities, group discussions, special pro-

grams on child rearing and other topics, and activities where children who lack a father or mother can be exposed to appropriate adult role models.

Other sources of assistance to the single parent are therapeutic groups conducted by local mental health departments or organizations. A number of researchers (Hiltz, 1975; Hozman and Froiland, 1976; Morris and Prescott, 1975) describe group therapy approaches in working with single parents. These approaches may attract those individuals who fail to find a sufficient degree of similarity between their needs and those provided by PWP chapters. The children may be in need of the objective guidance of individuals trained in these helping professions. The costs of such services are usually determined according to ability to pay.

Meeting child-care needs is often a major problem for both single fathers and single mothers. Most researchers report that the single parent cannot depend on relatives or in-laws to assist in providing child care because of the great distances between families or the inability or unwillingness of these individuals to provide the needed support. Day-care centers and other child-care facilities are used as community resources of child-care assistance. Locating quality facilities that are also convenient presents a major problem for single parents. Mothers who qualify for the Aid to Families of Dependent Children or Work Incentive programs administered through state social service departments receive financial assistance for child-care services as they prepare for vocations through training or are employed in the work force.

RECONSTITUTED FAMILIES

The high divorce rate in our country is accompanied by an equally high rate of remarriage after divorce. Glick and Norton (1973) state that the rate of remarriage among widowed and divorced women increased by 40 per cent during the 1960s and early 1970s. Plateris (1973) states that the proportion of divorced individuals with children under eighteen years of age is highest when they are in their late twenties and early thirties and declines thereafter with increases in age (see Figure 8-3). The remarriage of adults creates a *reconstituted* family or the restitution of the vacant adult role of a one-parent family. Occasionally two one-parent families will merge through the remarriage of the adults.

There is not a great deal of empirical evidence about the functioning or difficulties of reconstituted families. Jesse Bernard (1956) found in a comprehensive study of remarriage that both stepparents and stepchildren had predominantly accepting and favorable attitudes toward one another. The children were favorable in their attitudes toward the parents' remarriage and had friendly attitudes toward their new father. Both stepparents experienced favorable and affectionate attitudes about the children involved. These findings may help to alleviate the impressions we have that stepchildren are rejecting of the new stepparent. Bernard points out, however, that adolescents

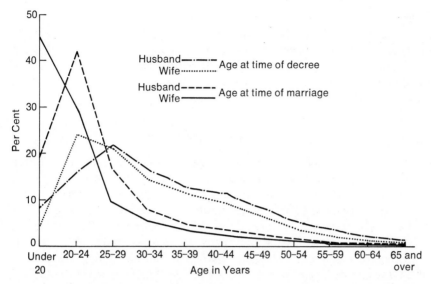

Figure 8-3. Distribution of individuals by age and sex at time of marriage and time of divorce in 1969. (Source: Plateris, A. Divorces: Analysis of changes, 1969. *Vital and Health Statistics,* 1973, *21,* 1–58.)

may be less accepting of the new parent than younger children or young adults.

In reviewing studies on the interpersonal relations of reconstituted families, Bowerman and Irish (1962), conclude that these families have a more stressful environment and are less organized or cohesive than intact families not broken by divorce or the death of one of the parents. Stepmothers are found to have more difficult adjustments and interactions, particularly when the children are teenagers upon her entrance into the family. Stepdaughters were found to have more difficult and extreme reactions than stepsons to the new stepmother.

The reconstitution of the family, however, generally seems to overcome some of the difficulties and impact on children of divorce or the death of a parent. Wilson, Zurcher, McAdams, and Curtis (1975) report that they could find only small and rather insignificant differences in children of reconstituted families and those from unbroken families. The differences that were found suggest to these investigators that a child who has lived in a family where the stepfather occupies the reconstituted role may have a predominantly positive, negative, or mixed experience in this family.

Special parenting problems may arise for the individual who occupies a reconstituted role in a former one-parent family. Both men and women who become stepparents may approach their new role with some trepidation or fear of the unknown. These individuals literally come into a family situation where they may be considered an outsider, and the entire family interaction pattern must accommodate to the new member's cognitive style and personality pattern. The single mother who marries or remarries is confronted with relinquishing her established authority in managing family affairs. Although some women experience this change with great relief and ease, others state that they must work hard to realign their role with that of their new spouse (Kogelschatz, Adams, and Tucker, 1972).

THE ADOLESCENT AND UNWED PARENT

Marriage between adolescents has never been an unusual occurrence in our culture, although the minority of people who marry have been in this age bracket. There has been a slow but steady increase in the percentage of teenagers who marry since 1890, although fewer marriages among teenagers were reported in 1970 than in 1950 (see Figure 8-4) (Hetzel and Capetta, 1973).

Although the median age at first marriage was 23.5 years for males and 20.6 years for females in 1974, one marriage in thirteen during this year involved a female between 14 and 17 years of age (U.S. Bureau of the Census, 1976). Statistics show that more teenage girls than teenage boys get married (see Figure 8-5). The teenage marriage rate in 1969 was 88 per 1,000 marriages for females and 35 per 1,000 marriages for males (Hetzel and Capetta, 1973). The reasons are the advanced development of girls and the cultural tendency for females to marry older males.

Individuals face the likelihood of having a "high-risk" relationship when they marry during adolescence. *High risk* refers to the probability of an unstable relationship that will end in divorce sooner than the average marital relationship. Divorce rates are considerably higher when one or both individuals marry before age twenty (deLissovoy, 1973; Hetzel and Capetta, 1973; Lorenzi, Klerman, and Jekel, 1977; Nye, 1976; Reiner and Edwards, 1974). Figure 8-6 shows the percentage of husbands and wives divorced in 1969 who had married as teenagers. Almost half of the women and one quarter of the men had married at some time during adolescence.

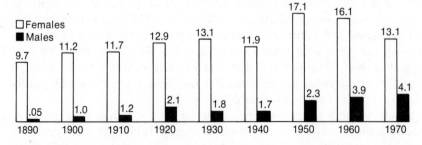

Figure 8-4. Per cent of adolescents ever married, by age and sex, United States, 1890–1970. (Source: Hetzel, A., & Capetta, M. Teenagers: Marriages, divorces, parenthood, and mortality. *Vital and Health Statistics*, 1973, 21, Whole No. 23.)

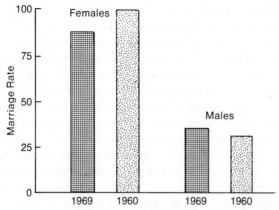

Figure 8-5. Estimated marriage rates of teenagers by sex per 1000 marriages in 1960 and 1969. (Source: Hetzel, A., & Capetta, M. Teenagers: Marriages, divorces, parenthood, and mortality. *Vital and Health Statistics*, 1973, *21*, Whole No. 23.)

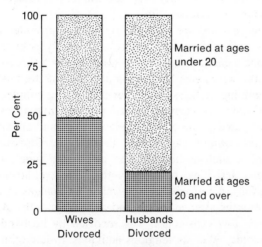

Figure 8-6. Per cent of husbands and wives who were divorced in 1969 and who had married during adolescence. (Source: Hetzel, A., & Capetta, M. Teenagers: Marriages, divorces, parenthood, and mortality. *Vital and Health Statistics*, 1973, *21*, Whole No. 23.)

Because marriage between teenagers has the statistical probability of being an unstable relationship, why does the marriage occur at all? The variety of reasons include (1) personality factors; (2) initiation of a pregnancy; and

(3) status recognition from peers. Reiner and Edwards (1974) report a study of fifty couples who married as teenagers. Almost all of these described their parents as being divorced, separated, alcoholic, or mentally ill. Severe conflict among the family members was mentioned by all the individuals in the study. Reiner and Edwards note that these same precipitating events can result in a teenager's running away from home. Although almost half of the couples were expecting a baby when they married, these authors point out that few couples felt that they were forced to get married. The individuals may have married to escape a poor home situation. It is also possible that they were more advanced in their psychosocial development, had pursued the development of their sense of intimacy, and had entered the sense of generativity stage before their age-mates. Another possible explanation mentioned by these investigators was that marriage represented an achievement of adult status and was an expression of independence and autonomy.

What kind of life can teenagers expect when they marry? Teenagers entering into marriage are rather naive in expecting life to be relatively free of problems. Romantic notions about marriage and parenthood are overemphasized in our culture, according to LeMasters (1974). Teenagers soon discover the unreality of their expectations when a baby arrives, the husband or wife has no job, and one or the other feels too immature, insecure, or "trapped" to maintain a marriage relationship.

A comprehensive study by deLissovoy (1973) provides an in-depth examination of the difficulties, adjustments, and life-styles of teenaged married couples. Sixty-one teenage couples were studied over a three-year period. The average age of the wives was 16.5 years and that of the husbands was 17.1 years at the beginning of the study. Over half of the couples were expecting a baby, providing the primary motivation of the marriages. A number of areas were investigated in the couples' relationships and are summarized here.

1. *Marriage adjustment* was studied through the individuals' reactions to a variety of topics, such as how income was spent, type and degree of religious and social activities, relations with in-laws, child-training methods, and sexual relations. Comparisons were made in changes in ratings on these topics at three months after marriage and at thirty months after marriage. In the initial ratings, low satisfaction was reported by husbands and wives on the spending income, whereas religious activities, in-law relations, and child-training methods were rated moderate to high in degree of satisfaction. The low ratings on spending income related to not having enough money to cover expenses because the median weekly income was $38. The majority of couples received some form of public financial assistance. Parents and other family members helped almost all the couples financially. Husbands rated sexual relations as low in satisfaction, whereas wives did the opposite. The husbands apparently wished for more frequent sexual intercourse, whereas the wives indicated a desire for more emotional and affectional expression and less frequent intercourse. The moderate to high ratings in other areas (religious

activities, in-law relations, and child training) reflect how these areas influenced the teenagers of the sample. The majority attended church regularly and felt that the church provided a sense of community and filled an emotional need for acceptance by others. Relations with in-laws presented few problems for most couples, showing the support of this primary reference group at the early stage of marriage. Few of the couples had had a child during the first rating period, and high ratings in satisfaction with child training reflected their idealized notions about parenthood *before* the arrival of their child.

When ratings were made by both husbands and wives thirty months after marriage and comparisons were made with the ratings taken at three months after mariage, differences were found in degree of satisfaction in the areas of social activities, mutual friends, child-training methods, and sexual relations among the husbands. Differences were found among wives' ratings in these areas as well as in the area of in-law relations. Spending family income continued to be rated low in satisfaction by both husbands and wives. The husbands lost interest in religious activities over this period, whereas the wives continued to find high satisfaction in this area. Satisfaction with social activities and mutual friends declined. The greatest change among both husbands and wives was in child-training methods. A significant decline in satisfaction ratings over this time period showed the impact of the realities of child care *after* having a baby. DeLissovoy notes that these changes reflect the general pattern in decline of marital satisfaction shown by other studies but that this occurred earlier in the marriages of the adolescents he studied because of their earlier age at marriage and their living conditions.

2. *Teenagers' preparation for parenting* is an area that is of special interest. Dr. deLissovoy questioned both husbands and wives who had a baby at the early stages of his study regarding their knowledge of developmental norms of child growth. Table 8-1 shows the responses of these young parents and compares these to the ages at which research shows the expected occurrence of developmental events in infancy. These young parents' lack of knowledge of when to expect an infant to show developmental progress has immense implications regarding the quality of these teenage parents' caregiving. Clearly these individuals may have failed to use behavioral and developmental clues from their child to guide their caregiving efforts, relying on highly erroneous impressions of when children achieve mastery of certain skills and when they should be developmentally ready to receive guidance and appropriate caregiving. The times given by the teenage parents for toilet-training (twenty-four weeks or six months of age) and obedience training (either twenty-six weeks or thirty-six weeks), for example, have serious implications that lead one to wonder how both parents and child reacted if such training actually did begin at these estimated times. One of the primary implications that deLissovoy mentions in reaction to these findings is the importance of school programs to provide training in child development principles and parenting skills for

Table 8-1. Teenage Parents' Knowledge of Developmental Norms

Developmental Event	Fathers' Estimate	Mothers' Estimate	Gesell Norms
First social smile	3 weeks	3 weeks	6 weeks
Unsupported sitting	12 weeks	6 weeks	40 weeks
Pull to standing position	24 weeks	20 weeks	40 weeks
Takes first steps	40 weeks	40 weeks	36–48 weeks
Achieves bladder control	24 weeks	24 weeks	48–96 weeks
Achieves bowel control	26 weeks	24 weeks	96–144 weeks
First meaningful word	32 weeks	26 weeks	36–48 weeks
Start obedience training	36 weeks	26 weeks	72–96 weeks
Recognizes wrongdoing	52 weeks	42 weeks	96–144 weeks

Source: V. deLissovoy. High school marriages: A longitudinal study. *Journal of Marriage and the Family*, 1973, *35*, 244–255. Copyright 1973 by the National Council on Family Relations. Reprinted by permission.

all teenagers and especially those who become married or pregnant during adolescence.

Dr. deLissovoy also administered a scale to measure the attitudes of teenage mothers toward children and child rearing. The results suggest that the mothers were generally impatient and intolerant with their children.

There is cultural pressure for teenage girls to marry the biological father of their child in the event that a pregnancy is initiated and carried to term. The results of a study by Lorenzi, Klerman, and Jekel (1977) suggest that this may not necessarily be the wisest course to take for several reasons. Of the group of adolescent girls in their study, only 23 per cent had married the fathers of their child, and 35 per cent either never saw the child's father again or had married another male. However, 23 per cent, still saw the child's father regularly and 18 per cent saw him occasionally. This suggests that the relationship is not a casual one between the teenage mother and father.

The general concerns of professionals regarding early marriage are the difficulties that can be expected by individuals, the impact of these marriages on the personal growth and development of the individuals involved, and the implications for the children of such marriages. Using Erikson's framework, one would expect that troubles would be encountered by teenagers who attempt to preempt developmental preparation for the sense of intimacy and generativity while still developing a sense of identity. Both statistics and findings of research on early marriage support this assumption. In spite of the decline in teenage marriages, communities need to face this problem. Recent judiciary rulings and legislation have forced school systems to discontinue their practice of discriminating against the participation of married teenagers in educational and extracurricular activities. Many professionals believe that community support through educational programs could alleviate much of the anxiety and dissatisfaction that teenagers face in marriage and in their family relationships. Examples of such programs will be discussed in a later section of this chapter.

Special Problems of Pregnant Teenagers

The decline in the number of teenage marriages has been replaced by an increase in both the number of teenage girls who carry a baby to term and retain custody of the child and by the number of abortions initiated by teenagers. There are two age groups of women considered to be at risk when pregnant: those under fifteen years of age and those over thirty-five years of age. The term *risk* applies to the health and well-being of both the mother and the infant. The teenage girl who becomes pregnant risks a number of complications of pregnancy that relate directly and indirectly to the successful delivery and survival of a healthy baby. The factors that place both the mother and the child at risk are discussed here.

Incidence and Cause of Teenage Pregnancies

Hetzel and Capetta (1973) report that in 1968 there were 600,816 recorded births among teenaged women, or 17 per cent of all births in the United States. Of the births to teenaged mothers in this particular year, 98 per cent were to women between fifteen and nineteen years of age. The majority of these (77 per cent) were the first child born to the mothers. Eighteen per cent of the teenagers were having a second child, and four per cent were having a third child.

As a group, teenagers have failed to show a significant decline in birth rates as compared with other age groups (see Figure 8-7). Zelnick and Kantner (1974) found that in 1971 almost three in ten teenaged women who experienced premarital intercourse became pregnant. Of these, 35 per cent married before delivery or abortion, and another 10 percent married after the birth of their child. The remaining 55 per cent did not marry. Of these, 60 per cent carried their baby to term, 19 per cent had abortions, and 8 per cent had miscarriages. These figures show that the usual outcome of teenage pregnancy is the illegitimate birth of a baby. This situation has numerous social, psychological, and economic implications for both mother and child.

The decline in marriage rates among teenagers partially accounts for the

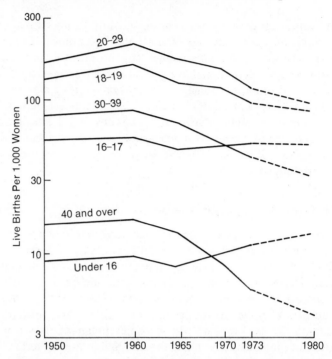

Figure 8-7. Fertility rates by age of mothers, United States, 1950 to 1980. (Source: Stickle, G., & Ma, P. Pregnancy in adolescents: Scope of the problem. *Contemporary OB-GYN*, 1975, *5*, 85–91.)

rise in illegitimacy rates. In 1968, for example, births among teenage women accounted for 49 per cent of the total illegitimate births for that year (Hetzel and Capetta, 1973), and in 1973, 53 per cent of the total illegitimate births occurred among women of this age group (U.S. Department of Health, Education, and Welfare, 1975).

The leading and most obvious cause of teenage pregnancy is lack of contraceptive use by either the boy or the girl. This lack of contraception has underlying motivations that can range from ignorance of what to use or how to use it to premeditated carelessness with the full intention of initiating a pregnancy if possible.

A number of studies trace the cause of teenage pregnancy to lack of adequate contraceptive knowledge and the inaccessibility of the various forms of birth control. Psychological motives are discussed as well in many studies (Aug and Bright, 1970; Furstenberg, 1971; Coblinger, 1974; Furstenberg, Gordis, and Markowitz, 1969; Johnson, 1974; Jurhasz, 1974; Sandberg and Jacobs, 1971; Sklar and Beckov, 1974; Zelnick and Kantner, 1974). Studies by Furstenberg and his associates (1969, 1971) find that most teenage pregnancies are unintentional and do not result from promiscuous sexual behavior or a casual, "one-night-stand" sexual encounter. Limited knowledge about female contraception and not having confidential access to these methods account for the majority of the pregnancies that were studied. Most of the girls had a stable, long-term relationship with the fathers of their babies and continued to see the father after delivery. The investigators also discovered that the girls generally did not want to become pregnant and saw this as interfering with their education and prospects for marriage in the future. Coblinger (1974) also found that misinformation about birth control methods as well as psychological factors resulted in pregnancies among the teenagers he studied. Only 17 per cent of his sample of 211 single adolescent girls who became pregnant made some attempt to obtain contraceptive knowledge, and only 10 per cent had used some method unsuccessfully or incorrectly. Another 11 per cent of the girls became pregnant under false information about and lack of understanding of the process of conception. For example, some believed that avoidance of orgasms prevented conception or that vaginal suppositories acted as spermicides. Others simply took a chance that they would not become pregnant when being sexually active.

Other reasons mentioned by pregnant adolescents that are more psychological in nature are discussed by Sklar and Beckov (1974). Some teenagers feel that the use of contraceptives constitutes a premeditated preparation for intended intercourse. They feel that such preparation is contrary to an ideal notion of sexual relations' occurring under natural or spontaneous circumstances. Others feel that these methods are unnatural and harmful to their health or that they are too young to become pregnant. Zelnick and Kantner (1974) also state that the teenagers in their study either wanted to become pregnant or did not mind becoming pregnant. This attitude probably reflects the idea that a pregnancy will result in marriage to the father of the child (Zelnick and Kantner, 1972).

Other studies, however, show that illegitimacy is neither desirable or intended as a consequence of intercourse by teenagers. Although much of the stigma attached to illegitimacy has lessened in recent years because of greater family and community acceptance of out-of-wedlock births, Johnson (1974) states that married and separated clients of the Aid to Families with Dependent Children program did not support illegitimacy among single adolescent girls but did approve of premarital sexual relations that occurred with correct contraceptive information and use of methods. In the sample that Butts and Sporakowski (1974) studied, single adolescent girls who chose abortion were significantly more satisfied with their decision compared with those who chose to carry their pregnancy to term. The girls who chose abortion may have realized the disruptive impact of pregnancy and motherhood on educational opportunities or their lack of emotional and personal preparation to assume the responsibilities of child rearing at this time in their lives.

Risks in Adolescent Pregnancy

There are many physical complications in adolescent pregnancy. Pregnant teenagers risk three times the normal probability of experiencing maternal toxemia (a condition characterized by high blood pressure, retention of body fluids, and rapid weight gains) and death (Aubrey and Pennington, 1973; Grant and Heald, 1973; Ruppersberg, 1973). Prolonged and precipitate (too quick) delivery were found by Semmens and Lamers (1968) to decrease with age among adolescents. Stevenson (1973) states that the incidence of anemia, postpartum infection, and hemorrhage is increased among pregnant teenagers.

Social and psychological factors that place the single adolescent mother at risk during pregnancy and after delivery include interrupted education, lack of adequate prenatal care, reduced earning potential, improper nutrition, and interrupted physical and psychological development. Sugar (1976) attributes many of these psychological complications of teenage pregnancy to race, marital status, unsuspected infection, self-induced abortion attempts, endocrine disorders, reproductive tract abnormalities, and disadvantageous psychological and socioeconomic conditions.

Adolescent girls are generally described as being ambivalent about assuming or conducting the mothering role (Sugar, 1976). A number of studies reviewed by this investigator point to conflicts of the adolescent girl in wanting to mother her baby and wishing for the continued nurturance of her own mother. Whether this is a cause or a result of pregnancy among teenagers is debatable. Sugar reports that the adolescent mothers he studied provided inadequate stimulation for their babies in the first six months after birth as compared with older mothers. Many adolescent mothers may very likely fail to develop adequate mothering skills because of the interference (whether well intentioned or not) from their own mothers, who often provide the primary care for the grandchild.

Risk Factors for Babies of Adolescent Mothers

The chances of a healthy life are not as good for infants of adolescent mothers as for those of older mothers. A variety of factors affecting the health and well-being of infants result from the interaction of age, race, and socioeconomic and nutritional status. During adolescence, all of these factors culminate in increasing the risks of not having a healthy baby—one who is free of congenital defects, can survive the birth, and continues to grow and develop normally after birth.

Two of the most consistent findings of the outcome of adolescent pregnancies are the high prematurity rate and the low birth weight of babies (Campbell, Clague, and Godfrey, 1973; College of Obstetricians and Gynecologists, 1974; Sugar, 1976) (see Figure 8-8). Age, life-style, socioeconomic

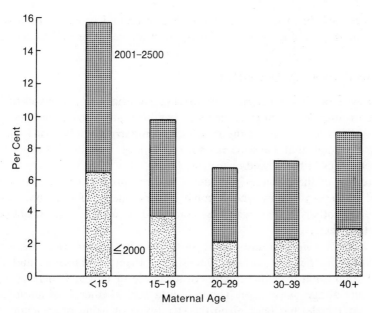

Figure 8-8. Per cent of live births weighing 2,500 grams or less by age of mothers. (Source: Stickle, G., & Ma, P. Pregnancy in adolescents: Scope of the problem. *Contemporary OB-GYN*, 1975, 5, 85–91.)

and nutritional status, and lack of adequate prenatal care are usually mentioned as the causes. Prematurity and low birth weight are associated with low survival rates, circulatory and respiratory difficulties, high incidence of brain damage, and prolonged hospitalization. The likely result for the baby is to be born defective. These infants can be born mentally retarded, diabetic, or physically handicapped, or may have other serious defects (Walters, 1975). The National Foundation/March of Dimes (1976) reports that the rate of birth defects in babies increases as weight at birth decreases. Of the babies weighing over 5½ pounds at birth, 6 per cent have defects of some type, whereas 30 per cent of babies weighing less than 4½ pounds at birth have defects. Teenagers who are fifteen years old or younger have the highest incidence of low-birth-weight babies resulting in an infant mortality rate that is twice as great as that for babies of women between twenty and thirty-four years of age (Stickle and Ma, 1975).

The seriousness of the incidence of birth defects in babies of adolescent mothers cannot be measured accurately in the terms that these figures try to convey. The loss of a baby's life; the impact of supporting, training, and educating a handicapped child; and the emotional impact of this situation on the parent cannot be measured accurately in monetary or any other terms. The optimistic prospect of dealing with these problems is that there are ways to prevent low birth weight and other health-related problems of both adolescent mothers and their babies. These are discussed later in this chapter.

The Adolescent or Unwed Father

The fathers of children born to adolescent girls have not received the same degree of attention from researchers as has been given to the mothers. Relatively little is known about the married or unmarried adolescent father, and the few studies that have been conducted have examined the personality characteristics of the unwed or teenage father.

A review of these studies provides a less comprehensive idea of the number of adolescent males who become fathers, their feelings about being a father, and other related factors as compared to what is known about adolescent mothers.

1. *There are no accurate figures on the number of age categories of teenage boys who become fathers.* One study (Pannor, Massarik, and Evans, 1971) found that over one quarter of a sample of unwed fathers were nineteen years of age or younger. The unwed father, whether he is an adolescent or an older male, has been given the stereotype of being promiscuous in his sexual behavior, and therefore it is too difficult to try to keep accurate figures on how frequently he fathers a child. Some teenage girls may not be able to identify the father of their child because of the number of sexual contacts that could have resulted in their pregnancy.

2. *The unmarried father is not a considerably older male who seduces a naive teenage girl.* The majority of fathers in the Pannor et al. study were within four years of the age of the unmarried mother. This finding is supported by other investigators (Lorenzi, Klerman, and Jekel, 1977; Young, 1954).

3. *He is probably an illegitimate child himself.* Robbins and Lynn (1973) found that more teenage fathers of their sample were illegitimate children themselves and had siblings who had illegitimate children than a comparison group of nonfathers of the same age.

4. *He may be less mature, have less self-control, and be more physically active than nonfathers his age.* Pannor et al. and Pauker (1971) report that the males in their studies had difficulties in interpersonal interactions because of a weak masculine identification and a great degree of irresponsible behavior.

5. *He maintains or has had a long-range relationship with the mother.* Several studies show that fathers and mothers dated or went together for six months or longer prior to the initiation of the pregnancy (Lorenzi et al., 1977; Pannor et al., 1977; Pope, 1967).

The explanation of why less attention has been paid to the unwed father than the mother involves both legal and social factors. It is difficult to prove the paternity of a child. The laws governing the custody of illegitimate children have long recognized the right of the mother over the father to the child. These laws, having come from English common law, have not been questioned until recently. Unwed fathers have not had any legal rights to the custody of their children, nor has their consent been necessary for abortion or for the release of the child for adoption. Two rulings by the United States Supreme Court (*Rothstein* vs. *Lutheran Social Services of Wisconsin and Upper Michigan,* 1972; *Stanley* vs. *Illinois,* 1972); were necessary to outline clearly the legal rights of unwed fathers regarding the guardianship of their illegitimate child. These decisions reverse the older pattern that the unwed mother is the only legal parent of an illegitimate child. Dukette and Stevenson (1973) note that social service and adoption agencies must now gain the unwed father's consent before an illegitimate child can be legally placed for adoption. These legal decisions have many implications regarding the responsibilities of unwed fathers toward their illegitimate children. These range from the child's rights to inheritance from the father and the availability of professional social work services to gaining custody of the child as the legal parent.

SUPPORT SYSTEMS FOR ADOLESCENT PARENTS

The adolescent parent currently receives more support from the community than in the past. A variety of social and human service programs are available in many communities. An example is the Aid to Families with Dependent Children program that provides child care and financial support as well as food stamps, maternal and prenatal care, payment of hospital costs, and limited provision of the necessary nursery equipment for adolescents who qualify under the federal poverty guidelines.

Programs have been developed recently to mainstream pregnant adolescents or those who are adolescent parents into schools (Cromwell and Gangel, 1974; Mackay and Milloy, 1974). Pregnant or married girls and married boys were formerly expelled from school or not allowed to participate in regular school programming. Recent government and judicial rulings have determined that school districts discriminate against these girls and boys by enforcing such policies. Many school districts in larger metropolitan settings have introduced special support programs for teenage mothers. These programs attempt to provide a therapeutic approach to helping teenage mothers to continue their psychosocial progress in meeting the developmental tasks of adolescence and to adjust to the impending change in their lives of becoming a parent. Instruction in required academic topics may take place in these programs or as a part of regular school attendance. Special instruction is given, however, on nutrition in pregnancy, child development principles, and parenting skills. Practicum experiences with infants and young children are sometimes incorporated into this specialized instruction to provide practical experiences with children. When teenagers participate in such programs, their return rate to regular school programs is greatly improved after the baby's birth (Adams et al., 1976; Ewer and Gibbs, 1977).

One of the most promising approaches to educating teenagers to the hazards and risks of pregnancy at this time in life is the "Healthy Babies: Chance or Choice" project. This program is jointly sponsored by the Future Homemakers of America and The National Foundation/March of Dimes (Teen Times, 1977). Both organizations have dovetailed their interests in bettering the quality of life by training groups of teenagers to conduct peer-education programs in their local junior and senior high schools. The FHA members provide the manpower and innovative ideas to reach their peer audiences, and the March of Dimes provides expertise in training, literature, and audiovisual materials. The goal of this project is to promote the prospects of a healthier next generation of children. The idea and approach of using peer education by adolescents to reach other adolescents is more effective than adults' performing these same functions because of the influence of peers during this developmental stage.

The March of Dimes also sponsors another project, "Operation Birthright," aimed at involving young adults in peer education. The program has been developed to educate young people regarding the causes of birth defects and is adaptable to many different audiences through workshops, conferences, and speeches sponsored locally by clubs and other groups that involve young adults.

POINTS TO CONSIDER

- Fathers and mothers react differently to the problems they encounter as single parents.
- Reactions of children in one-parent families are diverse, and adjustments differ according to the age of the child and the circumstances of family life.
- Supports for one-parent families are available in many communities and may be used more readily by women than by men.
- Little information is available on reconstituted families. Research generally shows that the reconstitution of adult roles in a family overcomes some of the children's problems associated with divorce or the death of a parent.
- Early marriage, particularly during adolescence, is characterized as a high-risk relationship having a high probability of divorce and requiring greater adjustments than marriages involving older individuals.
- Pregnancy in adolescence is characterized as high risk to both mother and infant in terms of physical, psychological, social, and economic hazards.
- Community supports for adolescent parents are essentially educational and therapeutic.

REFERENCES

ADAMS, B., BROWNSTEIN, C., RENALLS, I., and SCHMITT, M. The pregnant adolescent: A group approach. *Adolescence*, 1976, *11*, 467–485.

AUBREY, R., and PENNINGTON, J. Identification and evaluation of high risk pregnancies. *Clinical Obstetrics and Gynecology*, 1973, *16*, 3–27.

AUG, R., and BRIGHT, T. A study of wed and unwed motherhood in adolescents and young adults. *Journal of American Academy of Child Psychiatry*, 1970, *9*, 577–594.

BERNARD, J. *Remarriage: A study of marriage*. New York: Dryden Press, 1956.

BOWERMAN, C., and IRISH, D. Some relationships of stepchildren to their parents. *Journal of Marriage and the Family*, 1962, *24*, 113–121.

BRANDWEIN, R., BROWN, C., and FOX, E. Women and children last: The social situation of divorced mothers and their families. *Journal of Marriage and the Family*, 1974, *36*, 498–514.

BURGESS, J. The single-parent family: A social and sociological problem. *Family Coordinator*, 1970, *19*, 137–144.

BUTTS, R., and SPORAKOWSKI, M. Unwed pregnancy decisions: Some background factors. *Journal of Sex Research*, 1974, *19*, 110–117.

CAMPBELL, A., CLAGUE, A., and GODFREY, F. United States fertility rates. *Vital and Health Statistics*, 1973, *21*, Whole No. 24.

CARTER, H., and GLICK, P. *Marriage and divorce: A social and economic study*. Cambridge, Mass.: Harvard University Press, 1970.

CLAYTON, P. Meeting the needs of the single parent family. *Family Coordinator*, 1971, *20*, 327–336.

COBLINGER, W. Pregnancy in the single adolescent girl: The role of cognitive factors. *Journal of Youth and Adolescence*, 1974, *3*, 17–29.

College of Obstetricians and Gynecologists. *Nutrition in maternal health*. Chicago: The College, 1974.

CROMWELL, R., and GANGEL, J. A social "action" program directed to single pregnant girls and adolescent parents. *Family Coordinator*, 1974, *23*, 61–66.

DELISSOVOY, V. High school marriages: A longitudinal study. *Journal of Marriage and the Family*, 1973, *35*, 244–255.

DUKETTE, R., and STEVENSON, N. The legal rights of unmarried fathers: The impact of recent court decisions. *Social Service Review*, 1973, *47*, 1–14.

EWER, P., and GIBBS, J. School return among pregnant adolescents. *Journal of Youth and Adolescence*, 1977, *5*, 221–229.

FURSTENBERG, F. Birth control experience among pregnant adolescents: The process of unplanned parenthood. *Social Problems*, 1971, *19*, 192–203.

FURSTENBERG, F., GORDIS, L., and MARKOWITZ, M. Birth control knowledge and attitudes among unmarried pregnant adolescents: A preliminary report. *Journal of Marriage and the Family*, 1969, *31*, 34–42.

GASSER, R., and TAYLOR, C. Role adjustment of single parent fathers with dependent children. *Family Coordinator*, 1976, *25*, 397–401.

GLASSER, P., and NAVARRE, E. Structural problems of the one-parent family. *Social Issues*, 1964, *21*, 98–109.

GLICK, P., and NORTON, A. Perspectives on the recent upturn in divorce and remarriage. *Demography*, 1973, *10*, 301–314.

GRANT, J., and HEALD, F. Complications of adolescent pregnancy. *Clinical Pediatrics*, 1973, *83*, 119–123.

HETZEL, A., and CAPETTA, M. Teenagers: Marriages, divorces, parenthood, and mortality. *Vital and Health Statistics*, 1973, *21*, Whole No. 23.

HILL, R. Social stresses on the family. *Social Casework*, 1958, *39*, 139–150.

HILTZ, S. Helping widows: Group discussions as a therapeutic technique. *Family Coordinator*, 1975, *24*, 331–336.

HOUSE, G. Divorced women: How they fare financially. *Journal of Home Economics*, 1976, *68*, 36–38.

HOZMAN, T., and FROILAND, D. Families in divorce: A proposed model for counseling children. *Family Coordinator*, 1976, *25*, 271–276.

HUNT, M. *The world of the formerly married*. New York: McGraw-Hill, 1966.

JOHNSON, C. Attitudes toward premarital sex and family planning for single never-pregnant teenage girls. *Adolescence*, 1974, *9*, 225–262.

JURHASZ, A. The unmarried adolescent parent. *Adolescence*, 1974, *9*, 263–272.

KOGELSCHATZ, J., ADAMS, P., and TUCKER, D. Family styles of fatherless households. *Journal of American Academy of Child Psychiatry*, 1972, *11*, 365–383.

KRIESBERG, L. *Mothers in poverty: A study of fatherless families*. Chicago: Aldine, 1970.

LeMASTERS, E. *Parenthood in modern America* (rev. ed.). Homewood, Ill.: Dorsey, 1974.

LORENZI, M., KLERMAN, L., and JEKEL, J. School-age parents: How permanent a relationship? *Adolescence*, 1977, *12*, 13–22.

MACKAY, B., and MILLOY, M. The impact of teenage pregnancy on the professional educator. *Family Coordinator*, 1974, *23*, 15–18.

MARSDEN, D. *Mothers alone: Poverty and the fatherless family* (rev. ed.). London: Penguin Press, 1973.

MENDES, H. Single fathers. *Family Coordinator*, 1976, *25*, 439–444.

MORRIS, J., and PRESCOTT, M. Transition groups: An approach to dealing with post-partnership anguish. *Family Coordinator*, 1975, *24*, 325–330.

National Foundation/March of Dimes. *Facts: 1976*. White Plains, N.Y.: The Foundation, 1976.

NYE, I. Child adjustment in broken and in unhappy, unbroken homes. *Marriage and Family Living*, 1957, *19*, 356–361.

NYE, I. School-age parenthood: Consequences for babies, mothers, fathers, grandparents, and others. Extension Bulletin 667. Pullman, Washington: Cooperative Extension Service, Washington State University, 1976.

ORTHNER, D., BROWN, T., and FERGUSON, D. Single-parent fatherhood: An emerging family life style. *Family Coodinator*, 1976, *26*, 420–437.

PANNOR, R., MASSARIK, F., and EVANS, B. *The unmarried father*. New York: Springer, 1971.

PAUKER, J. Fathers of children conceived out of wedlock. *Developmental Psychology*, 1971, *4*, 215–218.

PLATERIS, A. Divorces: Analysis of changes, 1969. *Vital and Health Statistics*, 1973, *21*, 1–58.

POPE, H. Unwed mothers and their sex partners. *Journal of Marriage and the Family*, 1967, *29*, 555–567.

REINER, B., and EDWARDS, R. Adolescent marriage: Social or therapeutic problem? *Family Coordinator,* 1974, *23,* 383–390.

ROBBINS, M., and LYNN, D. The unwed fathers: Generation recidivism and attitudes about intercourse in California youth authority wards. *Journal of Sex Research,* 1973, *9,* 334–341.

Rothstein v. *Lutheran Social Services of Wisconsin and Upper Michigan,* 47 Wisconsin 2d 220, 173 N.W. 2d 56, vacated (4-17-72), 40 U.S. L.W., 3498.

RUPPERSBERG, A. Maternal deaths among Ohio teenagers: A sixteen year study. *Ohio State Medical Journal,* 1973, *69,* 692–694.

SANDBERG, E., and JACOBS, R. Psychology of the misuse and rejection of contraception. *American Journal of Obstetrics and Gynecology,* 1971, *110,* 227–236.

SCHLESINGER, B. The one-parent family: An overview. *Family Coordinator,* 1966, *15,* 133–138.

SEMMENS, J., and LAMERS, W. *Teenage pregnancy.* Springfield, Ill.: Charles Thomas, 1968.

SKLAR, J., and BECKOV, B. Teenage family formation in post-war America. *Family Planning Perspectives,* 1974, *6,* 80–90.

SOROSKY, A. The psychological effects of divorce on adolescents. *Adolescence,* 1977, *12,* 123–136.

Stanley v. *Illinois,* 405 U.S. 645, 31, L.Ed. 2nd 551, 92 Supreme Court, 1208, 1972.

STEVENSON, R. *The fetus and newly born infant.* St. Louis: Mosby, 1973.

STICKLE, G., and MA, P. Pregnancy in adolescents: Scope of the problem. *Contemporary OB-GYN,* 1975, *5,* 85–91.

SUGAR, M. At risk factors for the adolescent mother and her infant. *Journal of Youth and Adolescence,* 1976, *3,* 251–270.

Teen Times: Teenage parenting. Future Homemakers of America, Jan.–Feb., 1977.

U.S. Bureau of the Census. *Census of the population: General social and economic characteristics.* Washington, D.C.: The Bureau, 1970.

U.S. Bureau of the Census. *Statistical abstract of the United States: 1976* (97th ed.). Washington, D.C.: The Bureau, 1976.

U.S. Department of Health, Education, and Welfare. National Center for Health Statistics, Monthly Vital Statistics Report: Summary report, final natality statistics, 1973, *23,* 11, Jan. 30, 1975.

WALLERSTEIN, J., and KELLY, J. The effects of parental divorce: Experiences of the preschool child. *Journal of American Academy of Child Psychiatry,* 1975, *14,* 600–616.

WALLERSTEIN, J., and KELLY, J. The effects of parental divorce: Experiences of the child in later latency. *Journal of American Academy of Child Psychiatry,* 1976, *15,* 257–269.

WALTERS, J. Birth defects and adolescent pregnancies. *Journal of Home Economics,* 1975, *67,* 23–27.

WEISS, R. The contributions of an organization of single parents to the well-being of its members. *Family Coordinator,* 1973, *22,* 321–326.

WILSON, L., ZURHER, L., MCADAMS, D., and CURTIS, R. Stepfathers and stepchildren: An exploratory analysis from two national surveys. *Journal of Marriage and the Family*, 1975, *37*, 526–536.

YOUNG, L. *Out of wedlock*. New York: McGraw-Hill, 1954.

ZELNICK, M., and KANTNER, J. The probability of premarital intercourse. *Social Science Research*, 1972, *1*, 335–347.

ZELNICK, M., and KANTNER, J. The resolution of teenage first pregnancies. *Family Planning Perspectives*, 1974, *6*, 74–80.

9

The Challenge of Contemporary Parenthood

A number of ideas have emerged throughout this text regarding the nature, characteristics, and functions of contemporary parent–child relations. Parenting is a complex process that is shaped by a variety of factors. These factors can be summarized as follows:

1. People have greater freedom today to choose to become parents.
2. Parents continue to be a primary source of socialization experiences for children.
3. A competent parent today is one who acquires information about child growth and development as well as a variety of methods for guiding children's emotional and social development.
4. Parenting continues to become an androgynous social role in that the caregiving functions of mothers and fathers have more similarities than differences.
5. Children's behavior and development have a great impact on the style and conduct of parenting behavior.
6. The changing nature of children's developmental needs acts to modify and shape caregiving by parents through the child-rearing years of the family life cycle.
7. The structure of a family affects not only its functioning as a group but also the nature of parent–child relations.
8. The challenge of contemporary parenthood lies in the socialization of children for their future.

Several questions were raised in the first chapter of the text about this last summary point. The socialization of children has always been a primary caregiving function and continues to be for the contemporary parent. This is not the real issue today. The issue that concerns parents today is how children can be effectively taught those skills and abilities that will help them to cope with the rapidly changing and different society of the future.

The family unit of today is changing in response to changes occurring in the larger society. Strains that affect the culture are reflected in strains experienced within the family. In summarizing the influences of change in the larger society on family structure and functioning, Arlene and Jerome Skolnick (1971) list the characteristics of our postindustrial society that have produced changes within the family. Today's society is seen to have:

1. An increased degree of complexity where there is greater division of labor and longer, specialized training for specialized occupations.
2. An increase in the consumption of limited energy and resources.
3. The replacement of human labor by automation.
4. More problems in the distribution of goods and services than in their production.
5. Increased urban growth.
6. Increased, more efficient worldwide communications, which create the emergence of a "world community."
7. A rapid rate of social change.
8. The emergence of learning and knowledge as growth industries.
9. Scientific and technological advances that rapidly replace existing knowledge with new, more relevant information.

The Skolnicks suggest that the rapid pace of social change may present the most serious implications for family life in the future. The period of the 1950s and 1960s saw much rapid social change that has affected family functioning today. The social ferment of this period gave rise to the feeling, according to these writers, that "one generation's knowledge and perspectives are irrelevant for the next." If this is actually the case, then there is a partial explanation for the changes in attitudes toward parenting and the motivations people may have to become parents today. Certainly individuals are more unsure of how to function effectively as parents. The wide variety of strategies of parenting available to parents today is one indication that there is the need for educated guidance and assistance in this role. A greater curiosity about information on human development has also caused a wide exploration of these strategies. There has been a decline in the romantic complex attached to parenting described by LeMasters (1957). People seem to be increasingly disenchanted with the prospects of having a rewarding experience as parents, drawing their impressions and feelings perhaps from their own past experiences in growing up and their anticipated prospects for the future.

For those who do choose to become parents, the central problem of socialization may not be how to pass on to the new generation the culture and skills of the older generation, in the view of the Skolnicks. These writers suggest that the challenge of contemporary parenting is to keep the burden of obsolete knowledge of the past from interfering with the necessary changes that are occurring and will occur in the future. The question is raised by these writers of how parents can teach children to be open to new knowledge and experiences throughout their lives. The somewhat radical answer they propose is that the idea of adulthood should be considered as obsolete as other ideas that come from the past.

This suggestion may not seem very radical under closer examination. The discussion in Chapter 1 of the text shows how changes have occurred in the concept of childhood. The definition of childhood and the expectations of children have changed through the years. The length of this period in the life cycle has increased as well. The idea of adolescence has only recently been introduced into the organization of the life cycle and extends further and further as a stage of development into the years of adulthood. The Skolnicks argue that if the idea of childhood can change, then the idea of adulthood can change as well. We have traditionally defined adulthood as the culmination of growth and development. By its definition, adulthood implies stagnation of learning and unresponsiveness to change. As the Skolnicks note, this traditional idea of an adult is obsolete in the current era of rapid social change.

One of the major purposes of this text is to demonstrate the effects of children as well as parents on influencing the development of each during the years of a child's presence in the family and the adults' years of child rearing. Developmental interaction between parents and children stimulates adults to continue to progress in their psychosocial development. The concept of developmental interaction is in agreement with the position of the Skolnicks, who suggest that parent–child relations in the future may be characterized by each individual's sharing in the development of each other.

The goals of the various strategies of parenting available today stress a degree of equality between parents and children. One of the primary goals of these strategies is to reduce or equalize the power of parents in their relations with children. Parental power in itself may not be the villain in causing disruptions in relations with children. The issue is rather the parents' use of power to instill their thoughts, values, and attitudes in children rather than assisting them to be open in their learning and flexible in their response to change.

What will be the future result of these suggested "good" strategies in parent–child relations of today, which stress equality between parents and children? How will the consistent use of a variety of methods and techniques of parenting affect children's development? Will these humanitarian strategies really produce positive changes in parent–child relations by reducing parental power?

The crystal-ball gazing of social scientists is notoriously erroneous in making accurate predictions for the future. Many intervening variables can quickly change social attitudes and behavior. Clark Vincent (1972), however, provides a glimpse into the future regarding the effects of parenting styles of the past on the future parenting behavior of today's young people. Vincent reminds us that there have been wide, pendulumlike swings in child-rearing theories and methods during the first half of this century. These changes from child-oriented methods and theories to ones that are more parent-oriented and back again are shown in Figure 9-1. Vincent shows the period from 1950 to 1970 as a time when child-oriented methods were in effect. One study confirms this situation in that "good" child-rearing practices during this period advocated (1) training children for self-reliance; (2) recognizing the child as a person of worth; (3) emphasizing the healthy, positive development of children's self-concepts through humanitarian methods of guidance; and (4) using whatever methods of guidance worked best for both parent and child (Bigner, 1972).

The last line in Figure 9-1 represents Vincent's prediction of the future toward more restrictive, parent-oriented philosophies and practices in parent–child relations. The predicted swing back in this direction may come as a surprise and seems unreasonable based on the rationale and hopes of the current strategies of parenting to overcome inequities of the past in relations between parents and children.

Vincent bases his argument for this return to a more restrictive, conservative period of parent–child relations on the reactions of people in the past (see Figure 9-1). He outlines his reasoning for this change as follows:

A. Today's 35 to 55 year old parents:
   1. were born and reared during the restrictive "parents" era of 1915–1935.
   2. were strongly influenced by the economic depression and the work-and-save ethic of the 1930s.

HOWEVER

   3. They became and were parents during the permissive "children–youth" era of 1945–1965,
      a. which they helped to initiate and support as a reaction to the way they were reared; and

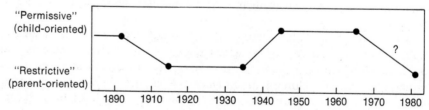

Figure 9-1. Trends in childrearing patterns and theories from 1890 to 1965 and prediction for the future. (Source: Vincent, C. An open letter to the "caught generation." *Family Coordinator*, 1972, *21*, 143–150. Copyright 1972 by the National Council on Family Relations. Reprinted by permission.)

   b. which they compounded by wanting to provide their children
      with the material advantages that they had been denied during
      the depression and that the affluence of the 1960s made pos-
      sible.
B. Tomorrow's parents, the 15 to 25 year olds in 1970:
   1. were born and reared during the permissive "children–youth" era
      of 1945–1965.
   2. are accustomed to having their wants regarded as "needs" to be
      satisfied here and now.

                            HOWEVER

   3. As parents during the seventies and eighties, they will usher in
      another restrictive "parents" era
      a. consistent with their experience of a high priority having been
         given their own needs and wants, and
      b. consistent with their emphasis, if not insistence, upon being
         heard and doing their thing. [Vincent, 1972, p. 148]

Other reasons that Vincent discusses for this return to parent-oriented strategies include (1) the increasing variety of family forms emerging in the 1970s
(communal living and marriages between homosexuals who also may be parents, for example); (2) an increase in behavior typical of college-aged individuals among high school students; (3) the trend toward conservatism
among young adults; and (4) a rejection of the humanitarian methods of
young people's own child-rearing experiences as demonstrations of caregiving by "weak" parents who could not provide psychological controls for
children.

The message of these views is that adults' socialization of children has been
based too much on the heritage of the past and too little on the promise of
the future. The manner and goal of children's socialization has been with
an eye to their future as ideal adults, of course. The process of teaching children what they need to know, however, has been rooted in the dogmas of
the past. One of these dogmas is that adults have the power and the responsibility to shape their child into an adult who reflects their own image of what
qualities constitute a mature individual. The heritage of the past leads us to
believe that the all-powerful adult is the only agent of socialization who can
provide the "right" kinds of experiences during childhood and adolescence
to produce this image of an adult with ideal traits.

This impression leads parents to ask, "What do children need to grow and
develop into normal, healthy adults?" This question actually implies, "What
kind of person do I want my child to be as an adult?" Although there can
be no complete agreement on an answer to this question, Kagan (1976)
suggests that children require no specific actions or behaviors from adults to
develop optimally. Kagan is not proposing that children can be neglected or
deprived of parental caregiving. Rather he is emphasizing that there is no
recipe for successful parenting behavior as today's strategies of child rearing

propose. Kagan notes that there is no formula for the proper amount of punishment, positive reinforcement, nurturance of children, and so on to produce the ideal adult. Kagan believes that children have definite psychological needs but that there is no known prerequisite set of parental behaviors that adequately fulfill these needs. The psychological needs of children in contemporary society, according to Kagan, include (1) knowing that they are valued by parents and a few other special adults (teachers, for example); and (2) developing autonomous attitudes and behaviors in making the decisions that affect the present and the future.

A comprehensive study of child rearing (*Raising Children in a Changing Society*, published by General Mills Corporation, 1977) keynotes the emerging changes in attitudes toward parenting and the challenges of parenthood in contemporary America. This study used a national probability sample of 1,230 families with children under thirteen years of age. A major finding of the study was that contemporary American families are divided into two basic groups, which believe either in traditional or in new values in child rearing. Both groups, however, feel that traditional values should be passed on to children through the experiences of child rearing (See Figure 9-2).

Parents who support the basic values by which they were raised constitute the majority (57 per cent) of the parents surveyed in the study. They are stricter disciplinarians and have higher expectations of their children. Although these parents basically support the values of the past, they are also adopting the newer values of contemporary society. For example, they do not believe that parents should remain married for the benefit of the children, and they believe that parents have a right to their own lives even if this involves spending less time with children.

Parents who have adopted newer attitudes were labeled as the "new-breed" parents and represented 43 per cent of the parents surveyed in the study (see Figure 9-2). These parents may represent the forefront of the "new" type of parent foreseen by Vincent (1972). The study by General Mills found these parents to be less child-oriented and more self-oriented. They regarded parenthood not as a social obligation but as an alternative that they freely chose to pursue as adults. They questioned the idea of self-sacrificing to ensure their children the best of everything. They were described as egalitarian in their belief in the equal rights of parents and children within the family unit.

The agreement of both groups that children should be socialized in traditional values is less of a dilemma for the traditionalist parents than for those of the new breed (see Figure 9-2). The new-breed parents' decision to support traditional values represents a compromise in their values and was explained as a way of preparing children to cope with a world that has not yet adopted values similar to their own. Vincent (1972), however, has predicted this occurrence using a different type of logic; he based the new-breed parents' child-rearing goals and objectives on their dissatisfaction with the manner in which they were raised as children.

THE NEW BREED—43%

Not Important Values
- Marriage as an institution
- Religion
- Saving money
- Patriotism
- Success

Characteristics and Beliefs:
- Parents are self-oriented— not ready to sacrifice for their children
- Parents don't punish their children
- Parents have a laissez-faire attitude—children should be free to make their own decisions
- Parents question authority
- Parents are permissive with their children
- Parents believe boys and girls should be raised alike
- Parents believe their children have no future obligation to them
- Parents see having children as an option not a social responsibility

THE TRADITIONALISTS—57%

Very Important Values
- Marriage as an institution
- Religion
- Saving money
- Hard work
- Financial security

Characteristics and Beliefs:
- Parents are child oriented— ready to sacrifice for their children
- Parents want their children to be outstanding
- Parents want to be in charge— believe parents should make decisions for their children
- Parents respect authority
- Parents are not permissive with their children
- Parents believe boys and girls should be raised differently
- Parents believe old-fashioned upbringing is best
- Parents see having children as a very important value

WHAT BOTH GROUPS TEACH THEIR CHILDREN
- Duty before pleasure
- My country right or wrong
- Hard work pays off
- People in authority know best
- Sex is wrong without marriage

Figure 9-2. Characteristics of today's parents and the values both groups agree should be transmitted to children. (Source: *Raising children in a changing society*. Minneapolis, Minn.: General Mills, Inc., 1977. Reprinted by permission.)

The majority of parents interviewed in the study (64 per cent) were satisfied with the quality of their family life and with how they were handling their problems. The remainder (36 per cent) felt uncertain, however, about their roles as parents and their efforts at child rearing. Those who expressed the greatest concerns in this respect were working mothers, single parents, and parents having low incomes. Most of the parents saw the major challenges of parenting coming from the larger society, as shown in Table 9-1. Five points particularly were seen as difficulties in raising children in today's society: (1) the pressures of a society where crime and violence are rampant; (2) the problems of coping with inflation and high prices complicated by advertising that encourages children to ask for more and more things; (3) the contradictions between old and new values; (4) the special demands on working mothers and minority, single, and economically disadvantaged parents and their children; and (5) the need for striking a balance between per-

Developmental Interaction: Implications for Parenting

Table 9-1. Major Influences in Society Which Make It Hard to Raise Children

	Per Cent
Drugs	34
Broken marriages	28
Inflation	28
Permissiveness in child raising	27
Crime and violence in the streets	25
Both parents having to work to get along financially	25
Breakdown of traditional values	22
Decline of religion	18
Parents being more selfish and less willing to sacrifice for their children	17
Insecurity about jobs and unemployment	16
Television	14
Quality of education	14

Source: *Raising children in a changing society*. Minneapolis, Minn.: General Mills, Inc., 1977. Reprinted by permission.

missiveness and strict discipline; sacrificing too much for one's children and not enough; and demanding too much of children and not enough.

Although these factors are seen as making parenting a difficult responsibility, the study by General Mills reports that 90 per cent of all parents surveyed would still have children again if given a second chance. They would appreciate having help, however, to make the job easier, as shown in Table 9-2.

Whatever the future may hold for parents in relating to children, we can rest assured that they will not be easily replaced by other cultural mechanisms

Table 9-2. Kinds of Help Needed by Parents to Do a Better Job

Type of Class/Group Study	Per Cent
Dealing with drug abuse among children	49
Understanding new classroom teaching methods	42
Convincing children not to smoke	37
Handling problems of discipline	36
Parenting and handling attendant problems	34
Dealing with children's medical problems	34
Feeding children more nutritiously	32
Teaching children about religion	32
Teaching children about sex	31
Balancing the family budget	27

Source: *Raising children in a changing society*. Minneapolis, Minn.: General Mills, Inc., 1977. Reprinted by permission.

for meeting the emotional needs and nurturance of children. The answers to the many questions about child rearing today must necessarily wait for evaluation. As Vincent notes, however, should his prediction prove correct, the grandparents of today have the consolation that their grandchildren will be more "respectful, appreciative, and well-mannered." The pendulum of social change perhaps will swing once more in response to new ideas and feelings about what children "need" to learn and what parents "need" to know about caregiving. As the Skolnicks conclude, Thomas Jefferson reminds us of an important point regarding the future and the challenge of contemporary parenthood:

> Freedom is the right to choose, the right to create for oneself the alternatives of choice. Without the possibility of choice and the exercise of choice, a man is not a man but a member, an instrument, a thing.
>
> [from Cuber, 1970, p. 11]

REFERENCES

BIGNER, J. Parent education in popular literature: 1950–1970. *Family Coordinator,* 1972, *21,* 313–319.

CUBER, J. Alternate models from the perspective of sociology. In H. Otto (Ed.), *The family in search of a future.* New York: Appleton-Century-Crofts, 1970. Pp. 11–23.

KAGAN, J. The psychological requirements for human development. In N. Talbot (Ed.), *Raising children in modern America: Problems and prospective solutions.* Boston: Little, Brown, 1976.

LEMASTERS, E. Parenthood as crisis. *Marriage and Family Living,* 1957, *19,* 352–355.

Raising children in a changing society. Minneapolis, Minn.: General Mills, 1977.

SKOLNICK, A., and SKOLNICK, J. *Family in transition: Rethinking marriage, childrearing, and family organization.* Boston: Little, Brown, 1971.

VINCENT, C. An open letter to the "caught generation." *Family Coordinator,* 1972, *21,* 143–150.

Name Index

(Entries in *italics* refer to pages on which bibliographic references are cited.)

263

Subject Index